INDO-EUROPEAN PH

Modern Languages

Editor

R. AUTY
M.A., Dr.Phil.
Professor of Comparative Slavonic Philology
in the University of Oxford

INDO-EUROPEAN PHILOLOGY

HISTORICAL AND COMPARATIVE

W. B. Lockwood

M.A., D.Litt.

Professor of Germanic and Indo-European Philology
in the University of Reading

Hutchinson of London

Hutchinson & Co (Publishers) Ltd
3 Fitzroy Square, London W1

London Melbourne Sydney Auckland
Wellington Johannesburg and agencies
throughout the world

First published 1969
Reprinted 1971, 1977

Printed in Great Britain by litho at The Anchor Press Ltd
and bound by Wm Brendon & Son Ltd
both of Tiptree, Essex

ISBN 0 09 095581 1 (paper)

CONTENTS

PREFACE

The discovery of the Indo-European family of languages and the consequent elaboration of the science of comparative philology rank among the highest achievements of the human intellect. As such, they are in no way inferior to the triumphs of man in any other branch of knowledge.

Comparative philology long ago, established itself as an academic discipline, but there has always been a dearth of introductory manuals. I therefore gladly accepted the General Editor's invitation to contribute a volume on Indo-European philology, and take this opportunity of thanking him for advice and help. I have attempted, in the space at my disposal, to illustrate the essential principles of the subject and give some idea of its results to date. The work assumes no previous acquaintance with comparative method, nor does it presuppose a knowledge of any given foreign language. It is intended to be complete in itself.

I have had in mind the general reader as well as the student following a regular course of instruction. It is my sincere wish that this little book may prove serviceable to both.

W. B. LOCKWOOD

ABBREVIATIONS

Anc. Gk	Ancient Greek	Mod. Fr.	Modern French
Av.	Avestan	Mod. Ger.	Modern German
Bret.	Breton	Mod. Ir.	Modern Irish
Bulg.	Bulgarian	OBrit.	Old British
Cl. Lat.	Classical Latin	OCS	Old Church Slavonic
Clt.	Celtic	OE	Old English
Co.	Cornish	OHG	Old High German
Eng.	English	OIr.	Old Irish
Fr.	French	OLat.	Old Latin
Gaul.	Gaulish	OLith.	Old Lithuanian
Ger.	German	ON	Old Norse
Gk	Greek	OPruss.	Old Prussian
Gmc	Germanic	OW	Old Welsh
Goth.	Gothic	Pr. Clt.	Primitive Celtic
IE	Indo-European	Pr. Gmc	Primitive Germanic
Ir.	Irish	Pr. Sl.	Primitive Slavonic
It.	Italian	Run.	Runic
Lat.	Latin	Russ.	Russian
Latv.	Latvian	Skt	Sanskrit
Lith.	Lithuanian	Sp.	Spanish
Low Ger.	Low German	VLat.	Vulgar Latin
MidIr.	Middle Irish	W	Welsh
MidW	Middle Welsh	WGmc	West Germanic
Mod. Eng.	Modern English		

I

LANGUAGE STUDY
BEFORE THE NINETEENTH CENTURY

One will not doubt that speculation on the relationship of languages must have exercised the intelligence and imagination of mankind for ages untold. Not without good reason is the story of the Tower of Babel related in Genesis xi. Yet it is hardly more than a century and a half since such speculation was finally transformed into science. The decisive change came when, through the comparative study of a large number of languages, ancient and modern, scholars at last learned to look for the right things. They had first to establish the true nature of linguistic evolution, and then to recognise those elements which demonstrate genetic affinity in languages. Only after this had been done, was the way clear for the solution of problems which had bewildered previous thinkers. All the same, the first great exponents of the new science of comparative philology, the Dane Rasmus Rask (1787–1832) and the Germans Jacob Grimm (1785–1863) and Franz Bopp (1791–1867), were building on the labours of predecessors. They were, in fact, the heirs of a long European tradition of linguistic studies which had, characteristically, begun in ancient Greece. One can best appraise the epoch-making significance of the new science in the light of achievements up to the turn of the eighteenth century.

GREECE AND ROME

The grammatical study of the mother tongue was early cultivated in Greece and the results have come down to us in summary form in the writings of Dionysios Thrax (first century B.C.) and Apollonios Dyskolos (second century A.D.). The Greeks, however, made no systematic study of foreign languages. They saw no point in occupying themselves with manifestations of the barbarian way of life, while their own high civilisation and the hellenisation of the eastern half of the Mediterranean basin gave the Greek language a uniquely pre-eminent place in the ancient world.

The Romans, too, had little time for the culture of the barbarian, but they were enamoured of things Greek. They made a careful study of the Greek language and pondered over the similarities and differences between this tongue and their own. Although the two were in no way mutually comprehensible, even a cursory examination would show obvious similarities. This is most apparent in the grammar. Both languages are highly inflected: their declensional systems are comparable, many of the endings being at least similar and occasionally identical, and the same applies to the terminations of the verb. Both Latin and Greek distinguish three grammatical genders, which in varying degrees affect the morphology of nouns, pronouns and adjectives, formation corresponding not only in a general way, but also in many points of detail.

However, there are important differences. The Latin declension, for instance, includes the ablative case, unknown in Greek. The overall classification of the verbs varies rather considerably, and there are important differences in the tense systems. Latin has three moods: indicative, imperative, subjunctive, Greek has a fourth, the optative, which expresses a wish. The Greek verb is altogether more complex than its Latin counterpart. Such formal differences naturally led to differences in syntactical usage; for example, the Latin ablative absolute has its analogue in the Greek genitive absolute. There are many other discrepancies: Greek has a definite, but no indefinite article; Latin has neither. Greek regularly uses the double negative, a construction which is an anathema in Latin.

The vocabulary of the two languages also presents many similarities, though many more dissimilarities. Nevertheless, there was abundant room for speculation here. In this connection we recall that the Romans, like the Greeks before them, were fully aware that their speech contained words borrowed from other languages.

In due course the Romans applied Greek learning in the field of linguistics to the analysis of their own language and, in view of the high degree of structural similarity between Latin and Greek, the process was not difficult. They raised the question of the origin of the Latin language, a widely held view being that it actually derived from Greek. We have already referred to the special status enjoyed by the Greek language in antiquity. The Romans also knew, of course, that Greek literature was much older than their own. They had, furthermore, legendary connections with Greece through Evander, believed to have come from Arcadia to settle by the Tiber at the foot of the Palatine Hill. It is reasonable to assume that such considerations fostered the notion that Greek was an older language than Latin and that the similarities between the two seemed best explained by a theory that Latin came from Greek. This opinion, which is at least as old as the first century B.C., was still being repeated in the early nineteenth century until finally superseded by the findings of the comparative philologists.

VARRO

But if it was the general view in Rome that Latin ultimately came from Greek, opinion was divided as to the interpretation of the details. As a sample of the philology practised by the ancients, we can do no better than refer to the work of Marcus Terentius Varro.

Varro (116–23 B.C.), the first important Roman grammarian known to us, composed a work *De lingua latina* in 25 books, of which books 5–10 are extant. Books 5–7 deal with the 'discipline of the origin of words'. It is at once apparent that the author understood that some words at any rate have a history, for they may change in various ways. Commenting on *meridies* 'midday', he notes that 'the ancients had *d* in this word, and not *r*, as I have seen at Praeneste, cut on a sun-dial'. He does not explain the change of *d* to *r*—a case of dissimilation—but he has the clue to the literal meaning of the word, since the older form *medidies* automatically calls to mind the adjective *medius* 'middle, mid-'. Varro also reflects on the fact that words may change their meaning in the course of time. He cites *hostis* 'enemy', by which word, however, 'they meant in olden times a foreigner from a country independent of Roman laws', and reminds the reader that the word for enemy was then *perduellis*. Varro proceeds to the analysis of groups of related words:

locus 'place' is where something can be *locatum* 'placed', or as they say nowadays *collocatum* 'established'. That the ancients used the word in this meaning is clear in Plautus: *Filiam habeo grandem dote cassam atque inlocabilem.| Neque eam queo locare cuiquam* 'I have a grown-up daughter, lacking dower, unplaceable. And I cannot place her now with anyone'. A *locus* 'place' is where everything comes to a standstill. From this the auctioneer is said *locare* 'to place', because he is all the time likewise going on until the price comes to a standstill on someone. Thence also is *locarium* 'place rent', which is given for a lodging or shop, where the payers take their stand.[1]

Having perceived the principle that related words are liable to considerable semantic and other variation, Varro goes on to connect words which are not in the remotest way related genetically.

Terra 'earth' is named from the fact that it *teritur* 'is trodden', and in older Latin always spelt *tera*.

Here Varro failed to appreciate that consonants were in any case never written double before Ennius (who is said to have introduced the practice); the oldest known occurrence is dated to 189 B.C., though consistency was not achieved for some decades afterwards. Not that Varro would really have worried about the differences of quantity implied by the later, more accurate spelling (*rr* denotes *r* pronounced twice, or rather lengthened, hence phonetically distinct from single *r*). At any rate, he whole-heartedly ignores the equally important question of vowel-length, having no hesitation, for instance, in recalling that

the poets have called the surface of the earth, which *sōla* 'alone' can be trodden upon, the *sŏla* 'soil' of the earth.

This, by Varronian standards, is by no means stretching the plausibility of linguistic change, and is not untypical, for as he says

a *palus* 'swamp', is a *paululum* 'small amount' of water as to depth, but spread widely *palam* 'in full sight'.

Sometimes, to be sure, Varro has recourse to Greek:

A *stagnum* 'pool' is from Greek, because they give the name *stegnós* 'waterproof' to that which has no fissure.

---

[1] The citations from Varro are taken from: Varro, *On the Latin Language*, 2 vols., Ed. R. G. Kent (Loeb Classical Library), London, 1938.

Varro's etymologising was therefore largely impressionistic. Generally speaking, he is only accurate when the relationship of the words considered is, on the face of things, fairly obvious. In practice, the great majority of the etymologies proposed are hopelessly wrong. But, however wide of the mark Varro so often was, he did at least seek, where he could, to derive Latin from Latin. His matter-of-fact approach, for all its vagaries, contrasts favourably with the efforts of other Roman writers who were for ever on the look-out for Greek sources. Such a predilection for Greek origins was evidently bound up with the preconception that Greek was the ancestor of Latin.

THE MIDDLE AGES

As to basic grammatical theory, it must be said that the Romans added nothing of consequence to the concepts they had themselves taken over from the Greeks, including the terminology which was mechanically transposed into Latin. In this way Greek linguistics was handed down through the Latin intermediary to the European Middle Ages, principally in the compilations of Donatus (fourth century) and Priscian (sixth century).

In the Middle Ages linguistic interest in Western Europe was chiefly associated with the study of Latin. This was the official language of the Church and the recognised medium of scholarship; law was promulgated and administration and business were carried on mainly in Latin. Greek, however, was now but little studied. Men had naturally become very much aware of Hebrew, which was held to be sacrosanct; but this language remained virtually unknown to Christian circles, for whom the Vulgate, the Latin version of the scriptures by Jerome (342–420), not the original Hebrew, was the canonical Old Testament text. Yet Hebrew had a mystical significance. There was a tacit, though scripturally unwarranted, assumption that it was the oldest of languages, indeed the language given by God to Adam. This was the view of the Fathers of the Church and remained general until Leibniz.

Surviving records tell us very little about what men in the Middle Ages said about the vernaculars spoken in their day, but doubtless observations were frequently made. A remarkable passage in the *Descriptio Cambriae* by Giraldus Cambrensis (1146– c. 1220) gives an idea of what a leading intellectual of the age might think. Giraldus states that Welsh, Cornish, then a living tongue, and Breton were descended from the single British source *antiquum linguae Britannicae idioma.* He saw connections between this and Latin and Greek, comparing among others the words for 'salt': Lat. *sāl*, Gk *háls*, Welsh *halen*.

DANTE

Towards the end of the Middle Ages the position of Latin was being somewhat weakened as the result of the increased literary cultivation of the vernaculars. There must have been many discussions on the merits and demerits of this development, for Dante (1265–1321) wrote, in Latin, a treatise justifying the use of Italian for poetry. The work *De vulgari eloquentia*—'vulgar eloquence' meaning something like 'composing in the mother tongue'—seems to have been hardly noticed by his contemporaries, but for us today it is an irreplaceable witness of medieval thought at the turn of the thirteenth century.

We are, first of all, amazed to learn that Dante did not realise that Latin was once the ordinary language of the ancient Romans and their Empire, afterwards superseded by Italian, Spanish, French and the rest. Dante recognises the Latinate quality of the modern languages just mentioned because, as he puts it, they all so very often use variations of the same word for the same thing. He comments on the fact that spoken languages fall into numerous dialects. He realises that the speech of today is different from that of yesterday, so that (he says) if the ancient Pavians were to rise from the dead they would find their dialect much altered. Dante's *leit-motiv* is the primacy of the spoken word. Now since Latin is not a normally spoken language, his argument goes, it is apparent that, in ancient times, men had deliberately invented Latin so as to have a uniform, unchanging language for the purpose of writing. This is called 'grammar'. Dante notes that the Greeks also possessed 'grammar', thus expressing in his medieval way the fact that, throughout the Middle Ages, Ancient Greek was still cultivated, Latin-like, as the ordinary literary medium in the east. A little before this, Roger Bacon (1214–94) had expressed himself in a similar strain. He referred to Aeolic, Doric, Ionic and Attic as the four main dialects of Greek comparable to Italian, Spanish, etc. as dialects of Latin.

MODERN TIMES

Dante's perspicacious views on the originality of the spoken word anticipate later developments when the living languages of the world would at last be investigated. But quite two centuries were to elapse before the first steps in that direction were taken. Meanwhile Latin, as codified by Donatus and Priscian, continued to be the main object of study until, with the Renaissance, the discovery of unknown classical works revealed new horizons. The publication of the newly found materials led to an immense amount of editorial activity involving no little philological acumen. Scholars became painfully aware of the appreciable difference between ancient and medieval Latin, even the hallowed diction of the Vulgate had now to be considered as a defection from classical standards.

The Renaissance did not only re-discover ancient Rome, it discovered ancient Greece as well. Greek became a favourite subject for advanced studies and again great experience was gained in the editing of texts, most of which had been unknown in Western Europe. A Greek grammar was published by Lascaris in 1476. Not long afterwards a third literary language was added: Hebrew. The appearance of a Hebrew grammar by Reuchlin in 1506 was something of a sensation. At last this mysterious tongue was easily accessible and, as it turned out, became of some consequence for linguistic studies generally. Here was a truly exotic language, in its structure fundamentally different from the familiar Latin or Greek, here traditional grammatical analysis showed itself most inadequate.

An obvious concept in Hebrew is that of the root, usually consisting of three consonants. From the root the various parts of speech are formed by inserting vowels according to definite patterns and by the use of various suffixes or prefixes. In the case of the persons of the verb, some of the suffixes are recognisably forms of the pronoun. From the root *šmr*, which incorporates the idea 'keep', are formed, e.g. *šāmartā* 'you (m.sg.) kept', *šāmart* 'you (f.sg.) kept', *šəmartem* 'you (m.pl.) kept', *šəmarten* 'you (f.pl.) kept'. Such endings, invariable for all verbs, are seen to be comparable with the independent pronouns: *attā* 'you' (m.sg.), *att* (f.sg.), *attem* (m.pl.), *atten* (f.pl.). Linguists were soon to adapt these notions to the analysis of Latin and Greek and the vernacular languages, too, which were now rapidly coming into their own as literary media. The grammarians of German, for example, expounded the theory that this language was reducible to monosyllabic roots, a view incorporated in J. G. Schottelius' pioneering *Deutsche Sprachkunst*, 1641.

EARLY STUDY OF THE VERNACULARS

By the sixteenth century Latin had been largely replaced by the vernaculars, except in the Church and as the language of scholarship and international correspondence. Apart from a few earlier publications, it is in this century that dictionaries and grammars of living tongues first make their appearance, including some which teach the language to foreigners. The chief European languages are represented as well as some of the less prominent ones, such as Polish and Czech. Even certain minor languages are treated, e.g. Basque. Curiously enough, no less than three separate grammars of Welsh appeared in the sixteenth century. The list does not stop in Europe. Several Semitic languages, including Arabic and Ethiopic, were described. The practical needs of the colonists in Central and South America led to the publication of about half-a-dozen grammars dealing with languages spoken in the New World.

In this way a corpus of material was being assembled and already one finds scientific observations of importance. One sees, for instance, how step by step the true relationship between Latin and the modern Romance vernaculars was established. J. C. Scaliger (1484–1558) considered the pronunciation of Latin in his day. He noted, for example, that *c* in a word like *cella* 'cell' was pronounced differently in Italy, Spain and France (i.e. It. [tʃ], Sp. [θ], Fr. [s]), but argues that only [k] is correct, since Latin *c* corresponds to Greek *k*. The historically significant development here is the discussion of pronunciation and the implication of the possible etymological identity of different sounds. P. Bembo (1470–1547) observed that *ĭ* and *ĕ* in Latin words appeared in Italian as [e] and [ɛ], i.e. closed or open *e*, respectively: Lat. *fĭdēs* 'faith', It. *fede* [e], Lat. *tĕmpus* 'time', It. *tempo* [ɛ]. With the application of such phonetic laws, etymologising became more rational and the old impressionistic procedure which had persisted since antiquity was more and more abandoned.

C. Gesner in *Mithridates*, 1555, derived Italian, Spanish and French from Latin with the same confidence as he derived Latin from Greek and all languages from Hebrew. Others, specialising in narrower fields, eventually confirmed Gesner's views on the Romance languages, at any rate. E. Pasquier in his *Recherches de la France*, 1560, sees French as a mixed language, the main constituents being drawn from the languages of the ancient rulers of the country, Gauls, Romans and Franks, together with some

Spanish and Italian admixture. But he emphasises that the Latin constituent is dominant. L. Castelvetro, who had done much research on the earlier Italian language, categorically declared in a work *Contra il Varchi*, 1572, that Latin was the parent of Italian, Spanish and French. It was not until the beginning of the next century, however, that the precise nature of this parenthood was carefully defined. B. Aldrete, *Del origen de la lengua castellana*, 1606, draws a distinction between the Latin the Romans wrote and the Latin they spoke. He then traces the spread of both forms of Latin in the wake of the conquering Roman armies and asserts that the differences observed between the living Romance languages are due in the first place to contact between colloquial Latin and the various indigenous populations. Italian, Spanish and French are thus sister languages, whose parent was spoken Latin. Aldrete considers the Gothic and Arabic words which occur in Spanish, and explains them as the linguistic legacy of Gothic and Arab invaders. In other words, he clearly classifies them as loan words.

By the beginning of the seventeenth century, thanks to the publishing activities already mentioned, the languages of Europe especially were becoming much better known. J. J. Scaliger (1540–1609) in an essay *Diatriba de Europaeorum linguis*, published in 1610, was able to distinguish eleven sorts of 'mother-tongue' spoken in Europe. The four major ones he classified according to their respective word for 'God', hence (1) the *Boge* tongue: Ruthenian (here = Russian), Polish, Sorbian, etc. (i.e. Slavonic languages, cf. Old Church Slavonic *Bogŭ* 'God'), (2) the *Godt* tongue: High German, Low German, Frisian, English, Scottish (= Scots English, Lowlands Scots), Danish, Swedish, etc. (i.e. Germanic languages), (3) the *Deus* tongue: Italian, Spanish, French, etc., (4) the *Theós* tongue: Greek in its manifold dialects. The minor 'mother-tongues' are (5) Albanian, (6) Tartar, (7) Hungarian, (8) Finnish with Lappish, (9) Irish and the language of the Scottish Highlands, (10) Old British (= Welsh) and Breton, (11) the speech of the Cantabrians (= Basque). This classification registers a great advance and accurately reflects the empirical facts ascertainable at the time.

Between these eleven groups, says Scaliger, there exists no relationship. But he will not have failed to notice that some of his groups nevertheless had much in common, especially when compared with some others. We have already referred to obvious structural similarities between Latin and Greek. Many of these are seen again, for instance in the Germanic or Slavonic languages, whereas others like Hungarian or Basque bear no such resemblance. The differences between the groups are clearly differences of degree.

LANGUAGE HARMONIES

Scaliger, as we have just seen, admitted no relationship between his eleven groups of European languages. Others, however, remained obsessed with the old notion that Hebrew was the mother of all tongues and that all languages were therefore somehow related. In order to prove this preconception, a number of writers produced compendious comparative dictionaries, the so-called language harmonies. But they could at best produce only a mere handful of serious correspondences. Some turned out to be fortuitous, like Hebrew *šiššā* 'six', now known to have arisen from an (unrecorded) ancestral form *sittā*, cf. Arabic *sitta*. Others are words which have been borrowed from one language to another, e.g. Eng. *sack*, Lat. *saccus*, Gk. *sákkos*, Heb. *śaq*. The likely explanation here is that the Phoenicians, whose language was very close to Hebrew, spread the use of the term through their trading operations. In this way the word would come to the Greeks and the Romans; the article ultimately became known in Northern Europe, too, and its name went with it, hence the English word. Loans like this, which pass from one language to another, can tell us absolutely nothing about any genetic relationship between given languages.

SEVENTEENTH CENTURY

While the harmonisers were diligently pursuing their almost fruitless labours, real progress was being made in the philologies of individual languages. Many older records of the vernaculars, which had hitherto often lain unnoticed in manuscript, were now printed and made avilable for general study. It became possible to outline, in some sort, the history of the better known languages and also to do some serious comparative work. It had been apparent from the first that certain languages were so closely related to each other that they formed easily recognisable groups. We have already referred to the progress of research in connection with the Romance group. Other obvious groups are Germanic and Slavonic. And now the comparative philology of these groups begins to make progress too. For instance, F. Junius (1589–1677) devoted the last years of his life almost exclusively to the study of the older forms of the Germanic languages, including Gothic. This latter was an extinct language known from portions of a translation of the Gospels preserved in a MS known as *Codex Argenteus*. G. Hickes (1642–1715) greatly advanced these studies. He drew up a genealogical tree for the Germanic languages on the analogy of that established for Romance. He distinguished three main divisions: English, German (in a wide sense, including Dutch) and Scandinavian (Danish, Swedish, etc.). These he regarded as descended from the language of the *Codex Argenteus*, just as Italian, Spanish, etc. were descended from Latin.

It goes without saying that more precise information was constantly accruing. Two Baltic languages, Lithuanian and Latvian, omitted altogether from Scaliger's list, were seen to form a group on their own, which, however, bore some resemblance to Slavonic. Scaliger had classified Welsh and Breton on the one hand and Irish on the other as two distinct types, but it now became clear that these were not two unrelated groups, but two moieties of a single Celtic group. The first synopsis of the vocabulary and grammar of the Celtic languages is found in E. Lhuyd, *Archaeologia Britannica*, 1707.

A great impetus to linguistic studies generally was given by G. W. Leibniz (1646–1716). Leibniz overcame the prejudice that Hebrew had been the primitive speech of mankind, arguing that language was not the product of a uniform plan, but had arisen and evolved as a consequence of man's natural needs. Leibniz did much to inspire the collection of linguistic data from all over the world. He was interested in origins and relationships, but it was left to a contemporary, the Semitic scholar J. Ludolf (1624–1704), to define the terms of genetic relationship unambiguously: in order to recognise given languages as related, it is not sufficient that they should have certain words in common, it is far more important that the grammatical structure of the languages concerned should correspond, as in the case of the Semitic languages, Hebrew, Syriac, Arabic, Ethiopic.

EX ORIENTE LUX

The eighteenth century saw a hitherto unparalleled accumulation of linguistic data. Philologists could not only familiarise themselves with all the tongues of Europe at the various stages of their recorded development, they now had access to exotic languages from all parts of the globe. Men were at last thoroughly aware of mighty and ancient civilisations in the east, and eastern languages became subjects of detailed study.

It is India which will concern us here. As early as the sixteenth century a few Europeans living in that country had obtained information about Sanskrit. P. Sassetti, who lived at Goa between 1581 and 1588, wrote that the sciences of the Indians were all written in Sanskrit, the people learning it as Europeans learnt Latin or Greek; no one knew when this language had been spoken, but it had many words in common with Italian, particularly in the numerals six to nine, in the names for God, snake, and many others. By the first half of the eighteenth century, certain missionaries had acquired an adequate knowledge of Sanskrit, and also of its archaic form Vedic, the language of the canonical books of the brahmins. In 1767, P. Cœurdoux asked the French Academy for an opinion on the reasons for the striking similarities between Sanskrit and Greek and Latin, especially the latter (as he says). He compares, for instance: Skt *dắnam* 'gift', *devás* 'god', *jắnu* 'knee', *mádhyas* 'middle', *vidhávā* 'widow' with Lat. *dōnum, deus, genū, medius, vidua,* and then the present tense of the verb 'to be': Sg.1 *ásmi,* 2 *ási,* 3 *ásti,* Pl.1 *smás,* 2 *sthá,* 3 *sánti,* Lat. *sum, es, est, sumus, estis, sunt.* Cœurdoux himself suggested that such words were relics of the primitive language of mankind after the confusion of tongues at Babel. The French Academy, apparently, did not get round to answering the question.

But the startling discovery that the classical language of India possessed elements of basic vocabulary and grammatical structure directly comparable to Greek and Latin called imperatively for a scientific explanation. To provide this, a new departure was necessary. In 1786 before the Royal Asiatic Society of Bengal, the orientalist Sir William Jones declared:

The *Sanskrit* language, whatever be its antiquity, is of a wonderful structure; more perfect than the Greek, more copious than the Latin, and more exquisitely refined than either; yet bearing to both of them a stronger affinity, both in the roots of verbs, and in the forms of grammar, than could possibly have been produced by accident; so strong indeed that no philologer could examine them all three without believing them to have sprung from *some common source,* which perhaps no longer exists. There is similar reason, though not quite so forcible, for supposing that both the *Gothick* and the *Celtick,* though blended with a very different idiom, had the same origin with Sanskrit; and the old *Persian* might be added to the same family.

The modern science of comparative philology had begun.

2

FOUNDATIONS AND DEVELOPMENT OF
COMPARATIVE INDO-EUROPEAN PHILOLOGY

THE FOUNDERS

William Jones did not live to elaborate his views further. The first significant development came from F. von Schlegel (1772–1829) in his famous work *Über die Sprache und Weisheit der Indier*, 1808. Schlegel, however, did not follow Jones exactly. He was so much impressed by a language 'more perfect than the Greek, more copious than the Latin' that he declared Sanskrit to be the parent language, of which Greek, Latin, Persian, and the members of the Germanic branch were the more or less degenerate descendants. More remotely connected were Armenian, and the Slavonic and Celtic languages. Schlegel based his conclusions on far-reaching, if unsystematic, comparisons of vocabulary and grammatical structure. His book provided a great stimulus to research. The epoch-making discoveries of the founders of comparative philology, Bopp, Rask and Grimm, already referred to (p. 11), were all published within the next decade or so.

Franz Bopp's first publication *Über das Konjugationssystem der Sanskritsprache in Vergleichung mit jenem der griechischen, lateinischen, persischen und germanischen Sprache*, 1816, laid the foundations of comparative Indo-European grammar. In the first place, Bopp correctly defined the position of Sanskrit:

I do not believe that Greek, Latin and the other European languages are to be considered as derived from Sanskrit . . . I feel rather inclined

to consider them altogether as subsequent variations of one original
tongue, which Sanskrit has preserved more perfectly. . . . But while the
language of the brahmins more frequently enables us to conjecture the
primitive forms of Greek and Latin . . . the latter may not infrequently
elucidate Sanskrit grammar.

He went on to compare the verbal systems in great detail and
attempted to explain historically the forms actually attested in
the languages considered. He took over from the German grammarians the theory that the root of the verb was monosyllabic, a
perfectly valid mode of analysis, in which he was supported by the
formulations of native Sanskrit grammar, and he sought for
traces of the pronoun thought to be incorporated in the terminations (p. 17).

Bopp's researches culminated in his *Vergleichende Grammatik
des Sanskrit, Zend, Armenischen, Griechischen, Lateinischen,
Lithauischen, Altslawischen, Gothischen und Deutschen*, the first
edition of which began to appear in 1833; the third and last edition
was published in 1868. In its day, this work was the most comprehensive exposition of the subject and its various editions document
the advance of knowledge in Bopp's lifetime. Bopp's great interest
had always been the elucidation of the origin of grammatical
forms and this interest led him to undertake the comparison of the
inflexional systems of the various Indo-European languages which
proved so fruitful for comparative studies generally. But the problem of origins all too often remained intractable. A sample of
Bopp's mode of analysis may give some notion of the stage
reached in his day. He compares, for instance, the *s*-element which
commonly appears in the Greek aorist and the Latin perfect, as
Gk. *é-tup-s-a* 'I have struck', Lat. *scrip-s-ī*, 'I have written', and
identifies it with the Sanskrit root *as-* 'be', seen in *ásmi* 'am', etc.
An *s*-element occurs in other tenses, for example commonly in
the Greek future: *túp-s-ō* 'I shall strike'. Bopp concluded that the
root of the auxiliary 'to be' had been employed in the formation of
tenses. He further inferred that the same element was present in
the Latin passive ending *-ur*, e.g. *scrib-it-ur* 'is being written',
since Latin frequently shows change of original *s* to *r*, as *honor*
'honour' from earlier *honōs*.

Not long afterwards, however, it was recognised that the Celtic
languages use a formation parallel to Lat. *-ur*, making it no
longer possible to appeal to secondary rhotacism. As to the
sigmatic element in the past tense of certain verbs, modern

scholarship does not doubt that Greek and Latin are comparable, but whether this *s* is identical with the *s* in the future tense is another matter. Nor is the conjecture that *s* in verbal forms represents an incorporation of the verb 'to be' any better supported than it was when Bopp first advanced it. In sober fact, the question of origin is quite unresolved. The same applies, too, to the theory that the terminations contain pronominal elements.

Although the knowledge of Sanskrit had been the key to real progress and had accordingly remained at the centre of Bopp's as of Schlegel's studies, another pioneering scholar made a very material contribution to the new science without actually incorporating the evidence of Sanskrit into his comparative work. This was Rasmus Rask whose *Undersøgelse om det gamle nordiske eller islandske Sprogs Oprindelse* (Investigation into the Origin of the Old Norse or Icelandic Language), completed in 1814, but not published until 1818, remained an unrivalled exposition of the methods of linguistic research for at least a generation. Rask described the affinities of the Germanic languages with the Baltic and Slavonic, and with Latin and Greek. He examined Celtic, but concluded that it seemed too different to be fundamentally akin— a view he retracted a little later. As we have said, Sanskrit was not included, much to the detriment of the work. Rask himself had no first-hand knowledge of the language at the time, though he was fully aware that this and other oriental languages could well be related. As it was, Rask examined hundreds of correspondences and provided a comparative statement of the groups of languages investigated, achieving results which make him one of the founders of the new science.

Rask attached special importance to sound changes, since an understanding of these may reveal the ultimate identity of words which at first sight seem unrelated. He compared, among others, the Icelandic words *faþir* 'father', *þrir* 'three', *horn* 'horn', *blaþ* 'leaf', *tamr* 'tame', *kona* 'woman', *ber* 'I bear', *dyrr* 'door', *gall* 'gall' with Gk *patér*, *treîs*, Lat. *cornū*, Gk *blastánō* 'I bud', *damáō* 'I tame', *guné*, *phérō*, Lat. *ferō*, Gk *thúrā*, *kholḗ*, and noted that the consonantal changes observed as between Germanic on the one hand, and Greek and Latin on the other, are regular, especially when the consonants occur at the beginning of the word. Rask's work in this direction was expanded and formalised by Jacob Grimm, Rask's occasional errors of detail being corrected as knowledge progressed. It was eventually realised, for instance, that Icel. *blaþ* and Gk. *blastánō* (above) are unrelated.

Jacob Grimm's earliest interest was medieval German literature, but later he devoted himself chiefly to German and Germanic linguistics. His *Deutsche Grammatik*, which is really a comparative Germanic grammar, appeared first in 1819. This work he recast and enlarged in 1822 when, inspired by Rask's *Undersøgelse*, he stated what subsequently became known as Grimm's Law. This law is a systematisation of the consonantal changes peculiar to Germanic. Not that Grimm was able to account for all the phenomena. There remained a substantial number of exceptions which were not explained until 1877 (below). Grimm further considered the regular vowel changes found in related words, e.g. Eng. *sing, sang, sung, song*. To denote this change he coined the expression *ablaut*, which may be used in English, though some writers prefer the hellenisation 'apophony'. It was eventually realised that ablaut was a primitive feature inherited by all Indo-European languages. The emphasis in Grimm's work was not only comparative, but also historic; he was, in particular, concerned with the history of German and the Germanic languages. It goes without saying that comparative and historic studies are eminently complementary.

The newly established family of languages received various names. The term *Indogermanisch* was introduced in 1823 by J. Klaproth, who is otherwise hardly significant in the history of the subject, and his term has become usual in works written in German. Bopp, however, considered *Indoeuropäisch* more suitable; this is the term generally preferred outside the German-speaking area. These names may also denote the postulated parent language itself, though in that case they are more usually qualified: Ger. *Urindogermanisch*, Eng. *Primitive* or *Proto-Indo-European*.

FROM POTT TO BRUGMANN AND DELBRÜCK

Bopp and Grimm had many followers, especially in their own country; indeed, comparative philology in the nineteenth century can be said to have been predominantly a German science. We mention first A. F. Pott (1802–87); his fundamental *Etymologische Forschungen auf dem Gebiete der indogermanischen Sprachen* (1833–36) may be regarded as the beginning of a thorough-going scientific phonology. Pott set up comparative sound tables embracing all the branches of the Indo-European family. He proved by his example that only the most rigorous application of the recognised sound laws could be scientifically profitable. Whereas

Bopp could once argue for a supposed sound change in Latin on the strength of developments in Armenian, such liberties were henceforth taboo; the peculiarities of Latin were first to be explained in terms of Latin. Pott foreshadowed the *Junggrammatiker* —so-called because they were still young at the time—who, from the seventies of the last century, upheld the precept that sound laws admit of no exceptions.

Another prominent figure was A. Schleicher (1821–68) whose most original contribution was his reconstruction of prehistoric Indo-European forms. Jones had long before spoken of the putative parent language, but this concept had rather been lost sight of. Bopp, for instance, had simply stated that the Greek aorist and the Latin perfect were sometimes formed with an *s*-element, whereas a more adequate statement would have been that these languages had inherited this formation from their common ancestor, Primitive Indo-European.

By comparing the recorded forms of a word, it is possible to imagine what the word looked like in Primitive Indo-European. Schleicher saw the matter something like this. The word for 'horse' (nom.sg.) in the three oldest Indo-European languages known at the time is: Skt *áśvas*, Gk *híppos*, also *íkkos*, Lat. *equus*, archaic *equos*. Other languages preserve this word, too. It is found in Gothic, though only as the first part of a plant name *aihwatundi* (*ai* = [e]) 'thornbush' literally 'horse-tooth', Goth. *h* representing IE *k*; further Old Irish *ech* 'horse', where *ch* likewise points to IE *k*. Schleicher concluded that the primitive word from which all were descended had been **akvas*—the asterisk indicating a reconstructed word not actually attested in any records. In view of its antiquity, Sanskrit was thought to have kept the vowels of the parent language. On the other hand, Skt *ś* and Gk *pp* are seen to be innovations peculiar to the two languages in question, the evidence of the others indicating the originality of *k*. By the same token, initial *h* in Gk *híppos* appears as a secondary development peculiar to that language. Lastly the Sanskrit, Latin and Gothic forms point to the presence of *v* or *w* in the parent tongue, the other languages having apparently lost the sound during the course of their separate evolution. It can, however, now be shown that Schleicher's postulated **akvas* is in part erroneous, particularly in respect of the vowels. A little after Schleicher's time (see next paragraph), it was realised that the evidence implied rather IE **ekwos*, since it had by then become clear that the vowel system of Sanskrit, far from faithfully reflecting the prehistoric stage, had in fact undergone sweeping changes which resulted in the transformation of both original *e* and *o* into *a*. Schleicher could not know this. But the practice of reconstructing Indo-European prototypes, first consistently applied in his main work, the *Compendium der vergleichenden Grammatik der indogermanischen Sprachen*, 1861, provided a necessary methodological advance. Comparative philology today is unthinkable without the asterisked forms.

It will be appropriate to mention now three important discoveries in the field of Indo-European phonology: Grassmann's Law (1863), Verner's Law (1877), and the Law of Palatals (about 1880). The first explained cases of parallel de-aspiration in Sanskrit and Greek (p. 90), the second accounted for the considerable number of exceptions to Grimm's Law and threw further light on the accentual system of Indo-European (pp. 118f.), while the third, arrived at by various linguists independently, demonstrated among other things that cases of palatalisation before Skt *a* were at once explicable on the assumption that *a* had replaced an earlier *e*. It was this prehistoric *e* which, as a front vowel, had led to the palatalisation of a preceding consonant, and which, moreover, corresponded etymologically to *e* in the languages of Europe, leaving no doubt that the latter were more archaic in this respect than Sanskrit. It also now became apparent that Sanskrit had innovated in cases where it had *a*, but the others *o* (pp. 90f.).

The discovery of the Law of Palatals was naturally a blow to the prestige of Sanskrit which philologists had hitherto assumed to stand close to the parent tongue. Now that this was obviously much less the case, new thinking about the character of Primitive Indo-European was urgently called for. A product of speculation in this direction was a new conception which divided the Indo-European languages into two moieties: a western *centum* group (Celtic, Italic, Germanic, Hellenic) and an eastern *satem* group (Albanian, Slavonic, Baltic, Armenian, Aryan), the latter being distinguished by the change of original palatal occlusives into sibilants as exemplified by the test word Avestan *satəm* 'hundred' contrasting with Lat. *centum*. This division, proposed by F. von Bradke in 1890, was generally accepted, though the position of Albanian appeared anomalous. One therefore supposed that the ancestors of the Albanians had at one time been established further east.

In 1879, an original thinker F. de Saussure (1857–1913) published a youthful, but profound study entitled *Mémoire sur le système primitif des voyelles dans les langues indo-européennes*. Having compared the structure of the various patterns of ablaut, he concluded that the presence of a long vowel was secondary, in certain cases to be explained as a reflex of an older short vowel and a lost sonant. He argued further, on the basis of vowel differentiation, that two distinct sonants were involved. This theory was at once welcomed by H. Möller who was endeavouring to show that the Indo-European family of languages was ultimately linked to the Semitic family. Since the Semitic languages contain as a basic feature a number of laryngeal sounds, Möller saw in de Saussure's lost sonants Indo-European laryngeals also. But even with the newly won (theoretical) laryngeals Möller's thesis remained too obscure to be convincing and soon the whole matter of laryngeals was as good as forgotten until it came up again, nearly fifty years later, as a consequence of newly discovered evidence.

Of other names becoming prominent in the second half of the last century, we should not forget that of Max Müller (1823–1900) who left Germany as a young man to teach at Oxford. He became the foremost populariser of his subject, his famous *Lectures on the Science of Language* going through nine editions between 1861 and 1891. It was he who introduced the term 'Grimm's Law'.

It goes without saying that then, as now, knowledge was rapidly increasing. New material was all the time being made available through the critical editions of texts. Then, as the corpus of traditional literary works was more or less exhausted, greater attention was paid to oral language and in particular to dialect speech, both of which had been relatively neglected in the initial period. The science of phonetics came into its own and we remember in this connection the pioneering work of Henry Sweet (1845–1912), alias Professor Higgins. The frank recognition of the primacy of the spoken word had far-reaching implications. It was recognised that the most fundamental laws of linguistic evolution are to be deduced, in the first instance, from living language, of which a given literary text may be a very biased reflection. Whereas comparative philology is especially concerned with origins and therefore supremely interested in the oldest documentary attestations of languages, it is nevertheless a fact that new concepts flowing from a study of contemporary language, notably in the field of phonetics, have led to progressive refinements in linguistic methods at all levels.

Meanwhile, work on the philology of the various branches of

Indo-European and on the constituent languages themselves was making great strides. Various historical grammars, often on a broad comparative basis, testify to progress in this sector. Comprehensive etymological dictionaries now begin to appear, suffice it to recall that the first edition of W. W. Skeat's *Etymological Dictionary of the English Language* was published between 1879 and 1882. At the same time, too, the fundamental dictionaries were under way: the *New (Oxford) English Dictionary* began to appear in 1888, the first edition being completed in 1928; the *English Dialect Dictionary* came out between 1898 and 1905. Similar works were produced for other languages. Such fundamental sources all contributed new data and led to an advance in comparative studies generally.

The closing years of the nineteenth century saw the consolidation of the discoveries of the previous decades. In this connection mention must be made of A. Fick (1833–1916), whose *Vergleichendes Wörterbuch der indogermanischen Sprachen*, 4th ed., 1890, is a monument both to his own genius and to the progress made by comparative studies in this field towards the end of the last century. There now existed a considerable body of widely accepted theory and this was systematically presented by K. Brugmann (1849–1919) and B. Delbrück (1842–1922) in their compendious *Grundriß der vergleichenden Grammatik der indogermanischen Sprachen* (1886–1916), in five volumes, from which Brugmann extracted a one-volume *Kurze vergleichende Grammatik*, 1904. Though in certain aspects inevitably antiquated, as for instance in the doctrine on the phonetic structure of the parent language, the *Grundriß* nevertheless remains an unequalled source of factual information and indispensable for serious work on Indo-European linguistics. In this respect, it differs from other comparative work dating from the nineteenth century, which is nowadays—usually—of historical interest only.

THE TWENTIETH CENTURY

With the new century came two discoveries which caused an unwonted stir on the philological scene: two entirely unknown branches of the Indo-European family suddenly came to light as the result of archaeological finds, first in Chinese Turkestan and then in Central Anatolia, the languages being Tocharian and Hittite respectively. These discoveries were destined to play a leading part in the modification of existing theory.

To begin with, both Tocharian and Hittite were clearly *centum* languages, which at once seriously questioned the validity of the conception of an ancient division of Indo-European languages into a western *centum* group and an eastern *satem* group. It now became more likely that the *satem* innovations were confined to more centrally placed dialects and took place before the emigration of the Aryans to the south and east.

But Hittite held the greatest surprises in store. One of these was, in due course, to call into question many of the classical reconstructions for Primitive Indo-European worked out by Brugmann and his contemporaries. In the meantime, however, Brugmann's postulates were broadly followed by the next generation of comparative philologists, as we find in the following representative works: A. Meillet, *Introduction à l'étude comparative des langues indo-européennes*, eight editions between 1903 and 1937, a most readable account, now reprinted (1964); H. Hirt, *Indogermanische Grammatik*, 7 vols., 1927–37; A. Walde / J. Pokorny, *Vergleichendes Wörterbuch der indogermanischen Sprachen*, 3 vols., 1927–32, entirely reworked as J. Pokorny, *Indogermanisches etymologisches Wörterbuch*, I, 1948–59. The general doctrine of these publications is summarised in two short volumes by H. Krahe, *Indogermanische Sprachwissenschaft*, 1962–63. But as Hittite studies progressed, it became evident that this very ancient language had continued to use one or more phonemes (in transcription ḫ, ḫḫ) of Indo-European age not admitted by Brugmann. Moreover, as pointed out by J. Kuryłowicz in 1927, ḫ, ḫḫ occur in a number of cases in positions where de Saussure had, for theoretical reasons, posited a lost Indo-European sonant. It is not certain what phonetic values exactly are to be ascribed to ḫ, ḫḫ, but the cuneiform signs employed are those used in Akkadian (an extinct Semitic language of Mesopotamia) to denote velar fricatives, sounds close to the types which were postulated by Möller for de Saussure's assumed sonants. In the nature of the case, the total amount of evidence adducible from Hittite is not great, and not all of it has been adequately accounted for, but it has been sufficient to provide a secure basis for research. This has not been easy, the necessarily abstruse character of many investigations has led to conflicting conclusions, but positive advances have been achieved. In particular, a number of unsuspected reflexes of the lost laryngeals have been either positively identified or at least made probable in various Indo-European languages apart from Hittite, and a number of apparent irregularities which had long puzzled philologists can be explained in the light of the new theory. American scholarship has been most prominent in this field; a representative publication is W. P. Lehmann, *Proto-Indo-European Phonology*, 1952.

The present century has seen the appearance of fundamental works dealing with the philology of the different branches of Indo-European in relation to the family as a whole. Some of these works have their genesis in the last century, others are new works replacing older accounts of the same subject, while not a few handle materials unknown before. The brief selection of titles below is intended to convey some idea of the scope of these studies in the present century.

The Indo-European languages are classified in Chapter 3 and the order of this classification is followed here; it will be noticed that German is still the language of the majority of fundamental publications:

Aryan or *Indo-Iranian:* J. Wackernagel/A. Debrunner, *Altindische Grammatik*, 3 vols., 1896–1954, *Nachträge*, 1957; T. Burrow, *The Sanskrit Language*, 1955; M. Mayrhofer, *Kurzgefaßtes etymologisches Wörterbuch des Altindischen*, 1953–; J. Bloch, *L'indo-aryen du Véda aux temps modernes*, 1934; R. L. Turner, *Comparative Dictionary of the Indo-Aryan Languages*, 1966; W. Geiger/E. Kuhn, *Grundriß der iranischen Philologie*, 2 vols., 1895–1904; I. M. Oranskij, *Vvedenie v iranskuju filologiju*, 1960.

Thraco–Phrygian: D. Detschew, *Charakteristik der thrakischen Sprache*, 1960; A. Meillet, *Esquisse d'une grammaire comparée de l'arménien*, 2nd ed., 1936.

Illyrian: A. Mayer, *Die Sprache der alten Illyrier*, 2 vols., 1957–59, E. Çabej, *Studime rreth etimologjisë së gjuhës shqipe*, 1960–.

Venetic: H. Krahe, *Das Venetische*, 1950.

Tocharian: H. Pedersen, *Tocharisch vom Gesichtspunkt der indoeuropäischen Sprachvergleichung*, 1941; W. Krause/W. Thomas, *Tocharisches Elementarbuch*, I, 1960.

Anatolian: J. Friedrich, *Hethitisches Elementarbuch*, I, 2nd ed., 1960.

Hellenic: E. Schwyzer, *Griechische Grammatik*, 3 vols., 1939–53; H. Frisk, *Griechisches etymologisches Wörterbuch*, 1954–.

Italic: F. Stolz/J. H. Schmalz, *Lateinische Grammatik*, 5th ed., 2 vols., 1925–28; G. Devoto, *Storia della lingua di Roma*, 1944; L. R. Palmer,

The Latin Language, 1954; A. Ernout/A. Meillet, *Dictionnaire étymologique de la langue latine*, 4th ed., 1959; W. D. Elcock, *The Romance Languages*, 1960; W. Meyer-Lübke, *Romanisches etymologisches Wörterbuch*, 3rd ed., 1935; C. D. Buck, *Grammar of Oscan and Umbrian*, 2nd ed., 1928.

Celtic: H. Pedersen, *Vergleichende Grammatik der keltischen Sprachen*, 2 vols., 1909–13, abridged as H. Pedersen/H. Lewis, *Concise Comparative Celtic Grammar*, 1937, *Supplement*, 1961.

Germanic: W. Streitberg, *Urgermanische Grammatik*, 1896, reprinted 1943; H. Hirt, *Handbuch des Urgermanischen*, 3 vols., 1931–34; E. Prokosch, *Comparative Germanic Grammar*, 1938; F. Stroh, *Handbuch der germanischen Philologie*, 1952.

Slavonic and Baltic: W. Vondrák, *Vergleichende slavische Grammatik*, 2nd ed., 2 vols., 1924–28; A. Meillet, *Le slave commun*, 2nd ed., 1934; A. Vaillant, *Grammaire comparée des langues slaves*, 4 vols., 1950–68; R. Nahtigal, *Die slavischen Sprachen*, 1961; H. Bräuer, *Slavische Sprachwissenschaft*, 2 vols., 1961–68; W. J. Entwistle/W. A. Morison, *Russian and the Slavonic Languages*, 2nd ed., 1964; E. Berneker, *Slavisches etymologisches Wörterbuch*, *A–M*, 1908–14; E. Fraenkel, *Die baltischen Sprachen*, 1950; C. S. Stang, *Vergleichende Grammatik der baltischen Sprachen*, 1967; E. Fraenkel, *Litauisches etymologisches Wörterbuch*, 1955–. ·

Greek and Latin have often been treated together, e.g. C. D. Buck, *Comparative Grammar of Greek and Latin*, 1946; A. Meillet/J. Vendryes, *Traité de grammaire comparée des langues classiques*, 2nd ed., 1948.

In addition to the works mentioned above, good modern etymological dictionaries exist for all the major languages of Europe and for several of the minor ones. Methods and results of etymological research are considered in A. S. C. Ross, *Etymology*, 1958.

Other publications contain the fruits of research into special fields of comparative studies, e.g. O. Schrader/A. Nehring, *Reallexikon der indogermanischen Altertumskunde*, 2nd ed., 2 vols., 1917–29; C. D. Buck, *Dictionary of Selected Synonyms in the Principal Indo-European Languages*, 1949; W. Porzig, *Die Gliederung des indogermanischen Sprachgebiets*, 1954; P. Thieme, *Die Heimat der indogermanischen Gemeinsprache*, 1954.

3

CLASSIFICATION OF
INDO-EUROPEAN LANGUAGES

ARYAN *or* INDO-IRANIAN

This branch falls into two well-known groups: Indian (*or* Indo-Aryan) and Iranian. Traces of Aryan in ancient Syria have recently come to light.

The oldest known form of Indian is Sanskrit. The earliest documents, in archaic language, are the religious texts known as Vedas, dating from about 1000 B.C. Vedic is followed by Classical Sanskrit, regulated in the grammar of Pāṇini (fourth century B.C.), and his language remained in use as a leading literary medium down to 1835 when Macaulay's minute inaugurated the era of of English. As a consequence of some three millennia of continuous cultivation, Sanskrit is the vehicle of an immense literature and the language itself is extraordinarily expressive. But Sanskrit in India today is regarded much as Latin now is in Europe. As a means of communication it is as good as defunct, but from its copious vocabulary it gives readily to the modern languages of India in the same way as Latin has enriched the living tongues of Europe. Sanskrit, Vedic and Classical, may be termed Old Indian.

The name Sanskrit 'polished (according to the rules of grammar)' contrasts with Prakrit 'unrefined', a term used in the first place to denote the popular spoken dialects which naturally evolved further and further away from the codified Sanskrit. The earliest stage of Prakrit is represented by Pali, which arose in the first centuries B.C. as the language of a school of Buddhism; it is still in use as the religious language of the Buddhists of Ceylon, Burma and Thailand. The various forms of the so-called Literary Prakrits reflect the speech of some centuries later. Prakrit may be termed Middle Indian. Finally, about the end of the first millennium, the period of Modern Indian begins with the earliest records of the living languages which have evolved from the Prakrits. Among the more important are Hindustani, now falling more and more into two culturally distinct forms, Hindi in the Indian Union and Urdu in Western Pakistan, further Bengali, Marathi, Gujarati, Panjabi. Romany, the language of the Gypsies, is likewise of Middle Indian origin.

In Vedic times, Indo-European speech was confined to northwest India, but subsequently spread over all the north and centre, generally obliterating the languages of the earlier inhabitants, of which today only small enclaves remain here and there in some less accessible areas. There is, however, one offshoot of our family far to the south. This is Sinhalese, the state language of Ceylon, introduced, it is thought, by immigrants from eastern India over two thousand years ago. Inevitably the indigenous languages have influenced the incoming Indo-European. Especially Later Sanskrit contains very many words recognised as borrowings from Dravidian, the family of languages now found chiefly in South India, but once widespread in the centre and north.

Old Iranian is recorded in an eastern and a western variety, known as Avestan (in older works often improperly called Zend) and Old Persian respectively. Avesta is the name given to the sacred writings of the Parsees, certain hymns of which, the Gathas, are attributed to Zoroaster c. 600 B.C. In linguistic form, however, the Gathas are so closely comparable to the Indian Vedas that verses from one can often be mechanically transposed into the other. Old Persian is less archaic; it is known from the monumental inscriptions of the Achaemenian kings of the sixth to fourth centuries B.C. The materials for the study of Old Iranian are thus not extensive, at any rate not when compared with Old Indian, but the records of Middle Iranian are much more considerable. Of these, Middle Persian or Pahlavi (third to eighth century) has been long known, while others have only come to light in the present century as a result of archaeological finds in Central Asia. Of the newly discovered languages, the most important are Sogdian and Khotanese, both eastern types. Modern Persian begins about 900; other modern languages are Kurdish and Pashto, the state language of Afghanistan. Ossetic, spoken in a small area in the Caucasus, is a relic of Alan, an Eastern Iranian language once current in South Russia.

Whereas, during the historical period, the Indian branch has been generally advancing, Iranian has suffered considerable territorial losses. In addition to South Russia, large tracts of Central Asia were lost to Turkish languages during the Middle Ages.

Archaeological discoveries in this century have revealed the presence of Aryans as far to the west as Syria where, about the middle of the second millennium B.C., they appear as a naturalised element in the (non-Indo-European) Hurrian-speaking kingdom of Mitanni. A few words of their language and some names are found on cuneiform tablets. Among their gods are *Indara* and *Mitrassil* (where -*ssil* is an exotic suffix), cf. Skt *Indras*, *Mitras*, Av. *Indras*, *Mithras*.

It may be assumed, as a working hypothesis, that the Aryans emigrated from Eastern Europe about 2000 B.Ç. When they finally entered India is unknown, but one thinks in terms of towards 1000 B.C. At all events, the Indus civilisation, brought to light by excavations in 1924, is pre-Aryan.

THRACO-PHRYGIAN

Thraco-Phrygian denotes a group of three languages, Thracian, Phrygian and Armenian, whose earliest known homeland was south-east Europe. The Ancient Greeks described the Armenian tongue as being similar to Phrygian, and the Phrygians, they said, were originally a Thracian people.

Thracian was spoken in the eastern half of the Balkan peninsula and in various districts in western Asia Minor. It was largely ousted by Latin and Greek, but seems to have survived in small areas on both sides of the Hellespont until the sixth century A.D. A little is known of the language from glosses and personal names. To the east of the Thracians in Asia Minor were the Phrygians, whose chief seat was Gordion. Their language is scantily preserved in glosses, personal names and also in inscriptions, the latest from the third century A.D., after which time the Phrygians will have been completely hellenised.

The Armenians are the most eastern of the Thraco-Phrygians. Armenian still survives, principally in the Armenian Soviet Republic, of which it is an official language. Old (or Classical) Armenian is the vehicle of a rich literature dealing mainly with religious subjects. The language of the period 1000 to 1500 is called Middle Armenian, though the classical language continued to be cultivated in this as in the modern period, too. From an early date Armenia was subject to Persian influence and the language contains an inordinate number of Persian loans. It was, indeed, once thought that Armenian was nothing more than an aberrant Persian dialect until, in 1877, Hübschmann showed that the Iranian element was due to wholesale borrowing. Many of the unexplained peculiarities of the language may be due to the influence of two ancient non-Indo-European languages, Hurrian and Urartian, which appear to have gone into the making of Armenian.

ILLYRIAN

Illyrian was spoken in the western half of the Balkan peninsula north of Greece. Romanisation began as early as 230 B.C., but the language appears to have survived sporadically until the seventh century, when it was finally eradicated by the invading Slavs. The language is known from a few glosses and a large number of names. Messapian, spoken in Apulia and (ancient) Calabria until replaced by Latin in the first century A.D., may be regarded as a colonial form of Illyrian. It is scantily represented in inscriptions beginning in the fifth century B.C.

From its geographical position, Albanian has been held to continue ancient Illyrian. Albanian also shows, however, lexical correspondences with Thracian. Research is hampered by the fact that Albanian is only known in its modern form, the earliest text being from 1462. The language has suffered much from phonetic attrition. Its lexicon is extensively romanised, but its grammatical structure is independent.

VENETIC

Venetic is the name given to the autochthonous language of the Roman province of Venetia. It is attested in some two hundred brief inscriptions dating from the sixth to the first centuries B.C. Though it shares some features with Italic, it is thought to have constituted a distinct branch of Indo-European.

TOCHARIAN

Archaeological discoveries made at the turn of the century in Chinese Turkestan brought to light a large amount of manuscript material, some of it in an unknown language written in the seventh and eighth centuries A.D. Decipherment was facilitated by finds of bilingual texts in Sanskrit and the new language, which received the name Tocharian. It was seen to fall into two considerably differentiated dialects; one could almost speak of separate languages, usually known as Tocharian A and B respectively. Its Indo-European character was demonstrated in 1908.

Tocharian contains many extraneous elements, but in spite of this and its relatively late dating, it preserves archaic Indo-European features valuable for comparative purposes. Tocharian is now extinct; at an unknown date it was replaced most likely by Uigur Turkish, the chief language of the region today.

ANATOLIAN

In 1906 the archaeologist's spade unearthed a huge collection of over 10,000 cuneiform tablets near Boğazköy in Central Anatolia. This was the archive of Hattusa, capital of the Hittite Empire, which had flourished from 1900 to 1200 B.C. Some tablets could be read at once since they were written in known languages, Sumerian and Akkadian, but the majority were in an unidentified language. Decipherment, however, progressed rather quickly and by 1915 the Indo-European character of the new language, Hittite, was first asserted and shortly afterwards generally recognised.

In spite of its antiquity—it is by far the oldest recorded form of Indo-European—Hittite is not as complex morphologically as Sanskrit or the other ancient Indo-European languages. Original Indo-European features are seen to have been partly obliterated by new developments due to the influence of exotic languages with which the Proto-Hittites came into contact after their arrival in Asia Minor. Significantly, the vocabulary is largely non-Indo-European. Nevertheless, Hittite preserves a respectable number of archaisms invaluable for the comparative study of Indo-European. Unfortunately, the imprecise nature of the cuneiform syllabary is often a hindrance to the full philological exploitation of the texts.

Another ancient language, closely akin to Hittite, was disclosed in the Boğazköy archive. This is Luwian which, in turn, is further affiliated to the language of the recently deciphered hieroglyphic script found in northern Syria, known since the 1870s as Hieroglyphic Hittite. The writers of this script were almost certainly the

Hittites known to the Bible. Hittite and Luwian represent an independent branch of Indo-European; it has been named Anatolian.

It is now realised that Anatolian survived into Greek and most likely also into Roman times. Lycian, a language from southwestern Asia Minor, recorded in inscriptions of the fifth and fourth centuries B.C., was proved to be Anatolian in 1957. There are reasons for supposing that Lydian, a language from the west coast of Asia Minor, known from inscriptions of a similar date, is also related. The existence of numerous minor languages in Roman times, like the 'speech of Lycaonia' (Acts xiv.11), is a historical fact. It is reasonable to suppose that some of these were of Anatolian stock.

The languages in cuneiform are termed Old Anatolian in contradistinction to New Anatolian which refers to languages recorded in classical times. The language of the hieroglyphs bridges the gap between the two.

HELLENIC

This branch is represented only by Greek. The famous works of the ancient or classical period are all written in regional forms of Greek, there being as yet no single standard for the whole country. Even more diverse are the inscriptional records which tend to follow local speech very closely. The dialects are variously classified; we here distinguish three main types: Aeolic, Doric, and Ionic with its offshoot Attic, the dialect of Athens and its immediate hinterland, which became the most influential form. From this emerged in the late fourth century B.C. the *koínē* or 'common' language of the Hellenistic Age. This is th; language of the New Testament and was the spoken standard when Greek became the lingua franca of the Near East. Much literature, however, was composed in an archaic or atticising form of the *koínē* and this austere style continued to be written, with variations, until the last century. It was soon very different from the evolving living language, which during the Middle Ages is usually known as Byzantine Greek. Modern Greek may be said to begin in the tenth century. Greek was early spread by colonisation notably to Sicily and southern Italy, where chiefly near Lecce something like 25,000 persons still speak as their patois a form of Greek.

It goes without saying that, by reason of its immensely rich records beginning with the Homeric poems *c.* 800 B.C., Greek is of the highest value for comparative Indo-European philology. Excavations at Crete and on the mainland especially at Pylos and

Mycenae have, in this century, brought to light over 4,000 clay
tablets inscribed with two forms of linear writing, A and B. In
1952, a decipherment of the latter was published, the language
being interpreted as an archaic form of Greek and named Mycen-
ean. The texts are chiefly inventories and date from 1500 to 1200
B.C. The syllabic system of writing, as deciphered, is so imperfect
and the material itself so problematic, that these early texts are
scarcely of value for comparative philology.

There are ample traces of a pre-Greek population in the place
names and in the ordinary vocabulary of Greek. The Greeks
themselves called these people Pelasgians. There is positive evidence of early connections with Asia Minor and future archaeological research may well throw light on the affinities of the Pelasgians.

ITALIC

The linguistic contours of Italy in the early period are highly
complex. Venetic was spoken in the north-east, Celtic in the Po
Valley. Between the Celts and the Tyrrhenian Sea lay the Ligur-
ians, of unknown origins. To the south were the non-Indo-European Etruscans, whose territory stretched from the sea to the
Apennines as far as the Tiber. East of them lived the Umbrians
and related peoples; south of the Tiber the Latins inhabited
Latium. The Samnites, whose language was Oscan, disputed the
southern half of the peninsula with Messapians and Greeks, immigrants of long standing. A people known as Siculi, of uncertain
connections, lived in Sicily side by side with influential colonies
of Greeks. Sardinia and Corsica seem to have held autochthonous
populations of unknown stock.

It was the speech of the minor province of Latium which was
destined to supersede all the multifarious languages of Italy and
many more beside. Latin is seen to have been originally one of a
group of closely related dialects, usually termed Latin-Faliscan
after the better known ones. This small group has much in common
with a larger group called Oscan-Umbrian. Both these latter languages are fairly well known from long inscriptions, the former at
any rate was an important language apparently having a standardised literary norm. The two groups are traditionally linked together as Italic, with the implication that they are members of a
single branch of Indo-European. But it is now argued that the
facts do not warrant such an implication, for while it is true that
the groups share many features, there are also a number of differ-

ences which seem more fundamental than the similarities. It is therefore possible that the similarities are relatively recent and due to the later co-existence in Italy of two originally distinct branches of Indo-European.

The Latin language everywhere followed the unprecedented expansion of Roman power. By the beginning of the Christian era, most of Italy had become thoroughly latinised. It is believed that by then Venetic, Celtic, Ligurian, Etruscan, Umbrian, Messapian, etc. were all extinct or moribund. Oscan may have survived a little longer, Greek certainly did, for it was still quite prominent in the Middle Ages and is even yet not extinct (p. 39). Carried beyond Italy, Latin established itself permanently in the Iberian peninsula, Gaul, and part of the Balkans. Until towards the end of the Middle Ages, Latin was the chief medium of law, administration and scholarship in Western Europe generally. Its position was particularly strong in those countries where vernacular forms of Latin were spoken. The cultivation of Latin necessarily meant a corresponding neglect of the vernaculars, all of which are recorded only from a relatively late date.

The principal modern descendants of Latin are Italian (recorded since the tenth century), Spanish (eleventh century), Portuguese and Catalan (both late twelfth century), French (ninth century), Rumanian (early sixteenth century). Though today reduced to the level of a spoken dialect, Provençal was an important medieval language with texts beginning in the tenth century. Minor forms include Romaunsch in south-east Switzerland, printed in as many as five divergent dialects, with an isolated early text from the twelfth century, Sardinian, normally only a spoken language, known since the eleventh century, and Dalmatian, once spoken on the eastern seaboard of the Adriatic, but extinct since the close of the last century. As a result of colonisation, creolised languages have come into existence. Several derive from French, of which the most important is Haitian, now often seen in print. Other creoles are based on Spanish and Portuguese. One of these, Papiamentu, combines elements of both. This is the colloquial language of Curaçao and Aruba; it has attained literary status and flourishes in journalism of all kinds.

CELTIC

The Celts are first mentioned in the fifth century B.C., when they are described as occupying territory from the Pillars of Hercules to the upper reaches of the Danube. Although a numerous and powerful people in antiquity, the continental Celts have left no literary records. The best known language is that of Gaul which survived into the fifth century A.D., but its records are only glosses, names and short inscriptions. Gaulish was very close to British spoken at the same time in Britain—Tacitus speaks of them as being óne language. This division of Celtic, often known as Brythonic or P-Celtic, lives on today in Welsh and Breton, the latter established by colonists from south-west Britain from the fifth to the seventh centuries A.D. The earliest monuments in these languages are glosses and a few short passages going back to the ninth century. Ample literary texts appear from about 1100, the Welsh tradition being by far the richer one. Cornish, closely related to Breton, became extinct about 1800, leaving a modest late medieval literature and a twelfth-century glossary.

A second division of Celtic, Goidelic or Q-Celtic, is first found in Ireland, but from the end of the fourth century A.D. was carried by conquest to Scotland and the Isle of Man. Speakers of this sort of Celtic call it Gaelic. Two types are distinguished: Irish and Scottish (or Erse), with Manx as a special development of the latter. The earliest Irish occurs in the Ogham inscriptions from the fourth to the eighth centuries. The first manuscript records are extensive glossaries, the earliest composed in the sixth century. The bulk of the vast corpus of Irish literature dates from the middle and early modern period, i.e. from 900 to 1650. Scottish and Manx Gaelic have no ancient documents; the former has been known only from the fifteenth, the latter from the sixteenth century. Manx, moribund since about 1870, must now be regarded as extinct.

In spite of the relative lateness of significant records, the Celtic languages, especially Old Irish, retain many archaic features of great interest and, taken together, these languages preserve a vast amount of Indo-European vocabulary. Insular Celtic appears to have been much influenced by the speech of the pre-Celtic inhabitants of Great Britain. Of such were, for instance, the Picts of the Scottish Highlands who spoke a language, now believed to have been non-Indo-European, until perhaps the tenth century A.D., when they were finally absorbed by the Gaels. The syntax of Gaelic in particular contains many exotic features.

There are, as yet, no means of determining when the Celtic speakers first reached Britain, but it is known that P-Celts were still moving across the channel into South-East Britain just before the Roman conquest of Gaul.

GERMANIC

The Germanic peoples were well known to the ancient world, but with one exception their languages are not found in literary texts until the Middle Ages. The exception is Gothic, preserved mainly in considerable fragments of a translation of the Bible made about 350 in Moesia (northern Bulgaria). The Goths are known to have reached their historical seats in eastern Europe as the result of migrations from Scandinavia, beginning perhaps in the first century B.C. Subsequently, a major part of the Gothic people moved into Italy and Spain. The language of the Goths is often described as East Germanic. It was in the main extinct by 700, but an enclave survived until modern times in the Crimea. A few words of Crimean Gothic were taken down in the sixteenth century.

Gothic is closely related to Scandinavian. Early Scandinavian is shadowly attested, in remarkably archaic language, in runic inscriptions beginning in the third century. On the other hand, literary Scandinavian is not older than the ninth century and is much advanced by comparison with runic. It seems that linguistic evolution was quickened in the Viking Age. At this time the language was carried to colonies overseas, but only Iceland and Faroe could maintain their Scandinavian character permanently. The language from the ninth century to 1500 is called Old Norse and is the vehicle of an extraordinarily extensive literature, most of it composed or written in Iceland, hence the term Old Icelandic. By the close of the Old Norse period, the modern Scandinavian languages have clearly emerged. They are: Swedish, Danish, Norwegian, Faroese, Icelandic. The first three are very similar, but the island languages are more divergent and also more archaic, Modern Icelandic in particular being still close to its medieval ancestor. The Scandinavian languages are classified as North Germanic.

South of the Baltic were other Germanic speakers whose languages appear in monuments from the eighth century onwards. These were the ancestors of the present-day Germans whose dialects fall into two moieties, the Low German of the north and the High German of the centre and south. The literary remains of the old period (to 1100) are fairly extensive, at least as far as High German is concerned, but much traditional vocabulary is not attested until the middle period (1100 to 1500) or even the modern period. By the end of the Middle Ages there had arisen in this area three literary languages: High German, Low German and Dutch (in Belgium called Flemish), the last being a local development at the western end of the Low German area. During the modern period High German replaced Low German, first as the literary medium and then largely as the spoken medium, too, so that today Low German is a vanishing patois. We note two further modern languages: Yiddish, the language of the eastern European Jews, which arose out of High German about the beginning of modern times, and Afrikaans, a more or less creolised form of Dutch which came into being at the Cape in the second half of the seventeenth century and subsequently spread with the Boers throughout South Africa.

Closely allied to German, especially Low German, is Frisian, its texts going back to the tenth century. The language survives today in the Dutch province of Friesland (West Frisian) and in a colonial form in Schleswig (North Frisian). English is of the same stuff as Frisian and German, with them forming the West Germanic division. Brought to Britain about the middle of the fifth century, English at first retained its traditional character, as seen in the ample records of Old English (Anglo-Saxon) from the late seventh to the eleventh centuries, but after the Norman conquest the vocabulary became heavily gallicised. Owing to this and other insular developments, English has grown very unlike the genetically related languages on the continent, while these, remaining in close contact with each other, have tended to develop on similar lines. The spread of English overseas in the age of colonisation led to the development of creole languages with an English base. Examples are Krio in Sierra Leone and Sranan in Dutch Guyana.

Evidence points to southern Scandinavia as the most likely homeland of Germanic. It is distinguished from other branches of the Indo-European family by far-reaching consonant changes, usually attributed to substratum influence, p. 123. Until about the Birth of Christ, Germanic may be regarded as comprising a single language.

BALTIC AND SLAVONIC

The Baltic group falls into two divisions embracing three languages: (West) Old Prussian, (East) Lithuanian, Latvian. The first was spoken between the mouth of the Vistula and the Memel, but has been extinct since about 1700. It is imperfectly known chiefly from a few short religious texts translated from German about the middle of the sixteenth century. The others are still flourishing languages; their oldest texts also date from the sixteenth century. The language of these texts may be termed Old Lithuanian, etc., though of course the languages have not changed greatly since then. Evidence of place names shows that Baltic dialects were once spoken as far east as Moscow. Even though they are only known from so recent a date, the Baltic languages, in particular Old Prussian and Lithuanian, are quite extraordinarily archaic, and therefore of first-rate significance for Indo-European philology. From them outlines of Primitive Baltic may easily be reconstructed.

The Slavonic tribes appeared earlier on the historical scene. In their original east European homeland they were, it is true, scarcely discernible to the Classical World, but their remarkable expansion from the beginning of the fourth century made them a well-known race.

Slavonic has been written since the ninth century. The earliest texts (gospels, liturgy) were composed in a dialect of Bulgarian, and this language, Old Bulgarian, was adopted as the official medium of the Orthodox Church in other countries; hence it is also known as Old Church Slavonic, sometimes simply as Old Slavonic. To be sure this language did not long preserve its purity. After the end of the eleventh century it becomes subject to a degree of geographical variation, so that one distinguishes, e.g. Russian, Serbian and Bulgarian types. In the orthodox countries, Church Slavonic was also the medium for literature in the widest sense down to modern times. This explains the paucity of medieval texts in the real vernaculars of the countries concerned.

The Slavonic languages fall into three divisions; the following are the literary forms in use today: (East) Russian proper or Great Russian, Ukrainian, formerly called Little Russian or Ruthenian, White or Belo-Russian, (West) Polish, Czech, Slovak, Upper and Lower Sorbian, sometimes known as Lusatian or Wendish, (South) Slovene, Serbo-Croatian, Bulgarian, Macedonian. Polabian, belonging to the Western branch, was the language of the Slavs on the Middle Elbe. It was superseded by German in the early eighteenth century, but is known in outline from glossaries and short texts. Another West Slavonic language is Kashubian; it has, however, now sunk to the level of a patois, its speakers employing Polish as their literary language.

One postulates a Primitive Slavonic language of the same nature as Primitive Baltic, from which the recorded Slavonic languages are descended. Old Church Slavonic is not far removed from

Primitive Slavonic and when first written was doubtless readily understood in all Slavonic-speaking lands. Although Slavonic speech today is considerably differentiated, the underlying genius is immediately recognisable. It may be stated, too, that the difference between some of the literary languages is not great, e.g. between Bulgarian and Macedonian, Czech and Slovak, or the two forms of Sorbian. By the same token, all the East Slavonic languages are very similar. Indeed, until modern times, Slavonic was essentially a dialect continuum, much as Aryan is in India to this day.

Between Baltic and Slavonic there are many similarities not only in vocabulary, but also in grammar. This led to the concept of a single Balto-Slavonic branch. Today it is more usual to think in terms of two independent branches of Indo-European drawn together by mutual influences as a result of their having occupied adjacent areas from time immemorial.

4

PRELIMINARIES

It goes without saying that the Indo-Europeanist is especially interested in the oldest forms of the languages he deals with since these naturally show a more archaic structure than the succeeding stages and are closer to the parent language. On the other hand, the subsequent history of the separate branches of the family or of individual languages is not without importance on a number of counts. It sometimes happens, for instance, that only a limited amount of vocabulary is preserved in documents written in the oldest forms of a given language. A case in point is Old Irish. By contrast with Middle Irish, it is from the point of view of its grammatical structure remarkably archaic, but since the number of texts in Old Irish is restricted, a large portion of ancient Irish vocabulary, a good deal of it Common Celtic, is not found until the copious records of the middle period. To be sure, much of the lexicon so preserved occurs in a more advanced form than it had in the old period. It is, however, usually possible to reconstruct its archaic shape and then the material can be used for comparative purposes with the same certainty as if it had actually been attested in the oldest texts.

Another example is Gothic, invaluable as the most anciently recorded Germanic language. As we know, Gothic is extinct and Biblical fragments its only monument. All the same, enough has been preserved to enable grammars to be written which reveal the essential structure of Germanic speech at this early date. On the other hand, only a small part of the traditional vocabulary is met with in the Gothic texts. More is not forthcoming until the appearance of documents in the Old West Germanic languages, and these in turn are supplemented by the profuse records of Old Norse. Although these languages are, grammatically speaking, in general considerably less archaic than Gothic, it is to them that one must constantly turn for lexical information lacking in Gothic. Since so much in our subject depends on etymology, the value of traditional material, even when recorded late, becomes obvious.

The study of the development of individual languages, i.e. their historical philology, leads to certain factual conclusions about linguistic evolution generally which are relevant to any discussion of the prehistorical stages of a language. It is well to bear such conclusions in mind when considering the possible nature of the parent Indo-European language. One important general consideration, for example, is the speed of linguistic change. The rate of change is seen to be more rapid at some periods than at others. Not surprisingly, changes are quicker in unsettled communities than in more stable ones. We noticed above (p. 43) that the upheavals of the Viking period ushered in far-reaching changes in the Norse language. During this period, Iceland was colonised and the Norse of the colonists there became appropriately known as Icelandic. When the days of the Vikings were over, Iceland sank into obscurity; it was remote and little disturbed by outsiders. The Icelandic language has remained so conservative that literature composed nearly a thousand years ago is, with the exception of a handful of obsolete words and phrases, immediately understood by a modern reader. How different is the position in England! To the Englishman of the present day the language of this country as it was a thousand years ago is quite incomprehensible, it has the character of a foreign tongue. We recall that Old English is separated from us by the Norman conquest, to mention only the most outstanding event to have provoked vast changes in our language.

We would add, too, that the rate of linguistic change is quicker among peoples who have no written language, for a literary form, which implies some sort of standard, exercises a stabilising influence, especially if literacy is widespread. In our reference to the remarkable conservatism of Icelandic (above), it would have been proper to add that the Icelanders have, it seems, always been a highly literate people. They created their own national literature in Old Icelandic times and have continued to draw on this heritage down to the present time.

Literary language not only exercises a stabilising influence on the spoken word, it also acts as a unifying force. Indeed, in most recent times literary standards, disseminated by such mass media as the press and radio, have in several countries created nation-wide spoken standards, before which dialect speech has either vanished or is rapidly waning. Elsewhere dialect is the most characteristic form of speech, in illiterate communities it is the only form. If we wish to reconstruct the prehistoric stages of the various branches of the Indo-European family or of their common ancestor, Primitive Indo-European, it is necessary to bear very much in mind that we will be dealing not with unified standard languages, but in every case with a cluster of dialects, as the evidence of the records themselves frequently confirms.

The history of known languages also gives evidence about the precise nature of linguistic changes. It is important for our present purpose to observe that the linguistic system at any given time contains petrified survivals of older systems. Take the English verbal forms *was, were*. They are unique in the language today, for every other verb has only one preterite form for both singular and plural. But, in fact, the distinction shown by *was, were* was at one time characteristic of scores of primary verbs. Present-day standard English has a single pronoun for the second person: *you*. Were it not for the dialects and the literary tradition or the possibility of comparison with related languages, it would never be known that the English had once used *thou* for the singular and that *you* was originally confined to the plural. Similarly in matters of pronunciation. The old-fashioned spelling of English bears witness to the one-time presence of sounds no longer current in the standard language. An outstanding example is silent *gh*, as in *night*, once the spirant [χ].

All such inferences as may be drawn from the history of known languages have to be taken into account when analysing the earliest records of a given language. This, too, will contain irregular features which may be relics of an older, but this time unrecorded, stage. As often as not, the problem is one of interpretation, and interpretations may vary from 'certain' to 'possible, but not proved'. To mention the case of Eng. *was, were* again, it would, on the strength of contemporary usage alone, be permissible to suggest that the forms could be survivals of a former (but of course unknown) verbal pattern, though it would not be possible to prove such a conjecture.

5

FROM LATIN TO MODERN ROMANCE

It has been shown in Chapter 2 how, during the second half of the sixteenth century, Latin at last came to be recognised as the parent of the living Romance (or Neo-Latin) languages. This discovery was not only significant in itself, it was also of consequence in that it introduced into linguistics the important concept of the family tree. This concept Hickes was later to apply to his classification of the Germanic languages, when he (erroneously, as we now know) derived the living languages from the extinct Gothic. He did not realise that the common ancestor of all the Germanic languages, including Gothic, was the unrecorded Primitive Germanic. Finally, Jones in his epoch-making statement on the affinities of Sanskrit, Greek, Latin and the rest, invoked the same concept

A. D.   L   A   T   I   N

            P R O T O - R O M A N C E

10th cent.

20th cent.   Italian   Spanish   French

when he spoke of a common source from which the languages mentioned must be supposed to have sprung, i.e. from the prehistoric language now termed Primitive Indo-European.

We may now consider further the nature of the relationship between Latin and its descendants. It will suffice for our immediate purpose to refer to three of these: Italian, Spanish, French. We set up the family tree (see p. 50), using dotted lines to indicate the preliterary periods of the modern languages, which imperceptibly merge into the spoken (i.e. Vulgar) Latin of the early Christian centuries.

PHONETICS

Latin used two related verbs with the meaning 'to sing': the primary formation *canere* and the secondary, originally iterative or intensive, *cantare*. The latter must have replaced the former in Vulgar Latin since the modern Romance forms are all derived from it, thus It. *cantare*, Sp. *cantar*, Fr. *chanter*. Italian is seen to be conservative, preserving the Latin infinitive unchanged, but not so Spanish and French. Spanish has discarded the final vowel. So has French, but this language has gone much further, changing the original termination into *-er*. The change is, indeed, greater than the spelling would suggest, for the actual pronunciation is [e]; we conclude that French spelling at this point is archaic. Orthographical convention also explains the presence of the letter *n*, for here again French has innovated, original [n] having been lost in the modern language, though evidence of its former existence is visible in the nasalisation of the preceding vowel [ã]. Finally, Lat. *c* has become Fr. *ch*, i.e. [k] > [ʃ]. There were undoubtedly intermediary stages in this change. Lat. [k] would first be palatalised and then become a fricative [kj], whence by a change of articulation [tʃ]. This stage is faithfully preserved in Eng. *chant*, borrowed from French in the fourteenth century. The modern French [ʃ] is a subsequent reduction of this sound.

In spoken Latin, *caballus* 'horse' replaced the usual classical term *equus*, hence It. *cavallo*, Sp. *caballo*, Fr. *cheval*. Thus none of the derivative languages preserves the Latin nom.sg. termination. But again the Italian and Spanish forms are more conservative than the French.

It is evident that there is some regularity in these changes. On the strength of what has been seen so far, one could formulate a sound law to the effect that Lat. [k] in initial position before [a] is preserved in Italian and Spanish, but becomes [ʃ] in French.

Other examples at once confirm this, as Lat. *carus* 'dear': It., Sp. *caro*, Fr. *cher*; Lat. *capra* 'goat': It. *capra*, Sp. *cabra*, Fr. *chèvre*. Conversely, one may argue that if a French word, regularly descended from Vulgar Latin, begins with *ch*, then its Latin prototype can be presumed to have had initial *c* followed by *a*.

Further laws describe the developments of Latin initial *c* before other sounds. Before *e* or *i*, its fate has been different in each of the three derivative languages. None retain the sound of Latin *c*, i.e. [k], though all of them preserve it in the orthography, as Lat. *cervus* 'stag': It. *cervo*, Sp. *ciervo*, Fr. *cerf* and Lat. *cinque* (< classical *quinque*) 'five': It. *cinque*, Sp. *cinco*, Fr. *cinq*—the pronunciations of the vernacular languages are It. [tʃ], Sp. [θ], Fr. [s], cf. p. 18. Before *o* or *u*, however, [k] remains unaltered, as Lat. *corona* 'crown': It., Sp. *corona*, Fr. *couronne*, and Lat. *currere* 'to run': It. *correre*, Sp. *correr*, Fr. *courir*. Initial *c* can also occur before *l* or *r*. In the case of the latter there is no change, thus Lat. *credere* 'to believe': It. *credere*, Sp. *creer*, Fr. *croire*, but the former is much less stable, thus Lat. *clavis* 'key': It. *chiave*, Sp. *llave*, Fr. *clef* (or *clé*). As far as the initial consonant cluster is concerned only French has remained conservative; in Italian the product is [ki], in Spanish [ʎ], i.e. palatal *l*. Lat. *c* is found in other environments, e.g. between vowels, as *amicus* 'friend': It. *amico*, Sp. *amigo*, Fr. *ami*, or *focus* 'fire' (originally 'hearth' replacing classical *ignis*): It. *fuoco*, Sp. *fuego*, Fr. *feu*. Again, the changes follow definite patterns.

An examination of the whole vast corpus of material available in Latin and the Neo-Latin languages reveals in great detail the evolution of the latter which has taken place essentially according to laws of the sort indicated above. It should be remembered, of course, that many of the correspondences recognised in Romance philology are based on highly complicated laws, and are by no means necessarily self-evident. This is particularly the case with French, where the phonetic changes have generally been the most far-reaching, as our examples have shown.

Nevertheless, with such correspondences as have been quoted above, it is often possible to infer from a word in one language its cognates in the others. Given It. *chiamare* 'to call', one could reconstruct Lat. *clamare* as the prototype and Sp. *llamar*, Fr. *clamer* as the parallel forms in the sister languages. It goes without saying that such cognates do in fact exist. On the other hand, it not infrequently happens that a postulated form is missing from one or other of the languages concerned. In the case of a derivative language this will be due to the word having been replaced by some synonym before the beginning of the vernacular records or to the fact that the word was probably never current in the speech of that part of Romania (cf. under 'Lexical Changes' below). But if the postulated form is absent from the parent tongue itself, the blame must be laid on the meagre records of Vulgar Latin. This language was never a recognised written medium. Its forms are known solely from solecisms in texts otherwise composed in literary Latin or from lists of common errors drawn up by the grammarians. As may be supposed, artless inscriptions and graffiti are among the best sources of Vulgar Latin. In point of fact only a minor portion of the vocabulary is attested in genuinely Vulgar form, though most of what is lacking can be inferred from literary Latin. When the exact prototype is missing altogether in the written sources, it can usually be reconstructed. For instance, a Neo-Latin word for 'needle', seen in It. *agucchia*, Sp. *aguja*, Fr. *aiguille*, presupposes Vulgar Lat. **acucula*, clearly a diminutive of the normal literary word *acus*.

It should be mentioned that Vulgar Latin abandoned the system of long and short vowels known to Classical Latin. In the latter, vowel length was etymological and phonemic: nom. *capra* 'goat', abl. *caprā*. But in Vulgar Latin quantity distinctions gave way to quality distinctions. The old long vowels were now pronounced closed, the old short ones open; long and short *a*, however, were reduced to a single phoneme. Lastly, the diphthongs of the classical language were monophthongised. Such is the basis from which the Neo-Latin vowel systems have evolved. Broadly speaking, the place of the accent has tended to remain unchanged, as exemplified in Italian and Spanish, but innovations in French intonation have today quite obscured the traditional stress patterns.

The operation of the regular sound laws may be disturbed by various fortuitous developments. One of the more significant is that known as dissimilation. Consider Lat. *arbor* 'tree' and the modern forms It. *albero*, Sp. *árbol*, Fr. *arbre*. The latter are obviously continuations of the Latin word, but the Italian and Spanish forms contain an *l* instead of an *r*. Unlike the Romans, the speakers of Italian and Spanish at some point felt the need to avoid the repetition of the consonant *r*. This they achieved by substituting the phonetically related, but acoustically distinct *l*, the Italians altering the first *r*, the Spaniards the second. At first sight, the French would seem to have tolerated the original arrangement, but this is not entirely so, for *abre* is commonly found in dialect and is a spelling met with in older texts. In other words, in some French at any rate, the first *r* was dropped. A parallel case is seen in the Vulgar Lat. *cinque* dissimilated from *quinque* (above).

The Neo-Latin languages under consideration have been attested since the Middle Ages and have, on the average, something like a millennium of recorded history. During this long period they have themselves changed considerably. It follows that the oldest forms, such as may be found in the earliest records, will be of particular importance for comparative purposes, especially when they are appreciably closer to the parent tongue than the present-day forms. Fr. *veau* 'calf' seems a long way from Lat. *vitellus*, but Old Fr. *veël* (cf. the fourteenth-century English borrowing *veal*) points unmistakably towards it. An original *l* is there and a consonant must have disappeared between the (separately pronounced) vowels. The closely related, but phonologically more conservative Provençal *vedel* preserves this consonant and thus represents a stage preceding the Old French form. And so the wide gap between the Modern French and its Latin source is effectively bridged.

MORPHOLOGY

Sparse as they are, the records of Vulgar Latin are sufficient to show how the morphological categories of the classical tongue were drastically reshaped in the spoken language of the early centuries of the Christian era. We shall refer to the fate of the nominal declension and to changes in the verbal system.

NOUNS

Phonetic changes prepared the way for the ultimate breakdown of the classical declension. Final *m* tended to disappear early, not surprisingly since it was already ignored in classical scansion. As a consequence the accusative and ablative often became identical, for example in the third declension singular: *monte* 'mountain'. With the loss of the classical vowel quantities (p. 53) the first, fourth and fifth declensions were likewise affected: *capra* 'goat', *motu* 'movement', *re* 'thing'. Unambiguous prepositions became more and more necessary; the prepositions in their turn then hastened the collapse of the traditional case system. Since possession could now be indicated by *de*, there was no further need for an inflected genitive. The dative could be circumscribed by *ad* and was eventually discarded as superfluous. The plurals kept pace with the singulars. Isolated relics of the lost cases could survive here and there, but by the fifth century Vulgar Latin nouns had only two functional cases: nominative and accusative. The declension of adjectives took the same course.

As the case system declined, the number of declensions contracted also. Already in the classical period there is evidence that nouns of the fifth declension tended to be drawn into the numerically stronger first declension, hence *materia* beside *materies* 'timber'. The continuance of this process of attraction in Vulgar Latin led to the virtual extinction of fifth-declension forms. Nouns of the small fourth declension were, in the main, readily absorbed into the second. The third declension preserved its identity, but largely generalised a parisyllabic pattern with nom.sg. in *-is*. Vulgar Latin had thus substantially three declensions:

	I	II	III
Sg.nom.	*capra* goat	*caballus* horse	*montis* mountain
acc.	*capra*	*caballu*	*monte*
Pl.nom.	*capre*	*caballi*	*montes*
acc.	*capras*	*caballos*	*montes*

By this time, too, the neuter gender had mostly disappeared. It was mainly absorbed by the masculine, a tendency detected in spoken Latin as far back as Plautus.

Then, in many places, the last case distinction broke down. The accusative form usually proved stronger, hence it is from this case that the great majority of Neo-Latin words are descended, cf. It. *capra, cavallo, monte*, Sp. *cabra, caballo, monte*. The accusative was often generalised in the plural, too, as in the often quoted tombstone inscription which runs *hic quescunt duas matres, duas filias, numero tres facunt* 'here lie two mothers, two daughters, that makes three'. Spanish has followed this principle, e.g. *cabras, caballos, montes*. But in other areas *s* was lost and vocalic endings came to indicate the plural, as It. *capre, cavalli, monti*. In Spain and Italy these developments were completed before the first vernacular monuments, but in France the two-case system persisted until the thirteenth century, so that it is amply attested in Old French. The three declensions of Vulgar Latin are, however, reduced to two:

	I	II	
Sg.nom.	*chievre*	*chevaus*	*monz* ($z = $[ts])
acc.	*chievre*	*cheval*	*mont*
Pl.nom.	*chievres*	*cheval*	*mont*
acc.	*chievres*	*chevaus*	*monz*

Subsequently the accusative forms were generalised, hence later French sg. *chèvre, cheval, mont,* pl. *chèvres, chevaux, monts.*

VERBS

The verb of the classical language was very considerably reshaped in Vulgar Latin. But the changes were not so sweeping as in the case of the noun, for a number of synthetic tenses were retained. The typological strength of these may be judged from the fact that new analytical developments were sometimes re-assimilated into the synthetic system, as follows. The Classical Latin future *cantabo* 'I shall sing' was everywhere replaced in the spoken style by periphrases, most commonly by *cantare habeo* originally 'I have to sing'. But in the derivative languages the infinitive and auxiliary are seen to have coalesced to give an entirely new synthetic tense:

	VLat.	It.	Sp.	Fr.
Sg.1	*cantare habeo*	*canterò*	*cantaré*	*chanterai*
2	*cantare habes*	*canterai*	*cantarás*	*chanteras*
3	*cantare habet*	*canterà*	*cantará*	*chantera*
Pl.1	*cantare habemus*	*canteremo*	*cantaremos*	*chanterons*
2	*cantare habetis*	*canterete*	*cantaréis*	*chanterez*
3	*cantare habent*	*canteranno*	*cantarán*	*chanteront*

By a similar process of agglutination VLat. (Italy) *cantare habui* or (Iberia, Gaul) *cantare habeba* originally 'I had to sing' evolved into the synthetic conditional of the modern languages, a tense without formal, or syntactical, parallel in Classical Latin: It. *canterei*; Sp. *cantaría*, Fr. *chanterais*, etc.

The following traditional synthetic tenses are kept in all the modern languages under consideration: present, imperfect and perfect indicative, present and pluperfect subjunctive. The syntactical use of the tenses in the modern languages need not, however, correspond in every case to Latin usage. In particular, the old pluperfect subjunctive has a different range of functions, having become the general past subjunctive; in French this tense is now but little used. The morphological development of the surviving tenses is illustrated in the comparative tables opposite. Spanish also preserves the future perfect: VLat. *cantaro*, Sp. *cantare*, etc., and the pluperfect indicative: VLat. *cantaram*, Sp. *cantara*, etc. The Spanish forms are, however, used as subjunctives, the so-called future imperfect and conditional imperfect respectively.

	VLat.	It.	Sp.	Fr.
Pres. indic.				
Sg.1	canto	canto	canto	chante
2	cantas	canti	cantas	chantes
3	cantat	canta	canta	chante
Pl.1	cantamus	cantiamo	cantamos	chantons
2	cantatis	cantate	cantáis	chantez
3	cantant	cantano	cantan	chantent
Imperf. indic.				
Sg.1	cantaba	cantavo	cantaba	chantais
2	cantabas	cantavi	cantabas	chantais
3	cantabat	cantava	cantaba	chantait
Pl.1	cantabamus	cantavamo	cantábamos	chantions
2	cantabatis	cantavate	cantabais	chantiez
3	cantabant	cantavano	cantaban	chantaient
Perf. indic.				
Sg.1	cantai	cantai	canté	chantai
2	cantasti	cantasti	cantaste	chantas
3	cantaut	cantò	cantó	chanta
Pl.1	cantamus	cantammo	cantamos	chantâmes
2	cantastis	cantaste	cantasteis	chantâtes
3	cantarunt	cantarono	cantaron	chantèrent
Pres. subj.				
Sg.1	cante	canti	cante	chante
2	cantes	canti	cantes	chantes
3	cantet	canti	cante	chante
Pl.1	cantemus	cantiamo	cantemos	chantions
2	cantetis	cantiate	cantéis	chantiez
3	cantent	cantino	canten	chantent
Pluperf. subj.				
Sg.1	cantasse	cantassi	cantase	chantasse
2	cantasses	cantassi	cantases	chantasses
3	cantasset	cantasse	cantase	chantât
Pl.1	cantassemus	cantassimo	cantásemos	chantassions
2	cantassetis	cantaste	cantaseis	chantassiez
3	cantassent	cantassero	cantasen	chantassent

Throughout the period of their recorded history the verbal forms of Italian and Spanish have generally remained conservative. French has innovated much more, but the archaic spelling of the modern forms suffices to give an approximate idea of the

sounds of the medieval stage. And here and there, in all the languages concerned, forms closer to Vulgar Latin may be found in
the older records. Thus final *t* of the pres.indic.sg.3 may be preserved as such in Old French and occurs in the oldest Spanish as *d*.
Besides standard Italian imperf.indic.sg.1 *cantavo*, the older language has the phonologically regular *cantava*, also in modern use
regionally. The standard form has evidently arisen after the analogy
of other tenses where the sg.1 ends in *o*, namely pres.indic. *canto*,
fut. *canterò*. Another analogical development is the French perf.
indic.pl.1 *chantâmes* (OFr. *chanta(s)mes*) following pl.2 *chantâtes*
(OFr. *chantastes*).

The imperative survives in the 2nd person only, as follows:

	VLat.	It.	Sp.	Fr.
Sg.	canta	canta	canta	chante
Pl.	cantate	cantate	cantad	chantez

As our examples show, the inherited system of verbal inflexions
is well preserved in Neo-Latin. Only in Modern French has phonetic attrition obscured many once distinct terminations, e.g.
pres.sg.1 *chante* (OFr. *chant*), 2 *chantes*, 3 *chante*, pl.3 *chantent*.
Though the spelling still largely reflects the actual pronunciation
of the medieval language, these forms are today all pronounced
alike. As a consequence, pronouns came into regular use and
were eventually generalised. In Italian and Spanish, on the contrary, where the distinct verbal endings have been much better
preserved, the pronouns are still used sparingly. For unambiguous
or non-emphatic contexts the verbal form alone is sufficient, just
as it was in Latin.

In the transition from Classical to Vulgar Latin, the number of
conjugations was, broadly speaking, reduced from four to three.
The first and fourth have kept their identity down to the present
day, e.g. Lat. *cantare* 'to sing', *dormire* 'to sleep': It. *cantare*,
dormire, Sp. *cantar*, *dormir*, Fr. *chanter*, *dormir*, but the second and
third tended to be confused. There were already certain correspondences between these two classes, which were increased with
the loss of the old system of vowel quantity. Forms might, however, still be distinguished by the position of the accent, and many
of these survive in the derivative languages. The distinction in this
respect between Lat. *debēre* 'to owe' (2nd conj., stressed on second
syllable) and *vendere* 'to sell' (3rd conj., stressed on first syllable)
is retained in the accentuation of It. *dovére, véndere*, and in the

different treatment of the endings seen in Fr. *devoir, vendre*. In Spanish, on the other hand, the two conjugations have quite fallen together: *deber, vender*, both with final stress.

The deponent verbs were eliminated in Vulgar Latin. Likewise the inflected forms of the passive disappeared, being replaced by the already existing analytical forms, which had changed their meanings, perfect and pluperfect becoming present and past respectively. This is the situation in the modern languages: contrast Cl. Lat. *laudatus sum* 'I have been praised' with Fr. *je suis loué* 'I am praised'. The participle also took on an active meaning. Classical phrases of the type *capram comparatam habeo* lit. 'I have a bought goat' were syntactically re-evaluated as 'I have bought a goat'. In other words, *comparatam* was now felt as belonging to the verb, not the noun. In this way, a new active periphrasis arose and led to that remarkable proliferation of analytical past tenses which sharply distinguishes the Neo-Latin languages from their common parent.

Other nominal parts of the verb were partly lost. The present infinitive remained: Lat. *cantare*, Fr. *chanter*, but the perfect was replaced by a circumlocution: *habere cantatum*, Fr. *avoir chanté*. The supine gave way to the gerund, *facile cantatu* being expressed *facile ad cantandum*. Then this construction in its turn declined and one said *facile ad cantare*, Fr. *facile à chanter*. Formally speaking the gerund does, however, continue into Romance. Having fused with the gerundive (Cl. Lat. *cantandus*) it has changed its function to become the regular present participle: It., Sp. *cantando*, Fr. *chantant*. The original participle (Cl. Lat. *cantans, -tis*) was thus forced out of the verbal system, but it often survives though only as an adjective. In French, phonetic evolution removed any formal distinction between inherited gerund and present participle, but the other languages keep them apart, e.g. Sp. *estaba corriendo* 'has just been running' (participle, old gerund), *agua corriente* 'running water' (adjective, old participle). The future participle of Classical Latin (*cantaturus*) vanished with the rest of the traditional future system.

SYNTAX

The sweeping morphological changes outlined in the previous section, involving as they did the collapse of the case system and many innovations in the structure of the verb, inevitably necessitated syntactical arrangements of a new order. It may be safely inferred that, as far as Vulgar Latin is concerned, the Neo-Latin new look was already there in essentials. If, therefore, a passage of literary Latin is compared with versions in modern Romance, one can obtain, by proxy, a fair notion of the nature of the syntactical developments which were at least well under way in Vulgar Latin. At the same time, of course, the Neo-Latin texts well illustrate the mutual affinities of the languages in question.

We take a passage (Gen.xxxix.6–12) from the Vulgate followed by renderings in the modern languages. While not classical, the style of the Latin is straightforward and unpretentious. It readily permits direct comparison between the highly synthetic parent tongue and its more analytically constructed descendants. Since the versions in the modern languages are essentially new translations from the Hebrew original, the wording of these texts and that of the Vulgate do not always agree in detail. Such differences scarcely detract from the value of the material for the present purpose.

LATIN

6 *Erat autem Joseph pulchra facie, et decorus aspectu.*

7 *Post multos itaque dies injecit domina sua oculos suos in Joseph, et ait: Dormi mecum.*

8 *Qui nequaquam acquiescens operi nefario, dixit ad eam: Ecce dominus meus, omnibus mihi traditis, ignorat quid habeat in domo sua:*

9 *nec quidquam est quod non in mea sit potestate, vel non tradiderit mihi, praeter te, quae uxor ejus es: quo modo ergo possum hoc malum facere, et peccare in Deum meum?*

10 *Hujuscemodi verbis per singulos dies, et mulier molesta erat adolescenti, et ille recusabat stuprum.*

11 *Accidit autem quadam die, ut intraret Joseph domum, et operis quippiam absque arbitris faceret:*

12 *Et illa apprehensa lacinia vestimenti ejus, diceret: Dormi mecum. Qui relicto in manu ejus pallio fugit, et egressus est foras.*

ITALIAN

6 *Or Giuseppe era formoso, e di bell' aspetto.*

7 *Ed avvenne, dopo queste cose, che la moglie del signore di Giuseppe gli pose l'occhio addosso, e gli disse: Giaciti meco.*

8 *Ma egli il recusò, e disse alla moglie del suo signore: Ecco, il mio signore non tiene ragione meco di cosa alcuna che sia in casa, e mi ha dato in mano tutto ciò ch'egli ha.*

9 *Egli stesso non è più grande di me in questa casa, e non mi ha divietato null'altro che te; perciocchè tu sei sua moglie; come dunque farei questo gran male, e peccherei contro a Dio?*

10 *E, benchè ella gliene parlasse ogni giorno, non però le accon- sentì di giacerlesi allato, per esser con lei.*

11 *Or avvenne un giorno, che, essendo egli entrato in casa per far sue faccende, e non essendovi alcuno della gente di casa ivi in casa;*

12 *Ella, presolo per lo vestimento, gli disse: Giaciti meco. Ma egli, lasciatole il suo vestimento in mano, se ne fuggì, e se ne uscì fuori.*

SPANISH

6 *Y era José de hermoso semblante y bella presencia.*

7 *Y aconteció después de esto, que la mujer de su señor puso sus ojos en José, y dijo: Duerme conmigo.*

8 *Y él no quiso, y dijo a la mujer de su señor; He aquí que mi señor no sabe conmigo lo que hay en casa, y ha puesto en mi mano todo lo que tiene:*

9 *No hay otro mayor que yo en esta casa, y ninguna cosa me ha reservado sino a ti, por cuanto tú eres su mujer; ¿cómo pues haría yo este grande mal, y pecaría contra Dios?*

10 *Y fué que hablando ella a José cada día, y no escuchándola él para acostarse al lado de ella, para estar con ella.*

11 *Aconteció que entró él un día en casa para hacer su oficio, y no había nadie de los de casa allí en casa:*

12 *Y asióla ella por su ropa, diciendo: Duerme conmigo. En- tonces dejóla él su ropa en las manos, y huyó, y salióse fuera.*

FRENCH

6 *Or, Joseph était beau de taille et beau de figure.*

7 *Après ces choses, il arriva que la femme de son maître porta les yeux sur Joseph, et dit: Couche avec moi.*

8 *Il refusa, et dit à la femme de son maître: Voici, mon maître ne prend avec moi connaissance de rien dans la maison, et il a remis entre mes mains tout ce qui lui appartient.*

9 *Il n'est pas plus grand que moi dans cette maison, et il ne m'a rien interdit, excepté toi, parce que tu es sa femme. Comment ferais-je un aussi grand mal et pécherais-je contre Dieu?*

10 *Quoiqu'elle parlât tous les jours à Joseph, il refusa de coucher auprès d'elle, d'être avec elle.*

11 *Un jour qu'il était entré dans la maison pour faire son ouvrage,
et qu'il n'y avait là aucun des gens de la maison, elle le saisit par
son vêtement, en disant: Couche avec moi. Il lui laissa son
vêtement dans la main, et s'enfuit au dehors.*

LEXICAL CHANGES

Despite their common origin, the Neo-Latin languages have considerably diversified vocabularies. For the concept 'more' Latin used *plus* and *magis*; the former was generalised in It. *più*, Fr. *plus*, the latter in Sp. *más*. Two verbs for 'weep' are commonly found in Latin—*plorare* and *plangere*; the one survives in Fr. *pleurer*, Sp. *llorar*, the other in It. *piangere*. Such differences are not exceptional.

The term for 'head' (as part of the body) in the modern languages is: It. *testa*, Fr. *tête*, Sp. *cabeza*. Thus only Spanish recalls *caput*, the usual term in Latin, the other words continuing Lat. *testa*, originally 'shell', then 'cranium'; this latter term is also found in Old Sp. *tiesta*, but since extinct. Now Italian and French also have the words *capo* and *chef* respectively, likewise meaning 'head', but which are used mainly in a figurative sense. The primary meaning is, however, amply attested in both languages, for example Fr. *chef* was so used until the sixteenth century and such use is still possible where reference is to relics: *le chef de saint Jean-Baptiste*. Spanish has this term, too: *cabo* 'headland', also one of the meanings of It. *capo*. There is further Fr. *cap* 'headland', but this cannot be a hereditary word, as its phonetic form shows; it must be a borrowing. It is, in fact, a late fourteenth-century loan from Provençal. Obviously, these forms are of the same stuff as Sp. *cabeza*. All the same, none of the modern words can be directly referred to Lat. *caput*. While Sp. *cabeza* goes back to a derivative *capitia*, peculiar to Iberian Latin, the other forms stem from *capum* which had replaced the morphologically unusual *caput*.

Consider the words for 'table': Sp. *mesa*, It. *tavola*, Fr. *table*. The Vulgar Latin prototypes are *mesa* (< literary Lat. *mensa*) and *tabula*, the latter properly meaning 'board'. It is not that the first of these survives only in Spanish, the second only in Italian and French. In fact, both survive in some sort in all three languages. Where *mesa* is used for 'table' today, *tabula* keeps its old sense 'board', as Sp. *tabla*; the same situation obtains in certain Italian dialects. Where *tabula* is used in the standard language for 'table', the old term either lives on in dialect use, as in Italian, or else takes on a specialised meaning as in Fr. *moise* 'cross-piece', a technical term in carpentry. Furthermore, scrutiny of these languages reveals a third word for 'table', based on Lat. *discus* (itself borrowed from Greek *dískos*); this is It. *desco*, Old Fr. *dais*.

A considerable part of the traditional vocabulary of Latin did not survive in Neo-Latin. We have already noticed the replacement of *canere, equus, ignis,* by *cantare, caballus, focus* respectively. Sometimes such vocabulary is absent from the contemporary literary languages, but may still live on in dialect or be attested in the older records. A case in point is Lat. *cras* 'tomorrow', its place being taken by It. *domani*, Fr. *demain*, Sp. *mañana*, neologisms formed from Lat. *mane* 'morning'. But Old Sp. *cras* preserves the original adverb, as does It. (dial.) *crai* to this day.

Borrowing of various sorts accounts for much lexical differentiation. Lat. *aratrum* 'plough' is continued in It. *aratro* and (with dissimilatory loss of the second *r*) in Sp. *arado*. But French has the entirely different word *charrue*, traced back to Gallo-Lat. *carruca*. It is a term confined to Gaul and recognised as a loan from the Gaulish language. To Lat. *canis* correspond It. *cane* and Fr. *chien*, but Spanish uses *perro*, a word of problematic origin, though presumably a relic of some indigenous, pre-Latin, language of the Iberian Peninsula. The borrowing of foreign words has taken place at all periods. By way of illustration we refer briefly to the Germanic element in Neo-Latin. Migrating Germanic peoples conquered at various times Gaul, Italy and Spain, when numbers of Germanic words were adopted by the emergent Romance dialects then spoken in these countries, e.g. Fr. *haie* 'hedge' from Franconian Ger. **haga* (cf. Mod. Ger. *Hag*), It. *strale* 'arrow' from Langobardic Ger. *strāla* (cf. Mod. Ger. *Strahl*), Sp. *gansa* 'goose', *ganso* 'gander' from the Gothic stem **gans-* (cf. Ger. *Gans*). Germanic influence was strongest in Gaul, from which a number of such words spread to other territories. Thus Franconian Ger. **werra* > Fr. *guerre* is also seen in It., Sp. *guerra*; there is no trace of Lat. *bellum* 'war' in the derivative languages.

Other lexical changes can likewise take place at all times. Vulgar Lat. *cecus* (< classical *caecus*) 'blind' is represented today in It. *cieco* and Sp. *ciego*, but the French synonym is the neologism *aveugle*, which since the sixteenth century has quite replaced the inherited *cieu*. It is held to continue a colloquial Late Lat. **aboculus*, a term developed in Gaul. This postulated form, based in the first place on phonological criteria, seems secure, but just how it came into existence is not entirely clear. One proposal is that it was coined from a contemporary medical expression **ab oculis* 'without eyes', but according to another suggestion it is a dissimilated form of **alboculus* from medical *album oculi* 'cataract' lit. 'white of eye'. Both explanations appear feasible, but in the absence of specific records from the period in question, the Merovingian Age, some doubt inevitably remains. This may serve as an illustration of one of the many problems which cannot be satisfactorily explained for want of adequate information.

The above example serves as a reminder that although the Romance languages evolved out of spoken Latin, they have nevertheless been continually influenced by literary Latin, which was for so long the sole or the chief written language of the Neo-Latin peoples (cf. p. 41). Throughout the centuries a stream of literary Latin words has passed into the derivative languages. Those borrowed early have naturally been more thoroughly assimilated than those taken up later. Fr. *aveugle*, as we have seen, is an early borrowing from Latin. French later had again recourse to Latin when in the sixteenth century it adopted *oculaire* 'eye-glass' after Lat. *ocularium*, obviously a conscious literary creation. Lat. *oculus* 'eye' has thus formed the basis for two different borrowings. The source of *oculaire* is seen at a glance, but the (hypothetical) Latin prototype of *aveugle* is not immediately apparent; it was, indeed, recovered only by the application in reverse of sound laws known to have operated since the early Middle Ages. But however much it may have been assimilated, it still contrasts very tangibly with the genuine folk words *oeil* 'eye', pl. *yeux*, which have always formed part of the basic stock of the language and which can be shown to go back regularly, in unbroken oral tradition, to Latin acc.sg. *oculum*, acc.pl. *oculos*. The presence of a single Latin word in a derivative language in as many as three shapes is exceptional, but doublets are commonly found, one form inherited through spoken Latin, the other taken later from the literary language, e.g. Fr. *frêle*, *fragile* (Lat. *fragilis*), Fr. *rançon*, *rédemption* (Lat. *redemptio*).

It is to be noted that words have not infrequently altered their meanings, and several examples have already been noticed in this chapter. Such semantic change is a permanent fact of linguistic evolution and the possibilities are well-nigh boundless. Lat. *captivus* continued into the daughter languages, but only Sp. *cautivo* preserves the original sense 'captive'; It. *cattivo* means 'bad, unkind', Fr. *chétif* 'paltry, puny'. The logic in the foregoing is fairly evident: the primary sense has suggested a secondary sense 'miserable, unfortunate', whence by further development the meanings found in Italian and French. (It goes without saying that Fr. *captif* 'captive' is a book word adopted from literary Latin; it has been used since the fourteenth century.)

Finally, shifts in gender are an established feature. Cl. Lat. *arbor* 'tree' is feminine, but the modern derivatives (p. 53) are all masculine; the change is clearly as old as Vulgar Latin. Lat. *mare* 'sea' is neuter. It would be expected to appear in the modern languages as a masculine (p. 55), and indeed it does so in It. *il mare*, Sp. *el mar*. But, surprisingly, French has *la mer*, presumably due to the attraction of its opposite *la terre* < Lat. *terra* f.

6

ENGLISH AND ITS GERMANIC RELATIVES

In 449, according to the Anglo-Saxon Chronicle, Hengest and Horsa met the Britons at Ebbsfleet and began the Germanic conquest of these islands. But if the formal history of the English language thus goes back to the middle of the fifth century, its roots lie further back in the territories from which its speakers had emigrated. Its closest congeners are the languages spoken in the old homeland on the Continent.

THE CHARACTER OF PRIMITIVE GERMANIC

A summary classification of the Germanic languages has already been given (pp. 43f.) and from this the family tree may be constructed. It is, however, at once noticeable that this family tree will differ in two important respects from that set up for the Neo-Latin languages. The origin of the latter is to be found in a single, dialectally undifferentiated parent speech—the language of Rome and its immediate environs. As the administrative medium of a unique Empire and the vehicle of an immense literature, this language had spread in a highly standardised form. And it is fully known to us. But the common ancestor of the Germanic languages, Primitive or Proto-Germanic, has not been handed down. It was never a written language, only the humble idiom of illiterate barbarians and died with those who spoke it. And further, unlike Latin, it was never a uniform language. The speakers of Primitive Germanic, which is dated to the first centuries B.C., were tribesmen subsisting at a low level of material culture. Tribal rivalries, often erupting in warfare, were a permanent feature of their unsettled society. Such a people could not evolve a unified language; Primitive Germanic must always have remained a cluster of related dialects. Since dialects must thus be assumed to have existed in the parent language, it follows that the forms of words met with in the derivative languages will not always be referable to a single, undifferentiated source.

We noticed above (pp. 43f.) that the Germanic languages fall into three main divisions: East, North and West Germanic. These are not to be understood as primary divisions of the parent language, but as later groupings which acquired their individualities as a consequence of geographical proximity after the end of Primitive Germanic. The speakers of East Germanic, for instance, were emigrants from Scandinavia. They spoke the same language as their kinsmen who remained behind and whose speech is called North Germanic. In other words, North Germanic is the product of local evolution after the so-called East Germanic tribes had left Scandinavia. We recall that the first considerable texts in North Germanic (i.e. Old Norse) date from the ninth century, very much later than the comparable records in East Germanic (i.e. Gothic, A.D. 350). If substantial North Germanic monuments from the fourth century were available, the difference between them and East Germanic would not be great, as the handful of early runic inscriptions strongly suggests.

West Germanic shares certain features with East Germanic, others with North Germanic. It also has some peculiarities of its own, but the close relationship between the West Germanic languages can, in large measure, be explained by their having co-existed for so long. It may be borne in mind, too, that the earliest documents in these languages are contemporaneous—from the seventh and eighth centuries—showing them at the same stage of evolution, a fact which naturally accounts for many common traits. The small number of West Germanic idiosyncrasies for which one would postulate Primitive Germanic age do not warrant the assumption of a corresponding ancient division of the parent tongue. Like their counterparts in the other groups, they are best regarded as reflexes of dialect variations within Primitive Germanic, the original contours of which are no longer recognisable.

EVIDENCE FOR PRIMITIVE GERMANIC

Documentary evidence for Primitive Germanic is not entirely lacking. The names of early Germanic notables occur in the writings of classical historians and preserve, in essentials, their Primitive Germanic form, e.g. *Chariomerus*. Indirect testimony is to be found in the oldest stratum of Germanic loan words in Finnish, e.g. *rengas* 'ring', which is seen to retain an original termination.

Apart from such attestations which are, relatively speaking, few in number, Primitive Germanic forms can be reconstructed theoretically. We saw in the previous chapter how it is often possible to infer the Latin prototype from a comparison of Neo-Latin forms. By the application of the same principles, it is possible to recover a good deal of Primitive Germanic from the evidence provided by the derivative languages, especially of course in their oldest stages. We quote below Gothic, Old Norse with Runic, if available and significant, and (as representative of West Germanic) Old English and Old High German. It will be noticed that the consonants of the last often differ from the others; such differences are due to regular innovations known as the High German Sound Shift.

MORPHOLOGY

DECLENSION OF NOUNS

Our first example is the word for 'day' (nom. case): Goth. *dags*; ON *dagr*; OE *dæg*, OHG *tag*. It is apparent that the East and North Germanic forms are more archaic than the West Germanic, since they keep a case termination: Goth. -*s*, ON -*r*. But which is primary? The evidence of Runic is here decisive, for instead of -*r*, Runic has a letter, transliterated *R*, which represents a consonant intermediary between *r* and *z*. Runic thus shows that ON -*r* is due to secondary rhotacism, and that therefore the sibilant, as in Gothic, is primary. It is also known (p. 118) that the sibilant was voiced in Primitive Germanic, i.e. *z*. And Runic tells us more. In inscriptions before the seventh century, the comparable ending is seen to have been -*aR*. In other words, early Runic contained a vowel lost in later Norse, as also already in Gothic. Comparative evidence thus indicates Pr. Gmc *daɣaz* 'day' (*ɣ* is a voiced spirant; *g* has this value in the forms of the derivative languages, except OHG where it is an occlusive).

The form just postulated is confirmed by the ending -*as* in Finnish *rengas* (above). The oldest Germanic forms for 'ring', a noun of the same class as 'day', are: ON *hringr*; OE, OHG *hring*. The word is not attested in Biblical Gothic, but Crimean *rinck* points to the expected **hriggs* (*gg*=*ng*), and there is no difficulty in postulating Pr. Gmc **hringaz*. But Finnish shows that this is not the most primitive form recoverable. Finnish is, phonetically, an exceptionally conservative language. In borrowing the word in Primitive Germanic times, Finnish naturalised it to some extent, i.e. it reduced the exotic *hr-* to *r-* and substituted *s* for *z*, a voiced sibilant being unknown in Finnish, but otherwise *rengas* must be held to represent faithfully the phonetics of the word at the time of borrowing. It demonstrates that Pr. Gmc **hringaz*, deducible from the oldest surviving forms in the derivative languages, was in fact preceded by the form **hrengaz*.

We may now analyse the name *Chariomerus* (above). The Latinised spelling represents Pr. Gmc **Harjamǣraz* 'famed throughout the army', i.e. nom. **harjaz* 'army'—attested in Goth. *harjis*; ON *herr*; OE *here* (still in the place name *Hereford*), OHG *heri*, older *hari*—and **mǣraz* 'famed', a side form of or dissimilated from **mǣrjaz*—implied by Goth. *mereis* (*ei*=closed *i*); ON *mǣrr*; OE *mǣre*, OHG *māri*.

Unlike Romance, the Germanic languages have preserved a fairly extensive case system. It is not possible to reconstruct the case endings of Classical Latin on the evidence of Neo-Latin because of the cataclysmic loss of these endings during the Vulgar Latin interregnum. But the Germanic languages, especially in their older periods, were much more conservative in this respect. They all regularly use four cases—nominative, accusative, genitive, dative—so that these can also be claimed for Primitive Germanic. But Primitive Germanic certainly knew the use of other cases as well, for Gothic preserves a vocative and in the earliest German, in particular, there are many examples of an instrumental case. Furthermore, vestiges of an ablative and a locative have been detected here and there. It is to be assumed that such cases as these were better represented in Primitive Germanic, though to what extent is unknown and unknowable.

By exploiting all the resources of comparative Indo-European philology (cf. pp. 100f.), the morphology of the Primitive Germanic cases—we ignore here occasional traces of vocative or instrumental—can in general be recovered without great difficulty, as follows:

	Goth.	ON	Run.	OE	OHG	Pr. Gmc
Sg.nom.	*dags*	*dagr*	*-aR*	*dæg*	*tag*	**dayaz*
acc.	*dag*	*dag*	*-a*	*dæg*	*tag*	**dayan*
gen.	*dagis*	*dags*	*-as*	*dægæs*	*tages*	**dayaza, -iza*
dat.	*daga*	*dege*	*-ē*	*dægæ*	*tage*	**dayai*

	Goth.	ON	Run.	OE	OHG	Pr. Gmc
Pl.nom.	*dagos*	*dagar*	(-*aR*)	*dagas*	*taga*	**daɣōz*
acc.	*dagans*	*daga*	(-*a*)	*dagas*	*taga*	**daɣanz*
gen.	*dage*	*daga*		*daga*	*tago*	**daɣōn*, ?-*ēn*
dat.	*dagam*	*dǫgom*	(-*umR*)	*dagum*	*tagum*	**daɣamiz*, ?-*umiz*

Except in the case of Gothic, which is virtually only known from one uniform text, the recorded languages show a degree of evolution even within their 'old' periods. In the above, the most ancient forms alone have been given, thus Early OE *dægæs, dægæ*, not the later *dæges, dæge*. The Runic endings in brackets, however, are more recent than the others, earlier plural forms chronologically parallel to those in the singular not being available owing to the scarcity of inscriptions.

Some of the forms point not to a uniform prototype, but to variants which reflect dialect differences within the parent language, as discussed in the previous section. Thus gen.sg. **daɣaza* is presupposed by all forms except Gothic which implies **daɣiza*. As it happens, gen.pl. **daɣōn* is likewise presupposed by all except Gothic. This time the Gothic form is altogether mysterious. If it is of Primitive Germanic age it must continue a variant **daɣēn*; on the other hand, it may be a later development native to Gothic alone. Tantalisingly, both postulates are philologically obscure as they involve an unparalleled ablaut change (p. 100). Other forms not transparent are nom.acc.pl. OE *dagas* (but compare p. 101), OHG *taga*. It is noticeable that both languages have this in common that they have generalised one form for both cases. Any such development is called syncretism. Goth. dat.pl. *-am* shows the original Germanic vocalism; the alternative vowel *u* found in the other languages may, however, be of Primitive Germanic age as well. The paradigms also contain various features which are definitely peculiar to the separate languages. ON dat.sg. *dege* and dat.pl. *dǫgom*, with change of root vowel, represent purely Norse developments, the former showing fronting of *a* to *e* before *ge*, the latter modification (or umlaut) of *a* to *ǫ* due to the influence of an original *u* in the desinence, seen in Run. *-umR*. Similarly, OE radical *æ* throughout the singular, contrasting with *a* in the plural, is explicable in terms of English philology, Pr. Gmc *a* regularly becoming OE *æ*, but remaining in open syllables when followed by a back vowel.

A large number of masculine nouns are declined according to the above paradigm. Since Pr. Gmc **daɣaz* is analysed into *daɣa-*

(stem) and -z (case ending), the former again into *daȝ-* (root) and
-*a*- (stem vowel), it is customary to refer to nouns of this class as
masculine *a*-stems. There are also neuter *a*-stems which differ
from the masculines only in that the nominative and accusative
are always alike. The example 'yoke':

	Goth.	ON	Run.	OE	OHG	Pr. Gmc
Sg.nom.acc.	*juk*	*ok*	-*a*	*geoc*	*joh*	**jukan*
Pl.nom.acc.	*juka*	*ok*		*geocu*	*joh*	**jukō*

Other important classes are:

ō-stems: (fem.) Goth. *wulla*; ON *ull*, Run. -*u*; OE *wulle*, OHG *wolla*—
Pr. Gmc **wullō* 'wool'

i-stems: (masc.) Goth. *gasts*; ON *gestr*, Run. -*gastiR*; OE *giest*,
OHG *gast*—Pr. Gmc **gastiz* 'guest', (fem.) Goth. *bruþs*; ON *brūþr*;
OE *brȳd*, OHG *brūt*—Pr. Gmc **brūðiz* (ð is a voiceless spirant) 'bride'.
OE and OHG retain a trace of a nom.acc. case ending in some words:
OE *wine*, OHG *wini* 'friend'; ON feminines do not usually retain -*r*:
ǫst—Pr. Gmc **anstiz* 'favour'

u-stems: (masc.) Goth. *sunus*; ON *sunr*, Run. -*uR*; OE, OHG *sunu*—
Pr. Gmc **sunuz* 'son', (fem.) Goth. *handus*; ON *hǫnd*; OE *hand*, OHG
hant—Pr. Gmc **handuz* 'hand', (neut.) Goth. *faihu* (*ai*=open *e*); ON
fē; OE *feoh*, OHG *fihu*—Pr. Gmc **fehu* 'cattle, money (fee)'

In addition to classes with vocalic stems, as above, there are
others in which the stem ends in a consonant. The most prominent
is the class of *n*-stems, often termed 'weak' in contradistinction to
the 'strong' vocalic stems; it includes all genders, e.g. Goth. *guma*
m. 'man', *augo* (*au*= open *o*) n. 'eye', *tuggo* f. 'tongue':

	Goth.	ON	OE	OHG
Sg.nom.	*guma*	*gume*	*guma*	*gomo*
acc.	*guman*	*guma*	*guman*	*gomon*
gen.	*gumins*	*guma*	*guman*	*gomen*
dat.	*gumin*	*guma*	*guman*	*gomen*
Pl.nom.	*gumans*	*gumar*	*guman*	*gomon*
acc.	*gumans*	*guma*	*guman*	*gomon*
gen.	*gumane*	*gumna*	*gumena*	*gomōno*
dat.	*gumam*	*gumom*	*gumum*	*gomōm*
Sg.nom.acc.	*augo*	*auga*	*ēage*	*ougo*
Pl.nom.acc.	*augona*	*augo*	*ēagan*	*ougun*

(otherwise as masculine)

	Goth.	ON	OE	OHG
Sg.nom.	*tuggo*	*tunga*	*tunge*	*zunga*
acc.	*tuggon*	*tungo*	*tungan*	*zungūn*
gen.	*tuggons*	*tungo*	*tungan*	*zungūn*
dat.	*tuggon*	*tungo*	*tungan*	*zungūn*
Pl.nom.acc.	*tuggons*	*tungor*	*tungan*	*zungūn*
gen.	*tuggono*	*tungna*	*tungena*	*zungōno*
dat.	*tuggom*	*tungom*	*tungum*	*zungōm*

Although the general outline of the Primitive Germanic forms is clear, the detailed reconstruction is frequently uncertain. The derivative languages have all innovated considerably, in addition to which it is most probable that the declensions already showed dialect variations in the parent language. A Primitive Germanic paradigm may have been: sg.nom. **gumō*, acc. **gumanun*, gen. **guminiz*, dat. **gumini*; pl.nom. **gumaniz*, acc. **gumanunz*, gen. **gumnōn*, dat. **gumanmiz*.

There is ample evidence that the different declensions affected each other. In particular, the numerically larger classes tended to attract the numerically smaller. In this way the whole singular of the masculine *i*-stems was reshaped to conform with the masculine *a*-stems. The *u*-stems, as in Latin never very numerous, were largely assimilated to the *i*- or *a*- stems in the case of masculines, to the *ō*-stems in the case of feminines. Eventually the number of traditionally distinct declensional types was reduced, the process of syncretism being in principle that already seen in Vulgar Latin (p. 55).

ADJECTIVES

The declension of adjectives was originally identical with that of the strong nouns, the most prominent group following the *a*-stems in the masculine and neuter, the *ō*-stems in the feminine. But already in Primitive Germanic the symmetry of nominal and adjectival declensions was largely destroyed by the tendency of adjectives of all classes to adopt uniform endings proper to the pronoun. In short, evolution was towards a single strong declension of adjectives, and by the time of the first records, traditional distinctions were almost obliterated, even in Gothic. But Primitive Germanic did not only simplify the inherited scheme of things, it added a new morphological category by creating the weak declension, so called since it followed the weak declension of nouns.

The opposition of two basic classes, strong and weak, is a

characteristic Germanic innovation. The difference involves meaning: the strong adjective denotes the indefinite, the weak adjective the definite. When this semantic distinction was subsequently reinforced by the use of articles, partly a development of the historical period, the indefinite article was naturally used with the strong adjective, the definite article with the weak one: OE (*ān*) *geong cild* 'a young child', (*þæt*) *geonge cild* 'the young child'.

The Germanic languages closely correspond in the formation of the degrees of comparison, e.g.

Goth.	*sutis* sweet	*sutiza* sweeter	*sutists* sweetest
ON	*sōtr*	*sōtare*	*sōtastr*
OE	*swēte*	*swētra*	*swētesta*
OHG	*suoʒi*	*suoʒiro*	*suoʒisto*

It is evident that suffixal *r* in the comparative in North and West Germanic has arisen from an earlier sibilant preserved in Gothic. This enables one to see that the comparative and superlative endings are related, the latter being a *t*-extension of the former.

PRONOUNS

A striking feature is the occurrence of dual forms in the 1st and 2nd person pronoun.

	Goth.	ON	OE	OHG
1.sg.nom.	*ik* I	*ek*	*ic*	*ih*
acc.	*mik*	*mik*	*mec*	*mih*
gen.	*meina*	*mīn*	*mīn*	*mīn*
dat.	*mis*	*mēr*	*mē*	*mir*
du.nom.	*wit* we (two)	*vit*	*wit*	—
acc.	*ugkis* (*gk = nk*)	*okr*	*unc*	—
gen.	*ugkara*	*okkar*	*uncer*	—
dat.	*ugkis*	*okr*	*unc*	—
pl.nom.	*weis* we	*vēr*	*wē*	*wir*
acc.	*uns*(*is*)	*oss*	*ūsic*	*unsih*
gen.	*unsara*	*vār*	*ūser*	*unsēr*
dat.	*uns*(*is*)	*oss*	*ūs*	*uns*
2.sg.nom.	*þu* thou	*þū*	*þū*	*dū*
acc.	*þuk*	*þik*	*þec*	*dih*
gen.	*þeina*	*þīn*	*þīn*	*dīn*
dat.	*þus*	*þēr*	*þē*	*dir*

	Goth.	ON	OE	OHG
du.nom.	*jut you (two)	it	git	(eʒ)
acc.	igqis (gq = nkw)	ykr	inc	(enc)
gen.	igqara	ykkar	incer	(enker)
dat.	igqis	ykr	inc	(enc)
pl.nom.	jus you	ēr	gē	ir
acc.	izwis	yþr	ēowic	iuwih
gen.	izwara	yþuar	ēower	iuwēr
dat.	izwis	yþr	ēow	iu

The German dual forms are not actually attested until MHG when
they are found in Bavarian texts; they have, however, the meaning
of the plural forms which they have replaced.

Whereas the 1st and 2nd persons are indifferent to gender, the
3rd person pronoun distinguishes masculine, feminine and neuter,
both in the singular and, except for Old English, in the plural too.
On the evidence of the other languages, one concludes that English
will have simplified its original morphology in this respect. Unlike
the 1st and 2nd persons, the form of the 3rd person varies considerably from language to language. Entirely different stems
occur, so that the forms clearly go back to various sources.

	Goth.	ON	OE	OHG
3.sg.nom.m.	is he	hann	hē	er
acc.	ina	hann	hine	inan
gen.	is	hans	his	sin
dat.	imma	honom	him	imu
nom.f.	si she	hon	hīo	siu
acc.	ija	hana	hīe	sia
gen.	izos	hennar	hiere	ira
dat.	izai	henne	hiere	iru
nom.n.	ita it	þat	hit	iʒ
acc.	ita	þat	hit	iʒ
gen.	is	þess	his	es
dat.	imma	þvī	him	imu
3.pl.nom.m.	eis they	þeir	hīe	sie
acc.	ins	þā	hīe	sie
gen.	ize	þeira	hiera	iro
dat.	im	þeim	him	im
nom.f.	ijos	þǣr	hīe	sio
acc.	ijos	þǣr	hīe	sio
gen.	izo	þeira	hiera	iro
dat.	im	þeim	him	im

	Goth.	ON	OE	OHG
3.pl.nom.n.	*ija*	*þau*	*hie*	*siu*
acc.	*ija*	*þau*	*hie*	*siu*
gen.	*ize*	*þeira*	*hiera*	*iro*
dat.	*im*	*þeim*	*him*	*im*

A 3rd person reflexive pronoun occurs in the languages in question, except English. It is indifferent to number or gender and inflects as follows:

	Goth.	ON	OHG
acc.	*sik*	*sik*	*sih*
gen.	*seina*	*sīn*	*sīn*
dat.	*sis*	*sēr*	—

In the OHG dative, non-reflexive forms were used. Old English substituted non-reflexive forms throughout, to which *self* could be added for emphasis.

CONJUGATION OF VERBS

The verbal paradigms of Primitive Germanic can also be reconstructed by comparative means. The Germanic verb is morphologically much simpler than its Latin or even Neo-Latin counterpart. There are two distinct types: strong and weak, each variously subdivided. The first, consisting of primary verbs, is the older type and forms its principal parts by ablaut (apophony). The second, consisting originally of secondary verbs, i.e. those derived from other parts of speech, is peculiar to Germanic and uses a dental suffix as a formative element. Both types are still commonplace: *sing, sang, sung*; *fish, fished*. The strong verbs are linguistic fossils, only the weak type is productive; in other words, newly created verbs are always weak: *televise, televised*. Strong verbs have not infrequently been assimilated to the weak type, e.g. *help, helped*, but OE *helpan, healp*, (participle) *(ge)holpen*, as still in Mod. Ger. *helfen, half, geholfen*.

Germanic has only two inflected tenses, present and preterite. Gothic, the earliest of the derivative languages, operates with these two alone, but Norse and West Germanic employ analytical tenses as well, especially for past time: (perfect) *has sung*, (pluperfect) *had sung*. Such periphrastic formations are, however, secondary and relatively recent. They will have arisen not long before the opening of the historical period of the languages concerned. It is likely that they are imitations of similar developments in Romance (p. 59), which would establish themselves first in West Germanic and then spread to Scandinavia. The evolution of analytical future tenses, e.g. *shall/will sing*, took place later still and is mainly a development of the historical period. Traditionally, the present tense suffices to express future time.

The exclusive two-tense system found in Gothic was doubtless characteristic of Primitive Germanic, cf. p. 123. This system is, however, a reduction of an older, more complex one. For this there is internal evidence. Analysis of the forms of the preterite indicative of most strong verbs shows that they go back partly to an aorist and partly to a perfect, pp. 121f. The strong preterite thus appears to be a conflation of two older tenses.

Each Germanic tense has an indicative and a subjunctive mood, the present tense has an imperative. There is a present infinitive, further a present and a past participle.

Since the weak verb is a purely Germanic innovation, it is from the comparative point of view of less interest than the strong verb which belongs to the deepest stratum and has Indo-European antecedents. We therefore concentrate here on the latter and begin with an account of its typical inflexions. We take the verb 'bear', again quoting the oldest recorded forms and reconstructing their Primitive Germanic prototypes. The reconstructions are, as in the case of the nouns, not entirely obvious, but dependent also on comparative Indo-European evidence.

	Goth.	ON	OE	OHG	Pr. Gmc
Pres.indic.					
Sg.1	*baira*	*ber*	*beru*	*biru*	**berō*
2	*bairis*	*berr*	*biris*	*biris*	**berizi*
3	*bairiþ*	*berr*	*biriþ*	*birit*	**beriði*
Pl.1	*bairam*	*berom*		*beramēs*	**beramiz*
2	*bairiþ*	*bereþ*	}*beraþ*	*beret*	**beriði*
3	*bairand*	*bera*		*berant*	**berandi*
	(*ai* = open *e*)				

Notes. ON sg.3 from sg.2, replacing morphologically regular Run. *-iþ* (lost by 800); change of radical *e* to *i* in OE and OHG caused by *i*, in OHG also by *u*, in the following syllable; OE *beraþ* historically pl.3 generalised for all persons pl.; OHG pl.1 has secondary suffix *-ēs* of unknown origin; ON, OHG pl.2 apparently influenced by subj. (below).

Pret.indic.					
Sg.1	*bar*	*bar*	*bær*	*bar*	**bara*
2	*bart*	*bart*	*bǣri*	*bāri*	**barta, *bēriz*
3	*bar*	*bar*	*bær*	*bar*	**bari*

	Goth.	ON	OE	OHG	Pr. Gmc
Pret.indic.					
Pl.1	*berum*	*bǫrom*	⎫	*bārum*	**bērumiz*
2	*beruþ*	*bǫroþ*	⎬ *bǣrun*	*bārut*	**bēruδi*
3	*berun*	*bǫro*	⎭	*bārun*	**bērun*
		(*ǫ* = open *o*)			

Notes. In general the sg. of the above tense derives from the IE perfect, the pl. from the IE aorist, hence the different radical vowels, but in the case of WGmc an aorist is also found in the sg.2; OE has generalised pl.3.

	Goth.	ON	OE	OHG	Pr. Gmc
Pres.subj.					
Sg.1	*bairau*	*bera*	⎫	*bere*	**berai*
2	*bairais*	*berer*	⎬ *berǣ*	*berēs*	**beraiz*
3	*bairai*	*bere*	⎭	*bere*	**berai*
Pl.1	*bairaima*	*berem*	⎫	*berēm*	**beraimē*
2	*bairaiþ*	*bereþ*	⎬ *berǣn*	*berēt*	**beraiδi*
3	*bairaina*	*bere*	⎭	*berēn*	**berain*
		(*au* = open *o*)			

Notes. Goth., ON sg.1 unexplained; Goth. pl.3 has -*a* after pl.1; OE has generalised sg.1,3 and pl.3.

	Goth.	ON	OE	OHG	Pr. Gmc
Pret.subj.					
Sg.1	*berjau*	*bǣra*	⎫	*bāri*	**bērī*
2	*bereis*	*bǣrer*	⎬ *bǣri*	*bāris*	**bērīz*
3	*beri*	*bǣre*	⎭	*bāri*	**bērī*
Pl.1	*bereima*	*bǣrem*	⎫	*bārim*	**bērimē*
2	*bereiþ*	*bǣreþ*	⎬ *bǣrin*	*bārit*	**bēriδi*
3	*bereina*	*bǣre*	⎭	*bārin*	**bērin*
	(*ei* = close *i*)				

Notes. Goth., ON sg.1 from pres.subj.; Goth. pl.3 has -*a* after pl.1; OE has generalised as in pres.subj.

	Goth.	ON	OE	OHG	Pr. Gmc
Imperative					
Sg.	*bair*	*ber*	*ber*	*ber*	**beri*
Pl.	*bairiþ*	*bereþ*	*beraþ*	*beret*	**beriδi* (cf. indic.pl.2)

Infinitive	*bairan*	*bera*	*beran*	*beran*	**beranan*

	Goth.	ON	OE	OHG	Pr. Gmc
Pres.part.					
(sg.m.)	*bairands*	*berande*	*berǣndi*	*beranti*	**berandaz, *berandjaz*

Note. Paradigms show many variations, for some of which Pr. Gmc age can be assumed.

	Goth.	ON	OE	OHG	Pr. Gmc
Past part.					
(sg.m.)	*baurans*	*borenn*	*(ge)boren*	*giboran*	**buranaz*

Notes. Pr. Gmc radical *u* postulated by ablaut pattern, changed to *o* before *r* in derivative languages; OE *ge-*, OHG *gi-*, a perfective particle usually found with past participles, especially in German, where it has been generalised in the modern language.

The Germanic languages have two numbers for the verb, except in the case of Gothic which has also dual forms for the 1st and 2nd person. Dual forms of the 1st and 2nd person pronoun are widespread in the Old Germanic languages (pp. 73f.), but they were construed with the plural verb, except of course in Gothic. The passive is generally expressed periphrastically, e.g. *is, was borne*, etc., a secondary development, again parallel to Romance. Gothic, however, preserves a synthetic present passive (indic. and subj.), though the forms are much reduced. Doubtless dual number and synthetic passive were not unimportant features of Primitive Germanic. The Gothic forms are:

Dual. Indic.pres.1 *bairos*, 2 *bairats*, pret.1 *beru*, 2 *beruts*; subj. pres.1 *bairaiwa*, 2 *bairaits*, pret.1 *bereiwa*, 2 *bereits*; imper. *bairats*

Passive. Indic.sg.1,3 *bairada*, 2 *bairaza*, pl. *bairanda*; subj.sg.1,3 *bairaidau*, 2 *bairaizau*, pl. *bairaindau*

Finally Gothic preserves, also uniquely among Germanic languages, a 3rd person imperative: sg. *bairadau*, pl. *bairandau*.

All strong verbs have the same endings as the above paradigms, but the root vowels are variable. Strong verbs are therefore classified according to the pattern of ablaut occurring in the principal parts (infin., 1st pret.sg and pl., past part.). The characteristic patterns are:

Class	Pr. Gmc vowel	Goth.	ON	OE	OHG
1	*ī*	*beitan* bite	*bīta*	*bītan*	*bīzan*
	ai	*bait*	*beit*	*bāt*	*beiz*
	i	*bitum*	*bitom*	*bitun*	*biẓẓum*
	i	*bitans*	*bitenn*	*(ge)biten*	*gibiẓẓan*
2	*eu*	*liugan* tell lies	*liūga*	*lēogan*	*liogan*
	au	*laug*	*lō*	*lēah*	*loug*
	u	*lugum*	*lugom*	*lugun*	*lugum*
	u	*lugans*	*logenn*	*(ge)logen*	*gilogan*

Class	Pr. Gmc vowel	Goth.	ON	OE	OHG
3	e	*hilpan* help	*hjalpa*	*helpan*	*helfan*
	a	*halp*	*halp*	*healp*	*half*
	u	*hulpum*	*hulpom*	*hulpun*	*hulfum*
	u	*hulpans*	*holpenn*	*(ge)holpen*	*giholfan*
4	e	*bairan* bear	*bera*	*beran*	*beran*
	a	*bar*	*bar*	*bær*	*bar*
	ē	*berum*	*bǫrom*	*bǣrun*	*bārum*
	u	*baurans*	*borenn*	*(ge)boren*	*giboran*
5	e	*giban* give	*gefa*	*giefan*	*geban*
	a	*gaf*	*gaf*	*geaf*	*gab*
	ē	*gebum*	*gǫfom*	*gēafun*	*gābum*
	e	*gibans*	*gefenn*	*(ge)giefen*	*gigeban*
6	a	*graban* dig	*grafa*	*grafan*	*graban*
	o	*grof*	*grōf*	*grōf*	*gruob*
	o	*grobum*	*grōfom*	*grōfun*	*gruobum*
	a	*grabans*	*grafenn*	*(ge)græfen*	*gigraban*

There is a 7th class in which Gothic, in sharp contrast to North and West Germanic, forms its preterite by reduplication. As in the 6th class, the preterite has the same root vowel throughout, and the past participle takes its root vowel from the infinitive. The phonology of these forms is difficult, making prehistoric reconstructions problematic. We confine ourselves to typical examples from the recorded languages:

Goth.	ON	OE	OHG
haitan call	*heita*	*hātan*	*heiʒan*
haihait, -um	*hēt, -om*	*hēt, -un*	*hiaʒ, -um*
haitans	*heitenn*	*(ge)hāten*	*giheiʒan*

Note. OE preserves a reminiscence of a reduplicating syllable in the alternative pret. *heht* (> *hight* 'called').

Other Gothic examples: *faldan* 'fold', *faifalþ*; *letan* 'let, allow', *lailot*; *slepan* 'sleep', *saislep*; *skaidan* 'divide', *skaiskaiþ*.

LEXICON

The lexicon of the Germanic languages is seen to be about as diversified as that of Romance. But the study of origins in the case of Germanic is more difficult since the parent tongue is to all intents and purposes a theoretical entity.

Each division of Germanic has elements of vocabulary peculiar to itself. Some may be ancient, as Goth *haihs* 'one-eyed', etymologically identical with Lat. *caecus* 'blind' (pp. 117f.) and hence obviously part of the Indo-European inheritance. But in most cases such isolated items are without known cognates, like Goth. *azets* 'easy', and therefore most probably borrowed. But from what language? The problem of origins is, in fact, much greater than this. A very large number of words common to all the Germanic languages, e.g. *sea, earth, blood, finger, hand,* the adjectives *evil, little, sick,* or the verbs *bring, leap, run* and many more, are also without known etymological correspondences outside Germanic. It has been estimated that as much as one third of the basic word stock of Germanic has no parallel in the other Indo-European languages. It is possible that in some cases cognates have not yet been detected, a few could be Indo-European words lost everywhere except in Germanic, but even after such allowances the great majority must be borrowings from an unknown, prehistoric, non-Indo-European substratum.

We know that a considerable part of the vocabulary of Latin did not survive in Neo-Latin. In turn the Neo-Latin languages, too, frequently allowed traditional words to pass out of use. Similar things are observable in the Germanic languages, so that we conclude that such losses are a permanent feature of linguistic evolution. In English, losses from the early lexicon have been exceptionally severe. Owing to the Norman interlude, with its cultivation of French, the specifically literary vocabulary of Old English has entirely disappeared. Moreover, a considerable number of everyday words were replaced by French synonyms, e.g. *andwlite* 'face', *ātor* 'poison', *earm* 'poor', *ieþe* 'easy', *nyttian* '(to) use', *wixlan* '(to) change', cf. Mod. Fr. *face, poison, pauvre, aisé, user, changer.* In the related languages the wastage, though notable, has not been so catastrophic. With one exception, correspondences of the Old English words just quoted are still current in German: *Antlitz, Eiter* 'pus', *arm,* (OHG *ōdi* 'easy'), *nützen, wechseln.*

Whereas the majority of etymological correspondences between the various Germanic languages are fairly obvious, a not inconsiderable number are only apparent after some philological analysis. We take a case involving consonantal dissimilation, a principle already discussed in connection with Romance. Consider the following: OE *heofon*, OHG *himal*, ON *himenn*, Goth. *himins*, all meaning 'heaven'. It is seen that Gothic preserves the nom.sg. ending *-s*, which is assimilated to *n* in Old Norse and regularly lost in the other languages. But can these forms be otherwise reduced to a common denominator? The paradigm of Old Norse is instructive, for in the syncopated forms it has *fn* as an alternative to the expected *mn*, e.g. dat.sg. *hifne* beside *himne*, both for **himene*. Such a group can be explained as dissimilation of the first nasal in the group *mn*. Assume the same change in prehistoric English, subsequently generalised, and the consonants of the recorded English form are seen to agree with the Old Norse and Gothic. There remains German with final *l* in the root as against *n* in the related languages. It seems permissible to invoke dissimilation again and suppose that *l* in German arose from an original *n*, a development seen, for example, in substandard Eng. *chimley* for *chimney*.

How old such differences may be is a moot point. Conceivably they came into being during the prehistory of the separate languages; on the other hand, they could reflect variations already present in the parent tongue. At any rate, indubitable traces of dialect differentiation in Primitive Germanic have been observed from time to time in the formation of words. We take an example. The West Germanic term for 'tooth' is seen in OE *tōþ* m., OHG *zant* m., both presupposing Pr. Gmc **tanþaz* m. (OE *ō* < Pr. Gmc *an* before voiceless spirants, cf. OE *gōs* 'goose', OHG *gans*; OHG *z-* < Pr. Gmc *t-*, a result of the High German Sound Shift). The Norse term, however, is *tǫnn* f. which implies Pr. Gmc **tanþuz* f., i.e. a different gender and declension. A still greater contrast is offered by Goth. *tunþus* m. < Pr. Gmc **tunþuz* m., for this form has a different grade of ablaut in the root. The contrast between West and North Germanic possibly goes back to dialect variation in Primitive Germanic, the contrast between Gothic and the others certainly does.

The Neo-Latin languages have always drawn heavily on the vocabulary of literary Latin. The derivative Germanic languages were naturally in a fundamentally different situation as regards their parent idiom, and so it came about that they, too, became dependent on literary Latin for many of their neologisms. Borrowing often took the form of loan translation. In this manner Lat. *conscientia* 'conscience', analysable as *con-* 'with' and *scientia* 'knowledge', became OHG *giwizzanī*, i.e. *gi-* was equated with *con-* and *wizzanī* rendered *scientia*; Mod. Ger. *Gewissen* is a form of this word. Actually, the Latin term itself is, as often, a calque on Greek. The Greek word is *syneídēsis* (*syn* 'with', etc.). Such loan translation from Latin or Greek has played a great part in the lexical enrichment of all European languages. In the present case we may compare further, for example, Welsh *cydwybod* (*cyd* 'with') or Old Church Slavonic *sŭvěstĭ* (*sŭ* 'with') > Mod. Russian *sóvest'*.

TEXTS

The character of the early Germanic languages can best be visualised from connected texts. We therefore append a version of Luke ii. 8–14 in the languages considered above. It should be noted, however, that early translations tend to be very literal, even to the point of becoming unidiomatic. Accordingly the Gothic version, made from Greek, betrays the influence of Greek idiom. The Old English and Old High German versions were prepared from the Latin Vulgate, as their diction frequently shows.

GOTHIC, c. 350

8 *Jah hairdjos wesun in þamma samin landa, þairhwakandans jah witandans wahtwom nahts ufaro hairdai seinai.*

9 *Iþ aggilus fraujins anaqam ins, jah wulþus fraujins biskain ins, jah ohtedun agisa mikilamma.*

10 *Jah qaþ du im sa aggilus: Ni ogeiþ; unte sai, spillo izwis faheid mikila, sei wairþiþ allai managein,*

11 *Þatei gabaurans ist izwis himma daga nasjands, saei ist Xristus frauja, in baurg Daweidis.*

12 *Jah þata izwis taikns; bigitid barn biwundan, jah galagid in uzetin.*

13 *Jah anaks warþ miþ þamma aggilau managei harjis himina-kundis, hazjandane guþ, jah qiþandane:*

14 *Wulþus in hauhistjam guþa, jah ana airþai gawairþi in mannam godis wiljins.*

Note. For *q* read '*qu*'.

CLASSICAL ICELANDIC

(Text restored with the help of the Icelandic version of 1540)

8 *Ok fjárhirþar vǫro þar í sama bygdarlage, vakande ok vak-tande yfer hjǫrþ sína of nóttena.*

9 *Ok engell dróttens stóþ hjá þeim, ok dýrþ dróttens ljómaþe kring um þá; ok urþo þeir mjǫk hrædder.*

10 *Ok engellenn sagþe til þeira: hræpest eige, því sjáeþ, ek boþa yþr mikenn fǫgnoþ, sem skal vera ǫllom folke,*

11 *því at í dag er yþr lausnarenn fæddr, sá er Kristr dróttenn í borg Davíþs.*

12 *Ok hafeþ þat til merkes, þér monoþ finna barnet í reifom vofet ok lagt í jǫto.*

13 *Ok jafnskjótt var meþ englenom fjǫlde himneskra hersveita, sem lofoþo Guþ ok sǫgþo:*

14 *Dýrþ sé Guþe í upphæþom, ok friþr á jǫrþo, ok mǫnnom góþr vilje.*

OLD HIGH GERMAN (EAST FRANCONIAN DIALECT), *c.* 830

(Text normalised, except for archaic *th*—usual OHG *d*— characteristic of this dialect)

8 *Wārun thō hirta in thero lantskeffi wahhante inti bihaltante nahtwahta ubar iro ewit.*

9 *Kwam thara gotes engil inti gistuont nāh in, inti gotes berahtnessi biskein sie; giforhtun sie im thō in mihhilero forhtu.*

10 *Inti kwad im thie engil: Ni kuret iu forhten, ih sagēn iu mihhilan gifehon, ther ist allemo folke,*

11 *bithiu wanta giboran ist iu hiutu heilant, ther ist Christ truhtīn in Davides burgi.*

12 *Thaʒ sī iu zi zeihhane, thaʒ ir findet kint mit tuohhum biwuntanaʒ inti gilegitaʒ in krippia.*

13 *Thō sliumo ward thār mit themo engile menigī himiliskes heres got lobōntiu inti kwedantiu:*

14 *Tiurida sī in thēm hōhistōn gote, inti in erdu sī sibba mannum guotes willen.*

OLD ENGLISH (WEST SAXON DIALECT), END OF TENTH CENTURY

(Spelling regularised and marks of length added)

8 *And hierdas wǣron on þām ilcan rīce, waciende and nihtwæccan healdende ofer heora heorda.*

9 *Þā stōd dryhtnes engel wiþ hī, and godes beorhtnes him ymbescān; and hī him micelum ege ādrēdon.*

10 *And sē engel him tōcwæþ: Nelle gē ēow ādrǣdan, sōþlice nū, ic ēow bodie micelne gefēan, sē biþ eallum folce,*

11 *forþām tōdæg ēow is hǣlend ācenned, sē is dryhten Christ, on Davides ceastre.*

12 *And þis tācen ēow biþ: gē gemētaþ ān cild hrǣglum bewunden, and on binne ālēd.*

13 *And þā wæs fǣringa geworden mid þām engle micelnes heofonlices werodes, god heriendra and þus cweþendra:*

14 *Gode sī wuldor on hēahnesse, and on eorþan sibb mannum gōdes willan.*

MIDDLE ENGLISH, WYCLIF 1389

In conclusion, a Middle English version to illustrate the great gulf between this later stage of the language and the preceding Old English period.

8 *And schepherdis weren in the same cuntre, wakinge and kepinge the watchis of the nyȝt on her flok.*

9 *And loo, the aungel of the Lord stood by sydis hem, and the clerenesse of God schynede aboute hem; and thei dredden with greet drede.*

10 *And the aungel seide to hem: Nyle ȝe drede; lo, sothli I euangelise to ȝou a grete ioye, that schal be to al peple.*

11 *For a sauyour is borun to day to vs, that is Crist the Lord, in the cite of Dauith.*

12 *And this a tokene to ȝou; ȝe schulen fynde a ȝong child wlappid in clothis, and put in a cracche.*

13 *And sudenly ther is maad with. the aungel a multitude of heuenly knyȝthod, heriynge God, and seyinge,*

14 *Glorie be in the hiȝeste thingis to God, and in erthe pees be to men of good wille.*

7

THE CLASSICAL LANGUAGES:

LATIN, GREEK, SANSKRIT

As we saw in Chapter 1, it was the confrontation of the classical language of India with the classical languages of Europe which led to the recognition of an Indo-European family and the rise of modern philology. New discoveries have not altered the central position of these languages in comparative studies: it will be appropriate to consider them together.

PHONOLOGY

First, some notes on pronunciation.

In any language, intonation is a mixture of pitch and stress, one or the other tending to be stronger. Accordingly a given language will have either a (predominantly) pitch or a (predominantly) stress accent. In the older Vedic Sanskrit and in Ancient Greek, pitch predominated. It was movable and could, according to certain rules, fall equally on prefix, root, or termination. In Greek, however, the accent was not completely free, for it could not occur further back than the third syllable from the end; compare Gk *epherómetha* 'we were borne' with Skt *ábharāmahi* 'do.'. Otherwise there was a large measure of agreement between Greek and Sanskrit as to the position of the accent: Gk *phéromen* 'we bear', *néos* 'new', *heptá* 'seven', Skt *bhárāmas*, *návas*, *saptá*. This will be the continuation of a common tradition.

There were two types of pitch accent: acute or rising tone, and circumflex or rising-falling tone, the latter being only possible with long vowels and diphthongs. In Greek these types came to be indicated by the familiar 'accents', e.g. *moũsa* 'muse', gen.sg. *moúsēs*, gen.pl. *mousõn*. They are still in use, though meanwhile the distinction between them has been lost, pitch having given way to stress. In Modern Greek, therefore, both acute and circumflex have the same function: they mark the new stress accent which, as a rule, occupies the same position as the old pitch accent.

In Sanskrit only the acute accent is usual, the circumflex having virtually disappeared. Some of the Vedic texts are accentuated, but accent signs are not otherwise shown in the native script; in transcriptions for philological purposes it is usual to denote by an acute the position of the ancient accent (where known). In later Vedic Sanskrit, however, an entirely new system of accentuation came into being. Now stress predominated, not following the old pitch as in Greek, but creating a pattern reminiscent of Latin. Here disyllabic words are stressed on the penultimate (*régō* 'I rule'), polysyllabic words on the penultimate if this is long by nature (*regāmus* 'let us rule') or by position, i.e. before two consonants (*regúntur* 'they are ruled'), otherwise on the prepenultimate (*régitis* 'you rule'). In Sanskrit, however, the accent can fall as far back as the fourth syllable if the third and second are short: *ábharathās* 'thou wert borne', contrast Lat. *feríminī* 'you are borne'.

Sanskrit *e* and *o* are always long, *c*, *j* represent palatal occlusives, approximately *t* + *y*, *d* + *y*, *r̥* denotes syllabic *r*, conventionally read *ri*, *ś* is a palatal variety of *s*, *ṣ* a retroflex variety, i.e. pronounced with the rim of the tongue behind the teeth ridge, a characteristic Indian innovation, similarly *ṭ*, etc., *ñ* stands for a palatal, *ṅ* a velar variety of *n*, and finally all occlusives can be aspirated, e.g. *th* = *t* + *h*, *dh* = *d* + *h*.

It is to be noted that Anc. Gk *th*, *ph*, *kh* were aspirated occlusives, i.e. *t* + *h*, etc., not fricatives as in the modern language and in the conventional English pronunciation of Greek.

In quoting words which take inflexions, it is at times advantageous to give the stem rather than, say, the nom.sg., e.g. Skt *pitár-* 'father' (nom.sg. *pitā̆*), cf. Gk *patḗr*, Lat. *pater*.

OCCLUSIVES

A large number of consonants belong to the occlusive class, e.g. (unvoiced) *p*, *t*, *k*, (voiced) *b*, *d*, *g*. These may be studied by comparing related words in the languages under consideration. For convenience, we take examples in which the consonants in question occur initially:

IE	Skt	Gk	Lat.
p	pitár- father	patḗr	pater
t	tráyas three	treîs	trēs
k	kravís raw flesh	kréas meat	cruor gore
b (see below)			
d	dámas house	dómos hut	domus house
g (see below)			

It is clear that the sounds compared will also have been present as phonemes in the parent language. One therefore speaks of Indo-European p, etc. Remarkably enough, IE b seems to have been a rare sound. An example is Skt bálam 'strength', Gk beltíōn 'better' lit. 'stronger', Lat. dēbilis 'weak' lit. 'away from strength', p. 133. There is no example of initial g, but compare Skt yugám 'yoke', Gk zugón, Lat. jugum.

In addition to the above, there is a third series of occlusives: voiced and aspirated. These sounds occur commonly in Sanskrit, but are absent elsewhere.

IE	Skt	Gk	Lat.
bh	bhrā́tar- brother	phrā́tēr clansman	frāter brother
	nábhas cloud	néphos	nebula
dh	dhūmás smoke	thūmós passion	fūmus smoke
	mádhu honey	méthu fermented drink	—
	rudhirás red	eruthrós	ruber
	vidhávā widow	—	vidua
gh	stigh- walk (vb.)	steíkhei walks	—
	váhati (where h is	wekhétō (dial.) let him	vehit conveys
	from gh, pp. 90f.)	convey	
	conveys		

Thus, in Greek, the consonants corresponding to Skt bh, etc., are uniformly unvoiced. Latin has f corresponding to both Skt bh and dh when initial, but medially has b and b or d respectively, while the counterpart of Skt gh is h. These phenomena can be explained if the Sanskrit sounds are regarded as original, i.e. of Indo-European age. We may therefore say that, in the examples under consideration, IE bh, dh, gh remain in Sanskrit, but become unvoiced in Greek. In Latin, IE bh, dh, when initial indifferently become f, when medial they lose their aspiration, though *dh* may also appear as *b*, *gh* is attested medially as *h*. One cannot fail to observe that the series IE *bh*, *dh*, *gh* is quite distinct from IE *b*, *d*, *g* (above), which remained unchanged in all three derivative languages.

Parallel to IE *bh*, *dh*, *gh* was a series *ph*, *th*, *kh*, but of much rarer occurrence. A few correspondences appear in Sanskrit and Greek: Skt *śaṅkhás* 'shell', Gk *kónkhos* (Skt *ś* can be equated with Gk *k*, p. 89), but aspiration is not found in Latin: Skt *ráthas* 'chariot' lit. 'wheeled (vehicle)', Lat. *rota* 'wheel'. In spite of difficulties caused by numerous exceptions, e.g. Skt *sthā-* 'stand', Gk *stē-*, these voiceless aspirates were formerly regarded as a primary component of the Indo-European consonantal system, but recent advances in theory have shown that they are secondary and due to a late coalescence of IE *h* with *p*, *t*, *k*. Otherwise IE *h* has not survived, except in Hittite (p. 93).

Other equations lead to the postulation of a distinct series of labiovelar occlusives, e.g.

IE	Skt	Gk	Lat.
k^w	*kás* who	*tís*	*quis*
	kím, *kát* what	*tí*	*quid*, *quod*
		póthen whence	

Further equations (*passim* below) confirm that Gk *t* before a front vowel, otherwise *p*, correspond to Skt *k*, Lat. *qu*. Here Latin must represent the most archaic form, of which Skt *k* and Gk *t*, *p* are later modifications.

IE	Skt	Gk	Lat.
g^w	*gárbhas* womb	*delphús*	—
	gam- go	*baínō* go	*veniō* come

Parallels to the treatment of IE k^w are apparent: Sanskrit again simply discards the labial component, Greek characteristically transforms the original sound into *d* or *b* according to the nature of the vowel following. But Latin is not so conservative this time; it has lost the occlusive component.

IE	Skt	Gk	Lat.
g^wh	*gharmás* warmth	*thermós* warm	*formus* warm
	ja-ghǎna slew (sg.)	*é-pe-phnon* struck (1.sg.)	—
	hánti slays (p. 91)	*theínei* strikes	*-fendit* fends (*dē-*, *offendit*)

As before, Sanskrit loses the labial component, Greek changes to *th* or *ph* depending on the following vowel. But Latin has uniformly *f*. Apparently the occlusive component was lost first, cf. IE *gʷ* > Lat. *w* (*v*), the ensuing group *wh* then combining to give a voiceless labial, whence *f*.

We now, in conclusion, list the three series of occlusive consonants basic to Primitive Indo-European:

$$p, \; t, \; k, \; k^w; \quad b, \; d, \; g, \; g^w; \quad bh, \; dh, \; gh, \; g^wh$$

Satem THEORY

On p. 87, the equation Skt *kravís*, Gk *kréas*, Lat. *cruor* was cited as evidence for IE *k*. In most other cases, however, Sanskrit has *ś*, thus *śvan-* 'dog', Gk *kúōn*, Lat. *canis*. To explain such differences it was formerly usual to ascribe to Primitive Indo-European two *k*-phonemes, namely a purely velar and a purely palatal *k* (the latter denoted by *k̂*). It was then argued that these had fallen together in Greek and Latin, but had evolved separately in Sanskrit, IE *k* remaining an occlusive (*kravís*), *k̂* becoming a sibilant (*śvan-*). It is also noticeable that Skt *j* quite often corresponds to Gk or Lat. *g*, as Skt *jắnu* 'knee', Gk *gónu*, Lat. *genū*. One assumed, therefore, for Indo-European velar *g* and palatal *g* (denoted by *ĝ*). It was further supposed that IE *gh* likewise had a twofold articulation with phonemic value. A number of other groups follow Sanskrit in having sibilants of various sorts instead of the original occlusives. These are the *satem* languages, as opposed to the *centum* languages which in all cases preserve the occlusives, p. 28.

The above theory meant that three contrasting phonemes, *k̂*, *k*, *kʷ*, had to be posited for Indo-European. None of the descendent languages, however, has more than two, e.g. Lat. *canis*, *quis* (*k*, *kʷ*), so that a phonemic contrast between *k̂* and *k* does not seem a very probable postulate for the parent language. A palatal and a velar are here much better regarded as allophones of a single phoneme, the one or other articulation depending on the given phonetic surroundings, e.g. *k* tending to be palatal before a front vowel, velar before a back vowel. Moreover, the *satem* languages do not always agree in shifting the occlusives. For instance, Lithuanian has *šun-* 'dog' comparable to Skt *śvan-*, but *akmen-* 'stone' contrary to Skt *áśman-*.

In these circumstances, it is more realistic to assume that in the emergent, but still contiguous (p. 31) *satem* groups, IE *k* and *g* developed a marked palatal quality before front vowels, becoming fricatives from which, by a further change, sibilants arose in some cases. The fricative stage is implied by Skt *janu*, the sibilant is seen in *śvan-*. Analogous developments are plentifully documented in the history of many languages: one could compare the evolution of Lat. *c* in Romance (pp. 51f.). As a result of such changes, it would often happen that the new fricative or sibilant occurred side by side with the old occlusive—we recall the frequent ablaut pattern *e/o*, pp. 95f. Subsequently levelling processes affected both the vowel and the consonant variation. Sometimes the new sounds prevailed, at other times the old, developments naturally varying somewhat in the different groups. Reflexes of such variations are identifiable in contrasts of the type Lith. *akmen-*, Skt *áśman-*.

GRASSMANN'S LAW

The discovery of a sound change which took place independently in both prehistoric Aryan and Greek was to be of great significance for Indo-European phonology. This change is known as Grassmann's Law, the essential part of which states that the first of two aspirates beginning successive syllables loses its aspiration. The phenomenon is a form of dissimilation. Thus the consonants in Skt *dádhāti* 'places' are seen to correspond exactly to those in Doric Gk *títhēti* on the assumption that these forms are reflexes of **dhádhāti*, **thíthēti*—we recall that Gk *th* regularly corresponds to Skt *dh* (p. 87). Evidence of dissimilation is especially plentiful in verbs, since these often take a reduplicating syllable. Thus the reduplicating *pe-* in Gk *é-pe-phnon* 'I struck' was at one time **phe-*, while *ja-* in the related Skt *ja-ghắna* (p. 88) goes back to **ge-* ('Law of Palatals' below) dissimilated from **ghe-*. Grassmann's Law naturally accounts for such contrasts as Gk *thríx* 'hair' beside gen. *trikhós*, originally **thrikhós*.

LAW OF PALATALS

During the prehistoric period of Aryan, *k*, *g*, *gh*, of whatever origin, followed by *e* or *i* became the palatal fricatives *c*, *j*, *jh*; in prehistoric Sanskrit, *jh* was reduced to *h*. After this shift, known as the Law of Palatals, Aryan *e* changed to *a*, see p. 28 Examples:

Aryan	Skt	Gk	Lat.
k	ca and	te	-que
	sácate associates	hépetai follows	sequitur follows
g	jīvás alive; life	bíos life	vīvus alive
gh	váhati conveys	wekhétō (dial.) let	vehit conveys
		him convey	
	hánti slays	theínei strikes	-fendit fends

Notes. Gk *hépetai* (with *p* before *e*) is analogically reformed after *hépomai* 'I follow' and similar forms where *p* is regular. Reason for Gk *b* in *bíos*, instead of expected *d*, uncertain. Skt *hánti*, Gk *theínei* may be contrasted with *jaghắna, épephnon,* p. 88.

THE SIBILANT *s*

The parent language contained the sibilant *s*, as is clear from the following correspondences:

IE	Skt	Gk	Lat.
s	sárpati creeps	hérpei	serpit
	ávis sheep	óis	ovis

It is true that Gk *hérpei* does not keep the IE *s*. We conclude that Greek has innovated; in fact, IE *s*, when initial before a vowel, regularly becomes *h* in Greek, cf. Gk *héx* 'six', *heptá* 'seven' beside Lat. *sex, septem*, etc., p. 191.

When *s* formed the first member of an initial consonant group it was an unstable sound, liable to disappear. Hence forms with and without *s* are found, e.g. Skt *tányati* 'thunders', Lat. *tonat*, but Gk *sténei* 'roars', further Skt *stanayitnús* 'thunder'; Lat. *specit*, Skt *páśyati* 'sees'. With Gk *méldei* 'softens' may be compared Eng. *melt*, contrasting with *smelt*, a borrowing from Low German.

A voiced allophone *z* arose when *s* came to stand before a voiced consonant, cf. **nizdos* for **nisdos* 'nest', p. 180.

SONANTS

The sonants can have two functions, since they may have either a consonantal or a vocalic quality. In the latter case they are syllabic.

Examples of the consonantal function:

IE	Skt	Gk	Lat.
m	mātár- mother	mḗtēr	māter
n	návas new	néos	novus
l	laghús light, meagre	elakhús small	levis light
r	rudhirás red	eruthrós	ruber
w	váhati conveys	wekhétō (dial.) let him convey	vehit conveys
y	yugám yoke	zugón	jugum

We notice that Gk zugón does not show the expected initial consonant, this language having made an independent change, p. 93. It may be also noted that, in Greek, IE w is only found in archaic dialect, it having otherwise disappeared, as in néos < *néwos.

Examples of the vocalic function:
It has been usual to postulate syllabic sonants to cover such correspondences as the following:

IE	Skt	Gk	Lat.
m̥	dáśa ten	déka	decem
n̥	tatás stretched	taṭós	tentus

Thus IE m̥, n̥ appear in Sanskrit and Greek indifferently as a, but in Latin as em, en.

IE	Skt	Gk	Lat.
l̥	mr̥dús soft	—	mollis < *moldvis
	pr̥thús broad	platús	—
r̥	mr̥tís death	—	mors, stem mort-
	—	kardíā heart	cor, stem cord-

Here the syllabic consonant is preserved in Sanskrit (original l > r by rhotacism common in this language), but is variously modified elsewhere, i.e. Gk al, la, ar, ra, Lat. ol, or.

The sonants w and y are seen to have occurred after the full vowels a, e, o. Since these combinations, when preserved, appear in the derivative languages as diphthongs, it is clear that in such cases w and y were vocalic. They are seen to be fully vocalised when occurring in the zero grade of an ablaut series, e.g. Gk élipon < IE e-lip-, aorist of leípō < IE leyp- 'leave', p. 97.

LARYNGEALS

As already mentioned (p. 31), clear documentary evidence for an Indo-European phoneme *h* first came to light in Hittite. It appears that this most ancient of known Indo-European languages preserved a laryngeal sound where the others had lost it, e.g. Hitt. *paḫḫur*, Gk *pǔr* 'fire'. On the other hand, IE *h* has now been recognised in the Sanskrit series *ph, th, kh*, p. 88. It is, therefore, reasonable to assume that other languages may also, at least here and there, show reflexes of this vanished sound. With this in mind, scholars have directed attention particularly to those unexplained irregularities which still abound in the various Indo-European languages and have sometimes attempted to account for them by postulating a former laryngeal. In the case of Skt *sthā-* 'stand' (*ti-ṣṭhati* 'stands', *sthitás* 'standing') referred to on p. 88, it is argued that the original root was composed of an initial *st* plus a vowel followed by *h*. In certain inflexional forms, however, the root vowel would be lost, so that the laryngeal came to stand directly after *st-* giving rise to the cluster *sth-*. It is supposed that this cluster was subsequently adopted throughout the verb. But no such development took place in Greek, where IE *h* was accordingly lost without trace, hence Gk *stē-* 'stand' (*hí-stēsi* 'stands', *statós* 'standing').

Other observations led to the conclusion that there had been more than one laryngeal in Primitive Indo-European. On p. 92 it was seen that the initial consonant of Gk *zugón* 'yoke' contrasts with that of Skt *yugám*, Lat. *jugum*, which presupposes IE *y*. In other correspondences, however, initial IE *y* may appear in Greek as *h*, e.g. Skt *yás*, Gk *hós* 'who' (relative). The contrast observed in Greek has been explained in terms of the laryngeal theory by assuming that in both cases IE *y* had been originally preceded by a laryngeal sound: in the first example the laryngeal was voiced, in the second voiceless. Thus, so the reasoning goes, IE *y* preceded by voiced laryngeal gave Gk *z*, preceded by a voiceless laryngeal it gave *h*. But in Sanskrit, as in Latin, both voiced and voiceless laryngeals vanished without affecting the following *y*. Some scholars reckon with four laryngeal phonemes, phonetically perhaps an aspirate [ḥ], a glottal stop [ʔ], a voiced and a voiceless velar fricative [ɣ, χ]. At any rate, it is to be noted that laryngeal in the present context does not necessarily mean a purely laryngeal sound in the strict phonetic sense. In some notations the postulated laryngeal is uniformly written H. Phonemes may then be distinguished as H_1, H_2, etc.

VOWELS AND DIPHTHONGS

The equations which follow indicate the presence of five short vowels in Indo-European.

IE	Skt	Gk	Lat.
a	ájati drives	ágei	agit
e	ásti is	estí	est
i	kím what	tí	quid
o	ásthi bone	ostéon	os
u	yugám yoke	zugón	jugum

We recall the regular change of IE e, o to Skt a (pp. 27f.) and note that this change equally affects long vowels:

IE	Skt	Gk	Lat.
ā	svādús sweet	hādús (Doric)	suāvis < *suādvis
ē	sāmi- half	hēmi-	sēmi-
ī	jīvás alive; life	—	vīvus alive
	pívān fat (adj.)	píōn	—
ō	āśús swift	ōkús	ōcior swifter
ū	mûs mouse	mûs	mūs

Note. Ionic-Attic Gk $ē$ < IE $ā$, hence hēdús 'sweet'.

In a few words, Skt i appears to correspond to Gk, Lat. a, e.g. Skt pitár- 'father', Gk patér, Lat. pater. To account for this variation, it has been very common to posit IE $ə$, i.e. a short indeterminate vowel, technically known from a term of Hebrew grammar as shwa. But, as some philologists have argued, this is a highly improbable postulate, expecially when one bears in mind that all other Indo-European languages have a in such cases, too. It is much more likely that the Sanskrit words should be differently analysed, thus not pi-tár-, but p-itár-, where -itar is an attested variant suffix before which the vowel of the root has disappeared. We have already stressed that the parent language was not homogeneous, but a continuum of dialects, and this fact has been incidentally illustrated in several of the equations quoted above. The Primitive Indo-European dialects showed, among other things, a degree of morphological diversity.

More recent research has attempted to penetrate beyond the

reconstruction of the vowel system given above. In particular, it now appears likely that phonetic vowel length is secondary, the Indo-European long vowels being in fact reflexes of an original short vowel and a lost laryngeal, cf. Saussure's 'sonants', p. 29.

The Indo-European vowels *a, e, o* are observed to have combined with the sonants *w, y*. Such combinations are preserved as diphthongs in Greek, but in Sanskrit, and partly in Latin, secondary long monophthongs are found.

IE	Skt	Gk	Lat.
aw	*ójas* strength	*aúxei* increases	*auget* increases
ew	*óṣati* burns	*heúei* scorches	*ūrit* burns
ow	—	*oureĩ* urinates	*ūrīna* urine
	lokás open space	—	*lūcus* grove

Notes. Gk *heúei* has irregular initial *h*, a not unusual feature; the original form was **eúsei*, intervocalic *s* regularly disappearing. Lat. *ūrit* for **ūsit* (compare perf. *ussī*, supine *ustum*) < **ousit*. The diphthongal stage is still present in OLat. *loucos*.

IE	Skt	Gk	Lat.
ay	*édhas* fuel	*aĩthos* fire	*aedēs* house, (orig.) hearth
ey	*deśás* country, (orig.) direction	*deíknūsi* shows	*dīcit* says, (orig.) points out
oy	*véda* knows	*oĩde*, (older) **woĩde*	—
	—	*oinós* one (on dice)	*ūnus* one

Note. Old Latin preserves the diphthongal stage: *deicit, oinos*, the former surviving into the Republican age.

It is further customary to postulate combinations of *w, y* with long vowels, e.g. *āw, āy*, but their occurrence is admittedly limited. An example is seen in Skt *naús*, Gk *naũs* 'ship', regarded as continuing IE **nāws*, cf. Lat. *nāvis*.

ABLAUT

It is very noticeable that etymologically related words are often distinguished by vowel changes which evidently follow recognised patterns. For instance, Gk *tréphō* 'I feed', *trophế* 'food', *légō* 'I speak', *lógos* 'speech; word'. Long vowels may also be involved: *rhḗgnūmi* 'I break', *rhōgmế* 'fracture, rent'. Similarly Lat. *tegō* 'I cover', *toga* 'toga' lit. 'covering'. The alternation of *e* and *o* can equally appear in the root of the word: Gk *dérkomai* 'I see', perf. *dédorka*, or in the inflexional endings: Gk *phílos* 'friend', voc. *phíle*, Lat. *amīcus* < OLat. *ameicos* 'do.', voc. *amīce*. In Sanskrit, however, no such differences are observable since IE *e*, *o* have there become *a*. In Latin, too, original patterns have been largely obscured by later phonetic evolution, which particularly affected the vowels in unstressed syllables, with the result that the phenomenon is not so prominent in Latin as it is in Greek. The change of vowel quality seen in the foregoing examples is termed qualitative ablaut. One speaks of *e*- and *o*-grades.

A second type of change involves vowel quantity; this is quantitative ablaut. In this case, a short vowel may alternate either with a long vowel or with zero. The short vowel is the normal grade, the others the lengthened or zero grades respectively. In the following all three grades are found together: Gk *patér* 'father', acc. *patéra*, dat. *patrí*; cf. also *eupátōr* (adj.) 'of a noble father', acc. *eupátora*. Quantitative ablaut is fully apparent in Sanskrit: *pitắ* (with loss of ancient -*r*), acc. *pitáram*, dat. *pitré*. There are no instances of the three grades together in Latin, but compare *pater*, dat. *patrī*, and *tegō* 'I cover', *tēgula* 'tile' lit. 'covering'.

Both types of ablaut are of Indo-European age. Qualitative ablaut is explained as a development of the period when pitch accent predominated; during this time *e* when not fully accented was modified to *o*. Later changes, not least those taking place during the prehistoric evolution of the separate languages, often obscured the original patterns. Consequently, *o* sometimes came to carry the main accent, as for example in Gk *lógos* (above), and naturally in Latin where the Indo-European system of accentuation was remodelled (p. 86). Quantitative ablaut, on the other hand, presupposes a strong stress accent such as could lead to lengthening under stress in certain conditions or to possible loss in the absence of stress. It is, therefore, assumed that the pitch accent of later Indo-European was preceded by a marked stress accent. As before, later developments may distort original patterns. Whereas Gk *patér* (above) shows ancient lengthening of final stressed syllable and dat. *patrí* regular loss in unstressed position, the compound *eupátōr* has generalised the accent on the root and also makes analogical dat. *eupátori*.

It frequently happens that a word in one language shows a grade of ablaut different from that found in the same word in another: Lat. *pēs* 'foot', gen. *pedis* contrasts with Doric Gk *pṓs*

(Attic *poús* is secondary), gen. *podós*. Nevertheless, Greek has such words as *pezós* < *pedyós 'foot soldier' and *pédē* 'fetter' showing that this language knew the *e*-grade as well. Both types of ablaut regularly occur together: Gk *pétetai* 'flies', *épteto* 'flew', *pōtãtai* 'flutters', *poté* 'flight', *pterón*, *ptérux* 'wing'; Skt *pátati* 'flies', *ápaptat* 'flew', *pātáyati* 'fells'; a Latin example—*sedeō* 'I sit', *sēdī* 'I sat', *solium* < *sodium (*l* < *d*, as *oleō* 'smell' beside *odor* 'odour') 'seat', *sīdō* < *si-sdō 'I sit down'. The series *e*/*o*/zero is sometimes found in the formation of tenses: Gk *leípō* 'I leave', perf. *léloipa*, aor. *élipon*, cf. also *édrakon*, aorist of *dérkomai*, perf. *dédorka* (above).

All in all, ablaut is seen to play a basic role of paramount importance in Indo-European inflexions and word formation. It is best studied in Greek, since this language has most faithfully preserved the inherited vowel system. Not all the multifarious forms observed have been explained or classified, which is hardly surprising seeing that the genesis of the changes lies so far back. Discussion of the problems has given rise to an immense literature, much of it dealing with fundamental issues, since questions of ablaut cannot be separated from a general theory of Indo-European phonology.

It will be realised that not every change superficially comparable to the above is to be attributed to ablaut. Each language exhibits a large number of phonological innovations of its own. Thus the vowel changes seen in the stem of Lat. infin. *velle* 'be willing, wish', sg.1 *volō*, or in the endings of *diēs* 'day', acc. *diem*, though reminiscent of Indo-European ablaut, are in fact secondary, purely Latin, developments. In these matters each case must be taken on its own merits.

MORPHOLOGY

The mutual relationship of the classical languages is also abundantly apparent from their morphology.

NOUNS

Classification

The category of nouns embraces both substantives proper and adjectives. There are three grammatical genders with inflexions for number and case, according to which the nouns are classified. Two main classes are distinguished: (1) stems ending in a vowel, (2) stems ending in a consonant.

The most significant vowel stems are:

ā-stems: (chiefly fem.) Skt *áśvā*, Lat. *equa* 'mare', Gk *chŏrā* 'country'

o-stems: (masc.) Skt *áśvas*, Lat. *equus*, Gk *híppos* 'horse', (neut.) Skt *dắnam*, Lat. *dōnum*, Gk *dŏron* 'gift'

i-stems: (masc.) Skt *pátis*, Gk *pósis* 'husband', Lat. *hostis* 'enemy', (fem.) Skt *ávis*, Gk *óis* (also masc.), Lat. *ovis* 'sheep', (neut.) Skt *vắri* 'water'

u-stems: (masc.) Skt *sūnús* 'son', Gk *pĕkhus* 'forearm', Lat. *gradus* 'step', (fem.) Skt *dhenús* 'cow', Gk *génus* 'chin', Lat. *manus* 'hand', (neut.) Skt *jắnu*, Gk *gónu*, Lat. *genū* 'knee'

The most significant consonant stems are:

n-stems: (masc.) Skt *rắjan-* 'king' (nom. *rắjā*), Gk *hēgemón-* 'leader', *poimén-* 'shepherd' (nom. *hēgemŏn, poimḗn*), Lat. *homin-* 'man' (nom. *homō*), (fem.) *hirundin-* 'swallow' (nom. *hirundō*), (neut.) Skt *nắman-* (nom. *nắma*), Lat. *nōmin-* (nom. *nōmen*) 'name'

s-stems: (masc.) Lat. *honor*, older *honōs* 'honour', (fem.) Skt *uṣas-* 'dawn' (nom. *uṣắs*), Gk *heŏs* 'do.', Lat. *arbor* < **arbōs* 'tree' (cf. *arbustus* 'planted with trees'), (mainly neut.) Skt *jánas*, Gk *génos*, Lat. *genus* 'sort, kind'

r-stems: (masc.) Skt *dắtar-* (nom. *dắtā*), Gk *dōtḗr* also *dotḗr*, *dŏtōr*, Lat. *dator* 'donor', (fem.) *mātár-* (nom. *mātắ*), Gk *mḗtēr*, Lat. *māter* 'mother'

stems ending in other consonants: Skt *marút* m. 'wind', *vắk* f. 'voice', Gk *gálakt-* n. 'milk', *lampád-* f. 'torch' (nom. *gála, lampás*), Lat. *rēg-* m. 'king', *op-* f. 'wealth' (nom. *rēx, ops*), *sōl* m. 'sun'

stems ending in alternating *r* (nom.acc.sg.) and *n* (other cases): (neut.) Skt *ūdhar* 'udder', gen. *ūdhnas*. Cognates are seen in synonymous Gk *oūthar*, gen. *oúthatos* (*a* < IE *n̥* with *t* suffix) and Lat. *ūber*. The latter has abolished the original alternation by generalising *r*, hence gen. *ūberis* for **ūbinis*, but compare *iecur* 'liver', gen. *iecinoris* for **iecinis*, further Skt *yákr̥t* (with *t* suffix), gen. *yaknás*, Gk. *hēpar*, gen. *hḗpatos* 'do.' Conceivably this very ancient alternation derives from phonetic change. Certain pronunciations of *r* and *n* come close together, so that sporadic change is found in many languages. A prominent instance of the regular change of *n* to *r* occurs in Albanian, where the northern dialects preserve *n* which has been changed to *r* in the South, thus N. *Shqypnia*, S. *Shqipëria* 'Albania'.

Declensions

The familiar three-gender pattern was evidently preceded by a two-gender system, animate and inanimate. A reflex of this former arrangement is seen in the morphology where the neuters, i.e. the older inanimates, have no special form for the accusative, nor do they ever have a separate vocative. A further trace of the archaic state is found in Ancient Greek, in the Avestan Gathas and in a few examples in Vedic Sanskrit, where a neuter plural takes a singular verb. The inference is that the neuter plural was originally a collective singular.

Sanskrit possesses eight cases: nominative, vocative, accusative, genitive, dative, ablative, locative, instrumental. Of these cases Latin retains six, Greek five, though both have relics of the locative. The vocative is often identical with the nominative, in the plural always so. In Latin, a formally distinct vocative occurs only in second-declension nouns. But even Sanskrit does not always distinguish eight cases morphologically, quite apart from the special matter of the neuters. Thus, except in the declension corresponding to the second declension of Latin and Greek, the genitive and ablative singular are always the same, while in the plural the dative and ablative are identical in all declensions, just as in Latin. These affinities must be ancient. Hence one sees, for instance, why in Greek the genitive has the functions of the missing ablative.

The collapse of the case system of Classical Latin has been illustrated above, pp. 54ff. Similar things happened in India. The Sanskrit inflexions began to decline in Pali and the process was accelerated during the remainder of the Middle Indian period. In the modern languages two cases only, nominative and oblique, are usual, postpositions functionally comparable to the prepositions of European languages playing a decisive role in the syntax. Greek, however, has been more conservative. Though the dative has disappeared from the living language and the nominative and accusative have often fallen together, a four-case system continues in full vigour.

Nothing is known about the origin of the case system as such, since no clue to.the provenance of the case endings has been found. One might imagine that they were once postpositions which became incorporated into the substance of the noun. But such an assumption cannot explain why the endings of the three numbers, singular, plural and dual, should be so divergent. It is noticeable, however, that an originally final *s* features in all cases of the plural except the genitive (and in the nom.acc.neut., as explained above); perhaps *s* was the primitive sign of plurality.

Paradigms

The morphology of the noun may be conveniently illustrated by considering the inflexions of a vocalic and a consonant stem. For the first, we select an *o*-stem, for the second an *n*-stem.

o-stems
(masculine)

	IE	Skt	Gk	Lat.
Sg.nom.	*ek^w-o-s* horse	*áśvas*	*híppos*	*equus*
voc.	*ek^w-e*	*áśva*	*híppe*	*eque*
acc.	*ek^w-o-m*	*áśvam*	*híppon*	*equum*
gen.	*ek^w-o-syo*	*áśvasya*	*híppoio*	*equī*
dat.	*ek^w-o-ey* > *ek^wōy*	*áśvāya*	*híppōi*	*equō*
abl.	*ek^w-o-od* > *ek^wŏd*	*áśvād*	(-*ō*)	*equō*
loc.	*ek^w-o-y*	*áśve*	(-*oi*)	(-*ī*)
inst.	*ek^w-o-o/e* > *ek^wŏ̃/ō*	*áśvā*	(-*ō*)	—
Pl.nom.voc.	*ek^w-o-es* > *ek^wōs*	*áśvās*	*híppoi*	*equī*
acc.	*ek^w-o-ns*	*áśvāṃs, -ān*	*híppous*	*equōs*
gen.	*ek^w-o-om* > *ek^wŏ̃m*	*áśvām*	*híppōn*	*equōrum*
dat.	*ek^w-o-ibh(y)os*	*áśvebhyas*	*híppoisi*	*equīs*
abl.	„	„	—	„
loc.	*ekw-o-isu/isi*	*áśveṣu*	—	—
inst.	*ekw-o-oys* > *ek^wŏ̃ys*	*áśvais*	—	—

Some of the details in the Indo-European reconstructions are dependent on more information than that given by the Sanskrit, Greek and Latin forms, as follows. The dat.sg. ending -*ōy* is conjectured to have arisen from earlier -*o-ey*, since -*ey* lies behind the dat.sg. endings in other declensions; it is preserved as such in the oldest forms, e.g. archaic Gk *Diweí-philos* 'dear to Zeus', OLat. *rēcei* 'to the king'. Similarly -*es* is regarded as the original ending of the nom.acc.pl. on the evidence of other declensions, e.g. Gk *pódes* 'feet' (nom.sg. *poús*, stem *pod-*). On the other hand, the long vowel of the gen.pl. -*ŏ̃m* appears to be of different origin. Its reflex in Vedic is frequently disyllabic, which coupled with the fact that, in Greek, the corresponding ending, when stressed, is always circumflex, has led to the postulation of earlier IE -*o-om*. In the same way, abl.sg. -*ŏ̃d* and inst.pl. -*ŏ̃ys* are regarded as contractions of

-o-od, -o-oys. In the case of the inst.sg., however, the evidence is ambiguous; we therefore give alternatives.

Notes. The forms are analysed as containing three morphemes: a root, a stem vowel (which together with the root comprises the stem), and a case ending. The vocative is exceptional in that case relationship is not involved; it is, in fact, a sentence in itself. The form is a survival of a pre-inflexional stage, *-e* ablauting with *-o-* of the other forms. Sanskrit and Greek preserve in composition the uninflected stem IE **ekw-o*, e.g. *aśvayúj-*, *Hippózugos* (proper name) 'yoking horses'. This seems to be another relic of a pre-inflexional stage.

Sanskrit. Forms quoted are those of the oldest language, hence sg.inst. *-ā* for later *-ena*, a new formation adopted from the pronominal declension, pl.gen. *-ām* occurring very rarely, normally replaced by *-ānām*, an Aryan innovation presumably carried over from the *n*-stems. Further, final *s* normally *ḥ*, but preserved in sandhi in certain positions; pl. acc. *-ą̄ṃs* (for **-āns*) only in sandhi before *t* (*-ą̄ṃś* before *c*), p. 158.

Sg.dat. *-āya* comparable only to Av. *-āyā*, unexplained.

Pl.nom. also ending *-āsas*, paralleled in Iranian, unexplained, but perhaps IE *-ōses* from which OE *-as* (*dagas* 'days', p. 70)?; acc. long vowel of termination borrowed from nom.; dat.abl. *e* < IE *o-i* in termination shows influence of pronominal declension, e.g. *ebhyás* 'to, from these', original thematic *o* found in Venetic *louder-o-phos* 'to children', cf. Lat. *-bus* in other declensions; loc. (*ṣ* is an Indian innovation due to preceding vowel) affected by pronoun, cf. dat.abl., but here the development is of IE age, witness Greek; inst. *-ais* regularly < IE *-ōys*.

Greek. Forms not further characterised are those of Homer. The exceptional roots *hipp-*, also dial. *ikk-*, are unexplained; **ep-* would be expected, cf. p. 88.

Sg.acc. IE *-m* regularly becomes *-n*; gen. *-oio* regularly < **-ohyo* < **-osyo*, later becoming *-oo*, whence Doric *-ō*, Attic *-ou*; dat. *-ōi* preserved until third to second centuries B.C., when *i* was dropped (subsequently restored in writing as iota subscript); abl. traced in a few relics, e.g. Delphic *woíkō* 'from home', final *d* not surviving in Greek; loc. occurring in some adverbs, e.g. *oíkoi* 'at home'; inst. only in a few petrified forms, as *episkherṓ*, i.e. *epí* +

skherŏ 'in turn, gradually', where on the evidence of comparative syntax the preposition is construed with the instrumental. Pl.nom.voc. *-oi* adopted from pronominal declension, cf. Doric *toí* 'these'; acc. *-ous* < *-ōs* < *-ons*, preserved in Cretan dialect; gen. *-n* from IE *-m* regular, cf. sg.acc.; dat. *-oisi*, becoming *-ois* about 450 B.C., apparently IE loc.

IE *-bh(y)os* has an approximate counterpart in Gk *-phi*, also found in the sg., e.g. *îphi* 'with strength' (nom. *ís*).

Latin. The forms are those of the classical language. Sg.nom.acc. OLat. *equos, -om* (phonetically regular classical forms were *ecus, ecum*, but *equus, -um* were later formed after analogy of other cases); gen. *-ī* unexplained; dat. OLat. *-ōi* (*Numasiōi* 'Numeriō' sixth century); abl. OLat. *-ōd* remaining until about 200 B.C.; loc. occasionally survives, e.g. *domī* 'at home' (nom. *domus*), *-ī*, older *-ei*, being the development of IE *-oy* in final position; inst. absorbed by abl.

Pl.nom.voc. *-ī*, older *-ei*, older still *-oe*, < IE *-oy* in final position (cf. sg.loc.), the termination itself having been taken over from the pronoun, as in Greek; acc. *-ōs* < IE *-ons* regular; gen. *-ōrum*, a Latin innovation, perhaps patterned on first declension (*mēnsa* 'table', pl.gen. *mēnsārum*) where it is of pronominal origin, the traditional ending being regular *-um* < IE *-ŏm* common in earlier Cl. Lat., i.e. *equum* (*ecum*), OLat. *equom*; dat.abl. *-īs* < IE *-ŏys* in final position, similar to pl.nom. and sg.loc., and thus formally the IE inst. (though doubtless supported by loc.) which replaced IE *-ibh(y)os* in this declensional class, but cf. Lat. *-bus* in other classes, e.g. *hostis* 'enemy', pl.dat.abl. *hostibus*.

Dual. Nom.voc.acc. share one form: Skt *áśvau* or *áśvā*, Gk *híppo* < IE **ekwo(u)* < **ekw-o-o(u)*. Skt gen.loc. *ásvayos*, dat.abl. inst. *áśvābhyām*, the origin of these terminations being problematic; thematic *ā* in the latter, however, will have been introduced from another declensional class. Gk gen.dat. *híppoiin*, archaic dial. *-oiun*, Attic *-oin*, where *-oi-* is comparable to Skt *-ay-*, the rest obscure.

(neuter)

Neuter nouns are distinguished morphologically as described on p. 99, hence sg.nom.voc.acc. Gk *dŏron*, Lat. *dōnum* (OLat. *dōnom*), Skt *dắnam* 'gift' < IE *-om*, pl.nom.voc.acc. *dŏra, dōna, dắnā* < IE *-ā*, i.e. formally identical with the (suffixless) nom.sg.

of the ā-stems, p. 98, also secondary Skt *danāni*, the termination
-āni having been taken over from the neut. *n*-stems (p. 104) and becoming exclusive in the classical language. In Greek, the dual
inflexions are as for masculines, but Sanskrit has nom.voc.acc.
dǻne < IE *-oy*.

n-stems
(masculine)

In the above examples from the *o*-stems, it was possible to quote
the same Indo-European word in all three derivative languages.
This is not possible in the following illustration, however, since
no word with exactly the same formation occurs in all the languages in question. Thus, while Skt *rǻjā* is comparable to Lat. *rēx*,
the former is an *n*-stem (*rājan-*), the latter a *g*-stem (*rēg-*). There is
no corresponding root at all in Greek, where the concept is expressed by the etymologically isolated *basileús*, regarded as a loan
word.

We briefly consider the inflexions of Skt *rǻjā* 'king', Gk *poimḗn*
'shepherd', Lat. *homō* 'man.'

	Skt	Gk	Lat.
Sg.nom.	*rǻjā*	*poimḗn*	*homō*
voc.	*rǻjan*	*poimḗn*	*homō*
acc.	*rǻjānam*	*poiména*	*hominem*
gen.	*rǻjñas*	*poiménos*	*hominis*
dat.	*rǻjñe*	*poiméni*	*homini*
abl.	*rǻjñas*	—	*homine*
loc.	*rǻjani, rǻjñi*	—	—
inst.	*rǻjñā*		
Pl.nom.voc.	*rǻjānas*	*poiménes*	*hominēs*
acc.	*rǻjñas*	*poiménas*	*hominēs*
gen.	*rǻjñām*	*poiménōn*	*hominum*
dat.	*rǻjabhyas*	*poimési*	*hominibus*
abl.	*rǻjabhyas*	—	*hominibus*
loc.	*rǻjasu*	—	—
inst.	*rǻjabhis*	—	—

Dual

Sanskrit: nom.voc.acc. *rǻjānau*, dat.abl.inst. *rǻjabhyām*, gen.loc.
rǻjños

Greek: nom.voc.acc. *poiméne*, gen.dat. *poiménoin*

As before, the forms contain three morphemes, but the

stem-forming element is more variable. It consists of the sonant *n* preceded by the vowel *e* or *o* (qualitative ablaut) subject to lengthening or loss (quantitative ablaut). The former is seen in the contrast between Gk *poimen-* and *hēgemon-* (p. 98), the latter is best preserved in Sanskrit, e.g. *rā́jā* for **rā́jān* (lengthened), *rā́jan* (normal), *rā́jñas* (lost). Lat. *homō* (with loss of final *n* as in Sanskrit) and *homin-* for **homen-* show a combination of both types of ablaut. Analogical levelling is also found, e.g. Gk *agṓn* 'contest', *agōn-*. In Skt *rā́jabhyas* etc., stem-forming *a* derives from IE *ṇ*, similarly Gk *poimési*, analogical for **poimási* (cf. p. 92).

Whereas each language has clearly innovated at certain points, the general correspondence between the terminations remains evident, as well as their overall affinity with the endings of the *o*-stems discussed in the previous section.

(feminine)

Feminines occur in Sanskrit and Latin. They follow the pattern of the masculines. In Latin, analogical levelling is a feature of the common type *ratiō* 'reason', *ratiōn-*.

(neuter)

Neuters show the usual morphological peculiarities of this gender (p. 99), the inflexional forms in question being sg.nom.voc.acc. Skt *nā́ma*, Lat. *nōmen* 'name', pl.nom.voc.acc. *nā́māni*, *nōmina*, du.nom.voc.acc. *nā́m(a)nī*. Skt *nā́ma*, Lat. *nōmen* presuppose IE **nōmṇ*, the cognate Gk *ónoma* (with prosthetic *o*) implies IE **nomṇ*. The Greek word, however, follows another declensional type involving a dental suffix, thus gen.sg. *onómatos*, except for dat.pl. *onómasi* answering to Skt loc. *nā́masu*.

ADJECTIVES

The classification and declension of adjectives is essentially that of the nouns. Originally the two parts of speech were not distinguished morphologically.

The commonest pattern shows a masculine and neuter *o*-stem combined with a feminine *ā*-stem: Skt *návas* m. 'new', *návā* f., *návam* n., Gk *néos*, *néā*, *néon*, Lat. *novus* (earlier *-os*), *nova*, *novum* (earlier *-om*). Reminiscences of the former two-gender system (p. 99) are widely found, e.g. in Greek, regularly in compounds, thus *rhododáktulos* m.f., *-on* n. 'rosy-fingered'. A few simplexes also belong here, as Gk *hḗsukhos* 'quiet'. It is evident that the development of a special feminine form was secondary.

Other, less frequent, combinations are:

i-stems, all genders, but with no special form for the feminine: Skt *súćis* m.f. 'pure', *súći* n., Gk *ídris* 'knowing', *ídri*, Lat. *trīstis* 'sad', *trīste* < **trīsti*.

u-stems, Sanskrit and Greek only, the feminine also taking an *i*-element: Skt *svādús* m. 'sweet', *svādvī́* f., *svādú* n., Gk *hēdús* 'do.', *hēdeîa*, *hēdú*. Note Skt *svādvī́* < IE **swādw-*, Gk *hēdeîa* < **hēdewiā* < IE **swādew-*, the stem-forming elements *w*/*ew* showing ablaut change (zero/*e*). Latin has given up this type, generally substituting the *i*-declension, hence *svāvis* 'sweet' < **svādvis*.

There are various types of consonantal stems, notably the present participles formed with *-nt*: Skt *bharant-* 'bearing', Gk *pheront-*, Lat. *ferent-* (nom.m. *bháran*, *phérōn*, *ferēns*).

Finally the type represented by the so-called adjectives of one termination, e.g. Gk *hárpax*, Lat. *rapāx* 'rapacious': it is presumed that this is the most archaic type going back to a time before the rise of grammatical gender. Such a stage is evidenced in compounds like Skt *pūrṇámāsas* (*r* < *l*) m. 'full moon', Lat. *plēnilūnium* (< **plēno-*) n. 'do.', Gk *akrópolis* f. 'citadel', lit. *ákro-* 'high', *pólis* 'fort'. The adjectival component is in every case invariable, taking no inflexions for gender, nor for number or case.

Comparison

The classical languages distinguish three degrees of comparison: positive, comparative, superlative. It is possible to postulate Indo-European age for many of the formations observed.

Comparative

This degree is seen to have been formed by two distinct suffixes. The first was an ablauting IE *-yos* added originally to the root, thus Lat. *mājor* m.f. < IE **mag-yōs*, *mājus* n. < **mag-yos* 'bigger', *magnus* < **mag-n-os* 'big'. The comparative is not derived from the positive stem, but is rather an associated formation: IE **mag-yos*, etc. meant in the first place something like 'biggish'. A Sanskrit parallel is *návyān* (stem *navyas-*) 'newer', *návas* 'new', cf. Lat. *novior*, *novus* 'do'. Besides the foregoing, Sanskrit also makes *navīyas-*, where the details of the formation are not transparent. However, *-īyas* became the more typical suffix, cf. *svādús* 'sweet', comp. *svā́dīyān* (stem *svā́dīyas-*). Greek makes use of the zero grade, i.e. the sonant *y* becomes the vowel *i*, in association with an ablauting *on*-suffix: *hēdús* 'sweet', comp. *hēdíōn* m.f., *hēdíon* n. < IE **swād-is-ōn*, *-on*. As in Sanskrit, an unexplained *ī* may appear, hence also *hēdíōn*, etc. There is only a two-gender system for comparatives using a *yos-* type suffix in Latin and Greek, but Sanskrit distinguishes a feminine: *návyān* m., *návyasī* f., *návyas* n.

The second comparative suffix IE *-teros* is found as such only in Greek and Sanskrit. It is attached to the masculine stem of the positive: Gk *deinós* 'terrible', comp. *deinóteros*, Skt *dūrás* 'far', comp. *dūrataras*. This is the commoner comparative suffix in the languages concerned. Originally, however, it was used to mark the second in a contrasting pair, hence Lat. *alter* 'other of two' as distinct from *alius* 'other of many'. It appears again in Lat. *dexter* 'right', *sinister* 'left', cf. Gk *dexiterós* beside *dexiós*, *aristerós* 'do.'. It is present in Skt *katarás* 'which of two'.

Superlative

Like the comparative, the superlative was also formed in two different ways. The first involves a suffix IE *-istos*, analysed as containing *-is*, (zero grade) of the comparative plus a dental element. This suffix is found essentially with those adjectives which use *-is* in the comparative. The formation appears in Greek regularly as *-istos*, but Sanskrit has *-iṣṭhas*, e.g. Gk *hḗdistos*, Skt *svādiṣṭhas* 'sweetest'.

Adjectives using IE *-teros* for the comparative, form the superlative with an equally distinctive suffix: Skt *-tamas*, Gk *-tatos*, e.g. Skt *dūramatas* 'farthest', Gk. *deinótatos* 'most terrible'. Since a superlative *m*-suffix is found in a number of words, as Skt *adhamás* 'lowest', *madhyamás* 'middlemost', also Lat. *extrēmus* 'most distant', *optimus* 'best', *prīmus* 'first', it is assumed that Skt *-tamas* is more original than Gk *-tatos*, presumably an expressive substitution for **-tamos*.

The so characteristic Latin suffix *-issimus*, e.g. *altus* 'high', super. *altissimus*, clearly contains the familiar *s-* and *m*-elements already mentioned, lengthening of the former perhaps emphatic. A related form is seen in *māximus*, older *māxumus* 'biggest', and in the type *facillimus* 'easiest' (positive *facilis*), from originals something like **mag-somos*, **facil-somos*.

PRONOUNS

While having a morphology in principle comparable to that of the noun and adjective, the personal pronoun shows a number of peculiarities, including such archaisms as forms without a case ending, e.g. Lat. *egō* 'I', *mē* 'me'. The inflexions in the separate languages vary considerably in certain instances, making Indo-European reconstructions problematic, sometimes impossible. Below we give a selection of nominative and accusative forms occurring in the three languages under consideration.

The 1st and 2nd person pronouns are indifferent to gender, another archaic trait. They may unite different roots in the same paradigm, the nominative often contrasting with the oblique cases.

1st sg.nom. Lat. *egō*, Gk *egṓ*, Skt *ahám* 'I', acc. *mē, emé, mǎm* 'me', pl.nom. *nōs, hēmeîs, vayám* 'we', acc. *nōs, hēmǎs, asmǎn* 'us', du.nom.acc. Gk *nṓi*, Skt *āvǎm* 'we, us two'

2nd sg.nom. Lat. *tū*, Gk *sú*, Skt *tvám* 'thou', acc. *tē, sé, tvǎm* 'thee', pl.nom. *vōs, humeîs, yūyám* 'you', acc. *vōs, humǎs, yuṣmǎn* 'you', du.nom.acc. Gk *sphṓi*, Skt *yuvǎm* 'you two'

There is a reflexive pronoun which naturally only occurs in the oblique cases, e.g. acc. Lat. *sē*, Gk *hé*. Sanskrit, however, has only the indeclinable *svayám* 'self'. The reflexive pronoun was originally indifferent to number as well as gender (as in Latin), so that Gk. pl.acc. *sphǎs*, etc., is a Hellenic innovation. This pronoun was not, in the first place, confined to the 3rd person, but was equally used with the 1st and 2nd persons also, p. 131.

Unlike the 1st and 2nd persons, the 3rd person pronoun varies for gender. This pronoun is also syntactically different from the others, for it can only refer to a subject already indicated. It is therefore essentially a demonstrative and, indeed, in many languages there is no hard-and-fast distinction between the personal and demonstrative pronoun. A number of stems are seen to have been in use. The most widespread is represented by Skt *sá(s), sǎ, tád*, Gk *ho, hē, tó*. An ablauting IE stem *ei-* is the ultimate source of Lat. *is, ea, id*. Other examples are Lat. *ille* 'that; he' (> Fr. *il*) and Gk *ekeînos* 'that; he', *autós* 'self; this, that; he', still living words in the language of today.

VERBS

An analysis of the structure and use of the verb in Sanskrit and Greek best reveals the essential character of the verbal system developed in the parent language. Latin is less archaic.

Voice

It is seen that the Indo-European verb had two voices: active and middle, the fundamental difference being that in the middle the subject was specially implicated in the result of the action, e.g.

Skt active *pácati* 'he cooks', middle *pácate* 'he cooks (a meal for himself)'. Semantic developments may lead to further differentiation between the voices: Gk active *lúei* 'sets free', middle *lúetai* 'ransoms'. Many verbs occur only in the middle, as Skt *sácate* 'associates with' and its congener Gk *hépetai* 'follows'. In some cases the active is transitive, the middle intransitive, cf. Skt *váhati* 'conveys', *váhate* 'rides (e.g. on a cart)', and from this latter it was but a short step to a passive interpretation 'is conveyed (on a cart)'. Thus out of the middle arose, in Late Indo-European times, a third voice, the passive. In Latin, the passive has replaced the middle, though the class of deponent verbs ('passive in form, active in meaning') is a reminder of the oldest state of affairs, e.g. *sequitur* 'follows', cf. Skt *sácate*, etc. (above).

Mood

There are four basic Indo-European moods: (1) indicative, the mood of factual assertion, (2) imperative, used in giving an order, (3) subjunctive, which expresses volition or expectation, (4) optative, which states a desire or contingency. Latin has no optative, but its subjunctive is a composite mood: formally it contains elements of both the Indo-European subjunctive and optative and combines the functions of both. Cl. Sanskrit has no subjunctive.

The different moods basically employ the same personal endings, but are distinguished by the vowel occurring between the root and the ending, e.g. Skt *bhárasi* (indic.) 'bearest', *bháres* (optat.), Gk *phéreis* (indic.), *phérēis* (subj.), *phérois* (optat.), Lat. *fers* (indic., p. 112), *ferās* (subj.). On the imperative, see p. 114.

Tense

Sanskrit and Greek distinguish the following tenses: (1) present, which may also be used for future or past time, the latter being the so-called historic present, (2) imperfect, which transfers present action to the past, (3) future, to express future or intended action, (4) aorist, as the expression of a momentary action, in the indicative used only of past time, (5) perfect, which expresses a state, (6) pluperfect, which transfers perfect state to the past.

Although these archaic languages distinguish six tenses, they make use of only four stems in their formation, the imperfect always deriving from the present, the pluperfect from the perfect. The pluperfect is furthermore not of Indo-European age, but a refinement developed independently in the languages concerned. In Sanskrit, it is very rare and disappears after the Vedic period.

It is most likely that the rise of the future is also post-Common Indo-European. An *s*-element frequently occurs in its formation. At times the formants appear to have been supplied by the subjunctive, for from its power of expressing volition, the subjunctive could develop a future sense, a semantic shift repeatedly observed in linguistic evolution; it has occurred in English, e.g. *he will go.* In considering the principal parts of the Indo-European verb, we may therefore ignore the future stems attested in the derivative languages.

Returning now to the basic stems: present, aorist and perfect, it is seen that a time relationship is not the only ingredient. Aspect, i.e. how an action took place regardless of when it took place, played a part too. In this way, the present stem represents a continuing action, thus contrasting with the aorist. Further, these tenses have no temporal reference in moods other than the indicative.

Closer analysis reveals that the aorist stem is ultimately a modification of the present. The most characteristic formation contains an obscure *s*-element added to the root ('sigmatic aorist'). The perfect stem, on the other hand, remains quite distinct from the foregoing. Thus there emerges an original division, corresponding to two divergent meanings: the present and its system which denoted an action, the perfect which denoted a state. The fundamental nature of this cleavage is underlined by the fact that each division had, in the first place, its own separate set of personal endings.

Latin modified the more original system kept in Sanskrit and Greek. In particular, the Indo-European aorist and perfect have coalesced to give the Latin perfect, which accordingly unites the functions of those tenses, and in fact comprises stems drawn from both. Latin evolved a two-aspect system, *imperfectum* and *perfectum*, for each of which was created a complete tense system, present, future and past. The temporal function was developed at the expense of the aspective, hence *inter alia* the familiar sequence of tenses.

The high degree of regularity obtaining in the Latin verbal system stands in contrast to the chaotic diversity of the Indo-European ancestor. Greek and Sanskrit represent an intermediary stage. This is why there are so few completely regular verbs in these languages. It is the irregular and defective verb which best reflects the prehistoric background. It follows that the concept of a conjugation, according to which numbers of verbs uniformly inflect, is not applicable to Indo-European. There were then only clusters of independent stems loosely linked by the meanings implicit in the root concerned. Since there was no appreciable systematisation, the presence of a given stem did not imply the presence of related forms.

Person and number

Verbs inflect for 1st, 2nd and 3rd persons, singular, plural and dual. The dual is a secondary refinement. It was fully developed, as seen in Sanskrit, but had declined in the other classical languages. Greek preserved a 2nd and 3rd person dual, but Latin had lost the number entirely.

Non-finite parts

Non-finite parts include verbal nouns (notably infinitives) and verbal adjectives (participles). These are not, in principle, any different from ordinary nouns and adjectives, except for their being closely identified with the verbal system.

Infinitives are, in origin, isolated case forms. The present infinitive ending -*re* in Latin, e.g. *amāre* 'to love', *regere* 'to rule', stands for -*se* which has been rhotacised in intervocalic position. The original form is preserved, for instance, in *esse* 'to be' (stem *es-*); it is regularly found in the perfect infinitive, e.g. *amāvisse* 'to have loved' (perfect stem *amāvis-*). This ending may be regarded as the locative of an *s*-stem, p. 98. The mode of formation of the passive infinitive, e.g. *amārī*, *regī*, remains, on the other hand, quite uncertain.

The common Greek pres.infin. ending -*ein*, e.g. *lúein* 'to loose', has not been explained beyond an assumed identification with the *n*-stems. The same element occurs in the infinitive in -*nai*, e.g. *lelukénai* 'to have loosed'. The termination -*ai* occurs in other infinitives, as *lûsai* aorist 'to loose' (*ū* for etymological *u* a secondary feature), or *lúesthai* pres.middle 'to ransom', but its origin is uncertain, though it has been interpreted as a petrified dative.

Vedic Sanskrit operated with a great variety of inflecting verbal nouns, but had no infinitive proper. Then, in the later language, one of the verbal nouns inherited from Vedic, petrified in the accusative, came to be used as an invariable infinitive. It ended in -*tum*, e.g. *bhártum* 'to bear', and is the only infinitive formation known to Sanskrit. It is at once noticeable that this same termination appears in the Latin supine *fertum* 'in order to bear'; the other form *fertū* 'in bearing' very likely represents an original locative.

Thus the evidence of Vedic strongly suggests that an infinitive was not a form occurring in the parent tongue. Participles, on the other hand, are definitely of Indo-European age. We have already referred to the pres.part.act. formed with ablauting -*ent*-, as in Lat. *ferēns, ferent*- 'bearing', p. 105. The same suffix is found with the Greek aor.act.: *lúsas, lūsant*- 'having loosed' and also with the aor.pass. *lutheís, luthent*- 'having been loosed'. By contrast, the perf.part.act. is formed with an ablauting *wos*-, *wot*- suffix: *lelukós, lelukot*- 'having loosed', cf. Skt *babhūvắn, babhūvus*- 'having been', another indication of the fundamental difference between this tense and the others.

Greek employs a distinctive termination to form all middle participles regardless of tense, e.g. aor. *lūsámenos* 'having ransomed'; the participles of certain tenses may have a passive meaning, e.g. perf. *leluménos* 'having been loosed'. A related formation appears as a pres.part.mid. in Sanskrit, as *vartamānas* 'turning' (*vártate* 'turns', cf. Lat. *vertit*), *bháramāṇas* (*ṇ* secondary) 'bearing (for one's self)' = Gk *pherómenos* (mid. and pass.). Latin preserves reminiscences of this formation in *alumnus* 'foster child' (*alō* 'nourish, rear') and *fēmina* 'woman' (*fēlō* 'suckle', cf. Gk *thēlḗ* 'teat', *thḗsthai* 'milk' (vb.), Skt *dhātrī* 'nurse', *dháyati* 'sucks', *dhenús* 'cow').

A perf.part. using an IE *no*-suffix is common and expansive in Sanskrit, e.g. *bhinnás* 'cloven' < **bhidnás*, root *bhid*- 'cleave'.

Last but not least, an IE *to*-suffix very often figures in perfect participles. It was generalised in Latin as the perf.part.pass., e.g. *amātus* 'loved', *rēctus* 'ruled'. The formation is common in Sanskrit and Greek, whose participles may therefore correspond to Latin, e.g. Skt -*stṛtas*, Gk *strōtós*, Lat. *strātus* 'strewn, stretched', cf. also Skt *śrutás*, Gk *klutós*, Lat. *inclutus* 'famous' lit. 'heard', cf. Skt *śṛnoti*, Gk *klúō*, Lat. *clueō* 'hear'. The suffix was neutral as to voice, hence Skt *sthitás*, Gk *statós*, Lat. *status* 'standing' lit. 'having come to stand'.

Terminations

One imagines that the personal endings will ultimately stand for postpositive pronouns which have combined with the verbal constituent proper. In this way one might explain IE **es-mi* 'I am', referring -*mi* to the oblique stem of the 1st person sg. pronoun, p. 107. Unfortunately, none of the other terminations are amenable to such analysis. Indeed, other possibilities must be reckoned with. It is a remarkable fact that the 3rd person pl. suffix -*nt* is paralleled in the formation of the pres.part., p. 111. How such similarity is to be interpreted is, however, not clear. The genesis of these things obviously lies far back. Changes that have occurred during, say, five millennia appear to have totally obscured the early evolutionary stages. This is the main reason why the problem of origins remains quite unsolved.

Verbal forms may be thematic or athematic. In the former the root takes a stem (or thematic) vowel before the ending, in the latter the ending is joined direct to the root. The former are numerically more significant. We have noted on p. 109 that the present-tense system and the perfect originally used different terminations and that such differences are fundamental. We now illustrate this statement from the forms of a (predominantly) thematic stem IE **bher-o-*, **bher-e-* 'bear'.

Pres.indic.active

	IE	Skt	Gk	Lat.
Sg.1	**bher-o-o* > **bherō*	*bhárāmi*	*phérō*	*ferō*
2	**bher-e-si* or -*is*	*bhárasi*	*phéreis*	*fers*
3	**bher-e-ti* or -*i*	*bhárati*	*phérei*	*fert*
Pl.1	**bher-o-mes/mos* or -*men*	*bhárāmas*	*phéromen*, -*mes*	*ferimus*
2	**bher-e-te*	*bháratha*	*phérete*	*fertis*
3	**bher-o-nti*	*bháranti*	*phérousi*, -*onti*	*ferunt*

Sanskrit. Sg.1 termination -*mi* proper to athematic type (Skt *ásmi*, Gk *eimí* for **esmí*, Lat. *sum* for **esmi* 'am' < IE stem *es*-) has been added to the regular ending (-*ā* < IE -*ō*) as always in Sanskrit; sg.3 also athematic (Veda) *bhárti* < IE **bher-ti*; pl.1 medial *ā* after analogy of sg.; pl.2 -*atha* regarded as innovation for **-ata*, cf. imperative, p. 114.

Greek. Pl.1 -*mes* (Doric), -*men* (both of IE age, cf. Hittite -*meni*); pl.2 also athematic (Homer) *phérte* < IE **bher-te*; pl.3 -*onti* (Doric) older.

Latin. Sg.2,3 formed athematically < IE **bher-si*, **bher-ti*; pl.1 -*mus* < OLat. **-mos* ablauting with IE -*mes* attested in Doric Gk; pl.2 -*tis* < **-tes*, i.e. *te* + *s* from sg.2.

Dual

Skt 1 *bhárāvas* (*ā* after analogy of sg.1) < IE **bher-o-wes/wos*, 2 *bhárathas*, 3 *bháratas*. The latter are differentiated solely by *th/t*, the general form being that of pl.2+*s*, as Lat. *fertis*.

Gk 2,3 *phéreton* < IE *-tom*, an ending attested in other tenses in Skt also, e.g. imperf.2 *ábharatam* = Gk *ephéreton* 'you two were bearing' (see below).

The endings illustrated above (except for Gk *-ton*) are known as 'primary' endings; they occur in the present and future indicative and, facultatively, in the tenses of the subjunctive. In the imperfect and aorist indicative, and in the tenses of the optative, sometimes also of the subjunctive, 'secondary' endings are found, as follows.

Imperf.indic.active

	IE	Skt	Gk	Lat.
Sg.1	*e-bher-o-m	ábharam	épheron	ferēbam
2	*e-bher-e-s	ábharas	épheres	ferēbās
3	*e-bher-e-t	ábharat	éphere	ferēbat
Pl.1	*e-bher-o-m .. ?	ábharāma	ephéromen, -mes	ferēbāmus
2	*e-bher-e-te	ábharata	ephérete	ferēbātis
3	*e-bher-o-nt	ábharan	épheron	ferēbant

Notes. The augment *e-*, found in association with past tenses of the indicative in Aryan and Greek (and Armenian: *eber* 'he was bearing'), is optional in Vedic Sanskrit as in Homeric Greek, though later becoming obligatory in both languages. Perhaps it was originally an adverb meaning 'at that time, then'.

Pl.1 IE reconstruction uncertain, though Skt *-ma* may reflect the oldest form; pl.3 IE *-nt* > regularly Skt, Gk *-n*.

Only Skt and Gk are of value for the IE reconstruction. Latin has substituted a periphrastic combination, *-bam* being in origin the preterite of the verb 'to be'; *ferēbam* is therefore structurally as well as semantically not unlike Eng. 'I was bearing'.

Dual

Skt 1 *ábharāva*, cf. pl.1, of which it appears to be a variant, 2 *ábharatam*, 3 *ábharatām*; Gk 2 *ephéreton*, 3 *epherétēn*. In both languages, the 2nd and 3rd persons appear as differentiations of a single form, most likely proper to the 2nd person, cf. pres.indic.

Comparison of the 'secondary' with the 'primary' endings shows that the terms have been misapplied, for the latter are no more than the former plus *i*. One may conclude that the function of this element was to indicate the present. In the Gk pres.indic. sg.2 *phéreis*, 3 *phérei*, it is joined direct to the stem. It has been inferred that the former must therefore originally have been **phérei*, i.e. identical with sg.3. If this analysis is correct, we have evidence for a stage of the verb which was still innocent of personal endings, i.e. Early IE **bher-e-i* 'bearest, bears'. It will be noted that Gk does not distinguish 'primary' and 'secondary' endings in the pl.1,2. Either Gk has generalised a single type, or else it reflects a stage before the two types were regularly differentiated.

The uninflected form of the verb is preserved in the pres.imper. active sg.2: IE **bher-e*, Skt *bhára*, Gk *phére*, Lat. *fer*. The pl.2 is identical with that of the indic.active: IE **bher-e-te*, Skt *bhárata* (on indic., see p. 112), Gk *phérete*, Lat. *ferte*. We note that Latin has athematic forms.

The corresponding endings of the middle voice are more heterogeneous, so that Indo-European reconstructions are often impossible or uncertain. Each language has innovated considerably, not least Latin which uses an *r*-element in the 1st and 3rd persons. Since a discussion of these developments and possible prototypes is necessarily very lengthy, we here simply list the recorded forms, leaving them to speak for themselves.

Pres.indic.middle

	Skt	Gk	Lat.
Sg.1	*bháre*	*phéromai*	*feror*
2	*bhárase*	*phérēi*	*ferris*
3	*bhárate*	*phéretai*	*fertur*
Pl.1	*bhárāmahe*	*pheróme(s)tha*	*ferimur*
2	*bháradhve*	*phéresthe*	*ferimini*
3	*bhárante*	*phérontai*	*feruntur*

Du.: Skt 1 *bhárāvahe*, 2 *bhárethe*, 3 *bhárete*; Gk 2,3 *phéresthon*

The middle voice, too, had a series of 'secondary' endings comparable to those of the active, but their philology is abstruse owing to the diversity of the recorded forms. A straightforward illustration, however, may be seen by comparing the 'primary' ending -*tai* contained in Skt *bhárate* (above) < **bháratai* = Gk *phéretai*, where *i* is the present-tense element already isolated in the active terminations (above), with sg.3 imperf.indic.middle *ábharata*, with 'secondary' ending -*ta*.

Perfect

The distinctive endings proper to the perfect are best preserved in Sanskrit, the other languages, Latin in particular, showing many innovations. Indo-European forms are only ascertainable for the singular. Etymologically identical verbs with chronologically typical inflexions are, however, not obtainable for all three languages. We take the perf. root IE *-dork-* (pres. root *derk-*, cf. Gk *dérketai* 'sees', Skt here substituting *páśyati*, p. 91) which occurs in Skt and, in the active, in Gk. For the Gk middle it must suffice to quote the regular terminations (as in *lélumai* 'I have ransomed'). Lat. has a synthetic perfect only in the active (as *vīdī* 'I have seen'), the passive being formed analytically (*vīsus sum* 'I have been seen'). However, the characteristic desinences of the Latin active are seen to be derived from the Indo-European middle.

		Active			Middle
	Skt	Gk	Lat.	Skt	Gk
Sg.1	*dadárśa*	*dédorka*	*-ī*	*dadṛśé*	*-mai*
2	*dadárśitha*	*dédorkas*	*-istī*	*dadṛśiṣé*	*-sai*
3	*dadárśa*	*dédorke*	*-it*	*dadṛśé*	*-tai*
Pl.1	*dadṛśimá*	*dedórkamen*	*-imus*	*dadṛśimáhe*	*-me(s)tha*
2	*dadṛśá*	*dedórkate*	*-istis*	*dadṛśidhvé*	*-sthe*
3	*dadṛśúr*	*dedórkăsi*	*-ĕrunt, -ēre*	*dadṛśiré*	*-ntai*

Notes. The Sanskrit tense has the regular perfect meaning 'I have seen, etc.', but in Greek, in this particular case, the perfect has assumed a present meaning 'I see, etc.'

The perfect was generally characterised by reduplication, as in Skt and Gk above. In Lat., the traditional system was greatly changed since here the IE perfect had fallen together with the aorist. But a number of reduplicating stems occur, e.g. *mordeō* 'I bite', *pellō* 'I drive', perf. *momordī* (OLat. *memordī*), *pepulī*.

Skt preserves typical ablaut of the root: IE *o*/zero, the former in the singular, the latter elsewhere.

Active. IE sg.1 **dedorka*, sg.2 **dedorktha* cf. Skt *vēttha*, Gk *oîstha* 'knowest' lit. 'hast seen' (non-reduplicating perfect), cf. Lat. *vīdisti* 'hast seen', supposed intrusive *i* in Skt apparently occurring in pl.1 also, sg.3 **dedorke*; Skt pl.1 Vedic also *-imá*; Gk sg.2 *-as* secondary (cf. *oîstha* above), pl. endings secondary.

Middle. IE sg.1 *-ay*: Skt *e* < older **-ai*, Gk *-m-ai*, Lat. *ī* < *ai*
(Faliscan dial. *peparai*, Cl. Lat. *peperī* 'I have given birth'); sg.2
-say: Skt *-se* < older **-sai*, Lat. *-istī* perhaps < **-is-thai* where *-is-*
would be a sigmatic formation (p. 109), *-thai* after the analogy
of (active) *-tha* found in Skt and Gk; sg.3 *-ay* identical with sg.1,
Gk and Lat. analogically innovating.

Lat. pl.3 *-ēre* with *r*-element found in Skt is the oldest form,
-erunt is from a new **-is-ont*, *-ērunt* presumably a mixture of both.

Dual

(Active) Skt 1 *dadṛśivá*, 2 *dadṛśáthur*, 3 *dadṛśátur*; Gk 2,3
dedórkaton

(Middle) Skt 1 *dadṛśiváhe*, 2 *dadṛśáthe*, 3 *dadṛśáte*; Gk 2,3 *-sthon*

Skt 1 intrusive *i*, as in pl.1

8

GERMANIC AND

THE INDO-EUROPEAN BACKGROUND

In reconstructing the antecedents of English and its Germanic relatives in Chapter 6, it was occasionally necessary to anticipate conclusions about the nature of Indo-European which could only be deduced by such a comparative study of Latin, Greek and Sanskrit as was undertaken in Chapter 7. We are now in a position to exploit these conclusions further and we shall see that they enable us to fit the Germanic languages closely into the Indo-European background.

PHONOLOGY

CONSONANTS

It is apparent that the Germanic branch of Indo-European is distinguished from other branches by far-reaching sound changes. Those affecting the Indo-European occlusive consonants are the most striking and the changes observed constitute the so-called Germanic Sound Shift, as follows:

$$\text{Indo-European} \begin{cases} p, t, k, k^w \\ b, d, g, g^w \\ bh, dh, gh, g^wh \end{cases} \begin{matrix} \text{become Primitive} \\ \text{Germanic} \end{matrix} \begin{cases} f, \flat, \chi, \chi^w \\ p, t, k, k^w \\ \beta, \delta, \gamma, \gamma^w \end{cases}$$

That is to say, the Indo-European voiceless occlusives were transformed into the corresponding spirants, the unaspirated voiced occlusives were devoiced, while the aspirated occlusives became voiced spirants. The sonants, on the other hand, and *s* remained unchanged.

This original Primitive Germanic consonant system was then modified to the extent that the voiceless spirants and *s* were voiced when the preceding vowel did not bear the accent. This is Verner's Law, also known as Grammatical Change. Another change concerned *β*, *δ* which initially or after *n* became the corresponding occlusives *b*, *d*. In most positions *χ* became *h*.

None of the recorded Germanic languages preserves this system exactly, since further changes took place in the prehistoric period of the separate languages, but comparative evidence leaves no doubt that the above formed the basis for all subsequent evolution. We may now illustrate this Common Germanic consonantal system by comparing cognates in Latin (see pp. 87f.) and Gothic, as representative of the oldest Germanic. The examples are in order of their initial consonants.

IE *p*, etc. > Gmc *f*, etc.

Lat. *pēs, ped-*, Goth. *fotus* 'foot', Lat. *tū*, Goth. *þu* 'thou', Lat. *canis*, Goth. *hunds* 'dog', Lat. *quod*, Goth. *hwa* 'what'

In combination with *s*, no shift took place (here we occasionally need a Greek example): Lat. *spuō*, Goth. *speiwan* 'spit', Gk *steíkhō*, Goth. *steigan* 'walk', Lat. *scindō*, Goth. *skaidan* 'cut'. IE *t* also remained after *p*, *k*: Gk *kléptēs*, Goth. *hliftus* 'thief', Lat. *nox, noct-*, Goth. *nahts* 'night'.

IE *b*, etc. > Gmc *p*, etc.

(On *b*, see below) Lat. *dūcere*, Goth. *tiuhan* 'lead', Lat. *genū*, Goth. *kniu* 'knee', Lat. *vīvus*, Goth. *qius* (*q=kw*) 'alive'. There is no certain correspondence between Latin and Gothic involving the rare IE *b*, but cf. OCS. *slabŭ*, Low Ger. *slap* 'weak'.

IE *bh*, etc. > Gmc *β*, etc.

Lat. *ferre*, Goth. *bairan* 'bear', Lat. *fēcī* 'I did', Goth. *ga-deþs* 'deed', Lat. *hostis* 'stranger, enemy', Goth. *gasts* 'stranger'; examples of IE *gwh* seem problematic, but cf. Lat. *-fendit* 'fends', Goth. **gunþs* (OHG *gund-*, OE *gūþ*, ON *guþr*) 'battle'.

The changes involved in Verner's Law are particularly noticeable in the parts of the strong verb which, in the earliest period of Primitive Germanic, retained the movable accent inherited from Indo-European. Thus OHG *werdan* 'become', sg.pret.1 *ward*, pl.pret.1 *wurtum*, past part. *giwortan*, and correspondingly OE *weorþan, wearþ, wurdon, geworden*. These forms presuppose Early

Primitive Germanic *wérþan-*, *wárþ-*, *wurðúm-*, *gawurðán-*, where voiced *ð* arose secondarily from voiceless *þ* < IE *t*, cf. cognate Lat. *vertit*, Skt *vártate* 'turns'. Except in Gothic (cf. *mizdo* below), voiced *s*, i.e. *z*, appears as *r* (rhotacism), e.g. OHG *firliosan* 'lose', *-lōs*, *-lurum*, *-loran*, OE *forlēosan*, *-lēas*, *-luron*, *-loren*. The modern languages tend to level out such differences, hence Mod. Ger. *verlieren* with *r* throughout, Mod. Eng. *lose* with *s* throughout. A relic of the change, however, remains in *forlorn*, now purely an adjective divorced from the verbal paradigm. Actually, levelling had already taken place in numerous cases before the earliest records. The phenomenon is absent from the Gothic verbal system, which must therefore have been adjusted in the prehistoric period.

Evidence that the position of the accent was indeed the cause of Grammatical Change is clearly seen when such examples as Goth. *broþar* 'brother' with voiceless spirant, and *fadar* (*d* = *ð*) 'father' with voiced spirant, are compared with their cognates in Sanskrit and Greek which preserve the original position of the Indo-European accent: Skt *bhrátar-*, *pitár-*, Gk *phrátēr* 'clansman', *patḗr*.

There are traces of IE *z* (allophone of *s*): Goth. *mizdo*, OE *meord* (rhotacism), Gk *misthós* 'reward, wages' < IE *mizdh-*.

SONANTS

The Indo-European sonants were well preserved in Primitive Germanic. We note that Germanic final *n* may stand for IE *m*. IE *m̥*, *n̥*, *l̥*, *r̥* appeared as *um*, *un*, *ul*, *ur* (in the derivative languages sometimes further changed to *om*, etc.): Lat. *decem*, Goth. *taihun* 'ten', OLat. *mentis* 'mind', Goth. *ga-munds* 'remembrance', Skt *vŕ̥kas*, Goth. *wulfs* (*f* irregular) 'wolf', Lat. *mors*, *mort-* 'death', Goth. *maurþr* (OHG *mord*) 'murder'.

VOWELS

The vowels of Primitive Germanic, as inferred from the earliest recorded Germanic languages, may be closely compared with those of the parent tongue. As before, we confine ourselves to the vowels of tonic syllables. The following may be regarded as typical of Common Germanic evolution.

The IE short vowels *a*, *e*, *i*, *u* were preserved, but *o* became *a*: Lat. *ager*, Goth. *akrs* 'field', Lat. *ferre*, Goth. *bairan* (*ai* = [e]) 'bear', Lat. *piscis*, Goth. *fisks* 'fish', Lat. *jugum*, Goth. *juk* 'yoke', but Lat. *octō*, Goth. *ahtau* 'eight'.

The IE long vowels *ī*, *ō*, *ū* were preserved, but *ā* became *ō*, while *ē* remains in Gothic, but appears as *ā* in N and WGmc (> OE *ǣ*): Lat. *suīnus* 'pertaining to pigs', Goth. *swein* (*ei* = [iː]) 'pig', Lat. *flōs*, Goth. *bloma* 'flower, bloom', Lat. *mūs*, Goth. **mus* (OHG, OE, ON *mūs*) 'mouse', but Lat. *frāter*, Goth. *broþar* 'brother', Lat. *sēmen*, Goth. *-seþs* (OHG *sāt*, OE *sǣd*, ON *sāþ*) 'seed'.

The IE combinations *aw*, *ew* were preserved as the diphthongs *au*, *eu*; parallel to the development of IE *o* to *a*, IE *ow* became *au*. The IE combination *ay* was preserved as *ai*, but IE *ey* became *ī*; IE *oy* became *ai*. Pr. Gmc *au*, *ai* are kept, for instance, in Early (Bavarian) OHG, but were monophthongised in Gothic to give open [o] and [e] respectively, and thus fell together with Pr. Gmc *o*, *e*. In using *au*, *ai* to denote these sounds, Gothic was influenced by contemporary Greek, where old *au*, *ai*, though still written as such, were no longer pronounced as diphthongs. That Goth. *au*, *ai* may appear as correct etymological spellings is due to this coincidence. Examples of the changes: (IE *aw*) Lat. *augēre*, Goth. *aukan* 'increase', (IE *ew*) Lat. *dūcere*, OLat. *douc-*, Goth. *tiuhan* 'lead', (IE *ow*) Lat. *rūfus*, Goth. *rauþs* 'red', (IE *ay*) Lat. *aes*, Goth. *aiz* 'bronze', (IE *ey*) Lat. *dīcere*, OLat. *deic-*, Goth. *ga-teihan* (*ei* = [iː]) 'say, tell', (IE *oy*) Lat. *ūnus*, OLat. *oinos*, Goth. *ains* 'one'.

It is to be noticed that vowel sounds apparently lost in Primitive Germanic reappear in the recorded languages as products of special changes, e.g. Goth. *waurms* (*au* = [o]) 'worm', where *au* never *u* is found before *r*, contrast OHG *wurm* with etymological *u*. In fact, in North and West Germanic (especially English) a complex vocalic system evolved, chiefly as a result of combinative changes.

MORPHOLOGY

DECLENSION

The Germanic languages have preserved IE **ekwos* 'horse' in more or less advanced phonological forms in OLG *ehu-*, OE *eoh*, ON *jōr* < Runic **ehwaR*; only Goth. *aihwa-* (*ai* = [e]) reaches back unchanged to Pr. Gmc **ehwa-*, older ** eχwa-*, immediately comparable to IE **ekwo-* (Skt *ásva-*, Gk *híppo-*). On the analogy of Pr. Gmc **dayaz* (p. 69) one has no hesitation in postulating analogous Pr. Gmc sg.nom. **ehwaz*, acc. **ehwan*, etc., the basic morphology of which obviously derives from the parent Indo-European (p. 100). A similar comparison may be made between the endings of the Germanic *n*-stems (pp. 71f.) and their Indo-European counterparts (pp. 103f.), and it goes without saying that the overall classification of Germanic nouns (pp. 69, 71) is a replica of Indo-European arrangements (p. 98). The same naturally applies to the adjectives.

It was possible, on internal evidence, to make inferences as to the nature of the comparative and superlative endings of the Germanic adjective. These may now be more fully understood in the light of Indo-European philology. The endings of Gk *hēdíōn* 'sweeter', super. *hédistos*, presuppose IE *-isōn, -istos*. These would regularly give Pr. Gmc *-isōn, -istas*, whence regularly Goth. *-iza, -ists*, etc., p. 73. The terminations of Greek and Germanic are entirely analogous.

The connection between the Germanic 1st and 2nd persons of the personal pronoun and those of Latin, etc., is self-evident. The 3rd person, however, is more problematic (pp. 74f.), but a knowledge of the Indo-European background helps one to interpret the Germanic forms. It was seen (p. 107) that the 3rd person pronoun is formed from a number of different, essentially demonstrative, stems. The same proliferation was clearly a feature of Germanic, too. The stem seen in Skt sg.n. *tád*, Gk *tó* is present in forms like ON *þat* 'it', also 'that', etc., the IE stem *ei-* occurs in Goth. *is*, etc., IE *ki-* (p. 162) is found in OE *hē* 'he', *hine* 'him' (acc.), etc., perhaps also in ON *hann* 'he', etc., but details here are elusive.

CONJUGATION

It is soon seen that the endings of the Germanic strong verb (pp. 76f.) bear the unmistakable stamp of its Indo-European origin. We interpose here that the weak verb, though not of Indo-European ancestry, operates with endings which are the same as, or similar to, those of the strong verb from which they ultimately derive.

The Indo-European connections of the Germanic (strong) verb are further apparent in the patterns of root ablaut used in their formation. The first pattern (or class), represented by Goth. *beitan* 'to bite', pret.sg.1 *bait*, pret.pl.1 *bitum* (p. 78), continues a Primitive Germanic ablaut series *ī, ai, i*, which has an exact parallel in Gk *leípō* 'I leave', perf. *léloipa*, aor. *élipon* (pp. 97, 92). It is noticeable that the ablaut grade of Gothic pret.sg. *bait* contrasts with pl. *bitum*, and that these grades correspond to those of the Greek perfect and aorist respectively. It thus appears that this type of Germanic preterite is, in origin, a conflation of two distinct Indo-European tenses, the perfect and the aorist.

Ablaut is, of course, a traditional feature of Indo-European tense formation. Germanic is seen to have evolved the principle with such consistency that virtually all its primary verbs came to be arranged in rigid ablaut series. These have proved most durable, so that the category of strong verbs has remained a central feature of Germanic speech down to the present day. Only creolised languages, such as Afrikaans, have destroyed these venerable formations.

Of the Indo-European moods, Germanic retains, as we saw, the indicative, imperative and subjunctive. The last includes the functions of the Indo-European optative; in fact, 'subjunctive' is here a misnomer, since the forms actually descend from the Indo-European optative.

Viewed against the Indo-European background, the Gothic dual forms and the synthetic passive voice appear as archaisms lost elsewhere in Germanic.

In the sphere of verbal nouns, the Germanic infinitive with its *n*-element invites comparison with Greek. However, the similarity seems to be deceptive. At any rate, the Germanic form, unlike the Greek, can be satisfactorily analysed. Thus Goth. *bairan* 'to bear' can be compared with Skt *bháranam* n. 'act of bearing' < IE **bher-o-nom* > Pr. Gmc **beranan* whence, with regular loss of -*an*, the recorded Gothic form.

The verbal adjectives also fit naturally into the Indo-European background. The present participle, Gothic *bairands* 'bearing', etc.(p. 77), are directly comparable with Lat. *ferēns, ferent-,* etc. (p. 105). The past participle of strong verbs, Goth. *baurans* 'borne', etc. (p. 78), is formed with an IE *no*-suffix in the same way as Skt *bhinnás* (p. 111). The past participles of weak verbs, on the other hand, are formed with a dental suffix, e.g. Goth. *fiskon* 'to fish', past part. *fiskops* 'fished'. It is clearly derived from the IE *to*-suffix found in Lat. *amātus,* etc. (p. 111).

Lastly we mention Goth. *berusjos* m. 'parents'. With only the resources of Germanic philology, one could scarcely analyse this word correctly. One might assume that it could contain the root *ber-,* the lengthened grade of *bair-* in *bairan* 'to bear', though even this would remain no more than a possibility. Only the knowledge that Indo-European formed a perf.part.act. with an ablauting *wos*-suffix (p. 111) enables the philologist to recognise in the present word a substantivised participle, originally feminine, with the literal meaning 'those having borne'. By a semantic shift, the term came to mean 'parents'. When this happened, it would change its gender to masculine. See further p. 184.

ORIGIN OF GERMANIC

Although Germanic naturally shares fundamental genetic features with other branches of the Indo-European family, it is distinguished by a number of prominent secondary features which lend it a marked individuality. The Sound Shift has already been referred to. Another significant phonetic development was the fixing of the (stress) accent on the root syllable, which took place after the operation of Verner's Law, p. 118. There are also lexical peculiarities. All Indo-European languages contain a contingent of words which cannot be etymologised, but the proportion of these in Germanic is exceptionally high, about one-third of the basic stock being of unknown origin. It may be that, owing to exceptional changes, the Indo-European affinities of some of these words are no longer recognisable, but this reservation will hardly hold for the great majority, which must therefore be attributed to an unknown source.

This unknown source is generally believed to have been the speech of an indigenous population linguistically assimilated by a group of invading Indo-Europeans. In the ensuing ethnic fusion, the Indo-European speech type prevailed, but at the price of a large admixture of autochthonous vocabulary. Moreover, its consonant system was entirely recast in accordance with the articulatory tendencies of the pre-Indo-European element. As the phonetic changes are as regular as they are sweeping, the fusion must have taken place at a time when there was no contact with other Indo-Europeans to disturb the process. This is a cogent philological reason for suggesting that Southern Scandinavia was most likely the birth-place of Germanic speech. But known historical facts give no guidance since the changes in question are prehistoric. One may think of them as taking place, perhaps, in the fourth or fifth centuries B.C.

One prehistoric development of Germanic, however, may be referred to a known source. Germanic has reduced the Indo-European tense system to two terms: present and preterite. This arrangement has an exact analogue in Finno-Ugrian. Since

Germanic was in contact with dialects of this family in antiquity, one may regard the Germanic two-tense system as a typological calque on Finno-Ugrian. Furthermore, this family of languages is characterised by initial stress. It is not unthinkable that Germanic stress is due to influence from the same quarter.

9

BALTIC AND SLAVONIC

I: LITHUANIAN

Lithuanian combines an exceptionally archaic structure with the rich documentation of a living language. It is pre-eminently fitted to represent the Baltic tradition.

PHONOLOGY

Notes on pronunciation:

č, š, ž, j are pronounced [tʃ, ʃ, ʒ, j]. Short and long vowels occur. Vowels with a subscript hook, e.g. *ą*, are long; they were formerly nasalised. *ė, ū, y* are pronounced [eː, uː, iː].

Accents are used in philological works since the type of accent varies and is not bound to a particular syllable. The accent is predominantly one of stress. If the stressed vowel is short it is marked with a grave: *galvà* 'head'. Stressed long vowels have either a falling or rising intonation. The former is marked by an acute, the latter by a circumflex: *vėjas* 'wind', *sēnas* 'old'. Stressed diphthongs are treated in the same way: *sáulė* 'sun', *piemuõ* 'shepherd boy'. The sonants *m, n, l, r* may form the second part of a diphthong (or 'half-diphthong') and take the accent, in which case they are lengthened: *šim̃tas* 'hundred'; 'half-diphthongs' can also contain a short stressed vowel: *pìlnas* 'full'. Accents may differ greatly within the paradigm of a single word, e.g. *galvà* (above), acc. *gálvą*, gen. *galvõs*, loc. *galvojè*. Lithuanian is particularly conservative in these matters. It not only preserves the free accent of

the parent tongue, but by distinguishing acute and circumflex
intonation it reflects, albeit in somewhat changed form, an ancient
Indo-European principle.

CONSONANTS

IE   *p*:Lith. *pilìs* 'castle', Gk *pólis* 'town', Skt *púram,* also *púr*
'castle, town'
t:Lith. *tamsà* 'darkness', Lat. *temere* 'blindly' lit. 'in the
dark', abl. of **temus,* gen. *-eris* 'darkness', a reconstruction confirmed by Skt *támas,* gen. *támasas* 'do.'
k:(1) Lith. *kálnas* 'hill', Gk *kolōnós,* Lat. *collis,* OE *hyll*
(2) Lith. *širdìs* 'heart', Gk *kardíā,* Lat. *cor,* gen. *cordis,*
Goth. *hairto*
kʷ:Lith. *keturì* 'four', Lat. *quattuor,* etc., pp. 191f.

IE   *b*:Lith. *dubùs* 'deep', Goth. *diups*
d:Lith. *dantìs* 'tooth', Skt *dán,* gen. *datás,* Gk *odốn (odoús),*
gen. *odóntos,* Lat. *dēns,* gen. *dentis,* OHG *zant,* OE *tōþ* <
Pr. Gmc **tanþaz*
g:(1) Lith. *glitùs* 'sticky', Lat. *glūten* 'glue', Gk *glitós*
'sticky'
(2) Lith. *žinóti* 'know', Skt *jānắti,* Lat. *co-gnōscō,* Gk *gi-*
gnōskō, OE *cnāwan*
gʷ:Lith. *gývas* 'alive', Skt. *jīvás,* Lat. *vīvus,* Goth. *qius* 'do.',
Gk *bíos* 'life'

IE   *bh*:Lith. *bedù* 'I thrust into', Lat. *fodiō* 'dig', Latv. *bedre* 'pit',
Goth. *badi* 'bed'
dh:Lith. *duktẽ* 'daughter', Skt *duhitắ,* stem *duhitár-,* Gk
thugátēr, Goth. *dauhtar*
gh:(1) Lith. *glodùs* 'smooth', Lat. *glaber,* OHG *glat* 'do.', OE
glæd 'shining, pleasant' > Mod. Eng. *glad*
(2) Lith. *žiemà* 'winter', Gk. *kheĩma,* also *kheimốn,* Lat.
hiems 'do.', Skt *himás* 'snow', ON *gemlingr* 'yearling' lit.
'winterling'
gʷh:Lith. *garếti* 'burn', OPruss. *gorme,* Skt *gharmás* 'warmth',
Gk *thermós,* Lat. *formus* 'warm'

The sibilant *s* is preserved: Lith. *sesuõ,* gen. *seseřs* 'sister', Skt
svásā, stem *svásar-* 'sister', Lat. *soror* < **sosor,* Goth. *swistar,* Gk
(Hesychius) *éor* ('daughter, niece') for **héor* < IE **swesor.* The
allophone *z* is likewise preserved: *lizdas* for **nizdas* 'nest', p. 91.

SONANTS

The IE sonants *m*, *n*, *r*, *l* are in general preserved, but in Pr.Baltic final *m* became *n*, still attested in Old Prussian, but in Lithuanian lost leaving a nasalised vowel in the older language, e.g. sg.acc. IE *sūnum* 'son', OPruss. *sunun*, Lith. *sūnų*.

The vocalised sonants appear regularly as follows:

IE *m̥*: Lith. *šim̃tas* 'hundred', Skt *śatám*, Av. *satem*, Gk *he-katón*, Lat. *centum*, OE *hund* (secondary change of *m* to *n* before dental)

n̥: Lith. *mintìs* 'thought', Lat. *mēns*, gen. *mentis* 'mind', Skt *matás* past part. 'thought', Gk *autó-matos* 'automatic' past part. lit. 'self-thought', Goth. *gamunds* 'memory'

l̥: Lith. *pìlnas* 'full', Skt. *-pṛṇas*, Goth. *fulls* < Pr. Gmc *fulnaz* (Other ablaut grades: Skt *pūrṇás*, Lat. *plēnus*; cf. also Gk *plérēs*)

r̥: Lith. *mirtìs* 'death', Skt. *mṛtís*, Lat. *mors*, gen. *mortis* 'do.', Goth. *maurþr*, OHG *mord* 'murder'

The sonants *w*, *y* are as a rule preserved, appearing as *v*, *j*: Lith. *vejù* 'I weave', Skt. *váyāmi*; Lith. *avìs* 'sheep', Skt *ávis*, Gk. *óis*, Lat. *ovis* 'do.', OE *ēowu* 'ewe'; Lith. *jùngas* 'yoke' (*n* from *jùngiu* 'I yoke', cf. Lat. *jungō*), Skt *yugám*, Gk *zugón*, Lat. *jugum*, Goth. *juk*. See further under 'Diphthongs' below.

VOWELS

Of the short vowels IE *a*, *e*, *i*, *u* are unchanged, but *o* appears as *a* or *ã*:

IE *a*: Lith. *ašìs* 'axle', Skt *ákṣas*, Gk *áxōn*, Lat. *axis*, OHG *ahsa*

e: Lith. *medùs* 'honey', Skt *mádhu* 'do.', Gk *méthu* 'wine', OE *medu* 'mead'

i: Lith. *miglà* 'fog', Gk *omíkhlē*

o: (1) Lith. *pàts*, OLith. *patìs* 'husband', Skt *pátis*, Gk *pósis* for *pótis* 'do.', Lat. *potis* 'powerful', Goth. *brup-faps* 'bridegroom'
(2) Lith. *ãvinas* 'ram', an earlier Baltic stage *ovinas* being represented in the Finnish borrowing *oinas*, cf. Lith. *avìs* 'sheep' above ('Sonants')

u: Lith. *rùdas* 'reddish brown', Skt *rudhirás*, Gk *eruthrós*, Lat. *ruber* 'red', OE *rudig* 'ruddy'

Of the long vowels IE *ē, ī, ū* remain, but *ā* changes to *ō*, while *ō* is diphthongised to *uo*:

IE *ā*:Lith. *móteris* 'woman', Skt *mātár-*, Gk *métēr*, OE *mōdor* 'mother'

  ē:Lith. *měnuo*, gen. *měnesio* 'moon, month', Gk *mén* 'month', *méně* 'moon', Lat. *mēnsis* 'month', Goth. *mena* 'moon', *menoþs* 'month', further Skt *mås-* 'moon, month'

  ī:Lith. *výras* 'man', Skt *vīrás* (With short vowel: Lat. *vir*; in Gmc, *i* broken to *e*: Goth. *wair*, OE *wer*, cf. Mod. Eng. *werwolf*)

  ō:Lith. *júostas* 'girt', Gk *zōstós*, Av. *yāstas*

  ū:Lith. *důmai* (pl.) 'smoke', Skt *dhūmás*, Lat. *fūmus* 'do.', Gk *thūmós* 'passion'

The IE combinations *aw, ew, ow* are reduced to the single diphthong *au*; there is no certain example of IE *ay*, but it doubtless fell together with *oy* as *ai*, IE *ey* remains as *ei*, but both *ai* and *ei* may be further altered to *ie*:

IE *aw*:Lith. *áugti* 'grow', Lat. *augēre*, Goth. *augan* 'increase'

  ew:Lith. *laũkas* 'having a white spot on the forehead', Gk *leukós* 'shining, white', Skt *rokás* 'lustre'

  ow:Lith. *laũkas* 'field', Skt. *lokás* 'open space', Lat. *lūcus*, OLat. *loucos*, OHG *lōh* 'grove', OE *lēah* 'wood, lea' (The basic sense of the prototype is 'clearing'; it is related to the foregoing word)

  ay:perhaps Lith. *priě* 'by, near', cf. Lat. *prae*, Oscan *prai* 'before'

  *ey:*OLith. *deivas*, now *diẽvas* 'god' (the older diphthong still kept in *deivě* or *deĩvě* 'goddess'), Skt *devás*, OLat. *deivos* (>Cl. Lat. *deus*), ON pl. *tīvar*

  oy:Lith. *snaĩgě* 'snowflake' beside *sniẽgas* 'snow', OPruss. *snaygis*, Goth. *snaiws*, OE *snāw* 'do.', OE *snīwan* 'to snow', presupposing IE ablaut change *o/e*, i.e. **snoigʷh-* (noun), **sneigʷh-* (verb)

MORPHOLOGY

We outline below some of the typical features of Lithuanian accidence. In considering the terminations, it will be seen that the Indo-European final consonants have been discarded except for *s*. It will be remembered, too, that the treatment of vowels in final syllables may be different from that found in root syllables illustrated in the previous section.

NOUNS

Vocalic formations of Indo-European age:

  ā-stems: (fem.) *rankà* 'hand'

  o-stems: (masc. only, the class of neuter substantives having been lost) *gaȓdas* 'pen, fold'

  i-stems: (masc.) *žvėrìs* 'wild animal', (fem.) *naktìs* 'night'

  u-stems: (masc.) *sūnùs* 'son'

Lithuanian has accommodated the overwhelming majority of its nouns in vocalic classes, but a few examples of consonantal inflexion survive:

  n-stems: (masc.) *akmuõ* 'stone', gen. *akmeñs*

  r-stems: now only *duktė̃* 'daughter', *sesuõ* 'sister', gen. *dukteȓs*, *seseȓs*; OLith. *mótė* 'woman', gen. *móteres*, but today reshaped after the *i*-stems: nom. *móteris*

  s-stems: only *mėnuo* m. 'moon, month', gen. *mėnesio*

Paradigm: IE *o*-stem

IE **ekwos* m. 'horse' is absent from Baltic (but cf. Lith. *asvà*, OLith. *esvà* f. 'mare' < IE **ekwā*); we take *vyras* m. 'man' < IE **wīros*, cf. Skt *vīrás*.

	Singular	Dual	Plural
nom.	*výras*	*výru*	*výrai*
voc.	*výre*	*výru*	*výrai*
acc.	*výrą*	*výru*	*výrus*
gen.	*výro*	—	*výrų*
dat.	*výrui*	*výram*	*výrams*
loc.	*výre*	—	*výruose*
inst.	*výru*	*výram*	*výrais*

Sg.nom. *-as* < IE *-os*; voc. *-e* < IE *-e*; acc. *-ą* < IE *-om*; gen. *-o* unexplained but presumably an original ablative ultimately identical with or related to IE *-õd* since the Lithuanian genitive includes functions of the ablative (an ancient trait, these cases often having the same ending in Sanskrit, p. 99), cf. OCS.; dat. *-ui* < IE *-ōy*; inst. *-u* < IE *-ō*; loc. *-e* unexplained, an expected *-ie* < IE *-oy* occurs in adv. *namiẽ* 'at home'.

Du.nom.voc.acc. *-u* < IE *-õ*; dat.inst. *-am*, cf. OCS. *-oma*, Skt *-bhyām*, see pl.dat. below.

Pl.nom.voc. *-ai* < **oi*, pronominal ending, cf. Gk, Lat., OCS.;
acc. *-us* unexplained (OPruss. *-ans* < IE *-ons*); gen. *-ų* < IE *-õm*;
dat. *-ams*: Baltic, in common with Slavonic and Germanic, has
a termination containing *m* where other languages have regular
reflexes of IE *bh*, as Skt *-bhyas*, Lat. *-bus*, also Gk *-phi*, cf. du.dat.
inst. above; loc. *-uose*, older **-ōsu*, after the analogy of the *ā*-
stems, i.e. *-ose*, OLith. *-osu*, older **-āsu*, the final *e* of the modern
endings being due to contamination by the singular; inst. *-ais* < IE
-õys.

ADJECTIVES

ā-/o-stems form the bulk of Lithuanian adjectives: *naũjas* m.
'new', *naujà* f. (< IE **newyos*, **newyā*, cf. Skt *návyas*, Gk *neîos*,
beside *návas*, *néos* < IE **newos*). *u*-stems are represented: *saldùs* m.
'sweet', *saldì* f., but the old *i*-stems have disappeared. Present participles are formed with *-nt*: *dìrbąs* or *dìrbantis* 'working' (infin.
dìrbti).

Broadly speaking, the neuter has been lost, but adjectives may
have a neuter form in the nom.voc.acc.sg., as *naũja* (form unexplained), *saldù*.

A Baltic innovation, paralleled in Slavonic, is the development
of a pronominal declension of adjectives, so called since the
(former) demonstrative pronoun *jìs* 'that' (now 'he') was added
enclitically to the simple adjective, both inflecting. This is the
definite form of the adjective, the enclitic demonstrative having
the function of a definite article: *jáunas vaĩkas* '(a) young child',
jaunàsis vaĩkas 'the young child' (*-is* regularly for *-jis*).

Lithuanian is remarkable in having entirely regularised the
forms of comparison: *-èsnis* m., *-èsnė* f. and *-iáusias* m., *-iáusia*
f. being the exclusive terminations of comparative and superlative
respectively: *gẽras* 'good', *gerèsnis*, *geriáusias*. Only the former,
however, is of Indo-European age, being analysable as the product of IE *-yes-nos*.

PRONOUNS

The Lithuanian pronoun reflects the general Indo-European
pattern as may be seen from the following nominative and accusative forms:

1st sg. *àš* 'I', *manè* 'me', pl. *mẽs* 'we', *mùs* 'us', du. *mùdu* m.,
mùdvi f. 'we, us two'

2nd sg. *tù* 'thou', *tavè* 'thee', pl.nom. *jũs*, acc. *jùs* 'you', du. *jùdu* m., *jùdvi* f. 'you two'

The second element of the dual forms is simply the numeral 'two': *dù* m., *dvì* f.

The reflexive pronoun occurs in the oblique cases, e.g. acc. *savè*. It refers not only to the 3rd person subject, as in Latin, etc. (p. 107), but equally to the 1st or 2nd person, doubtless an original Indo-European feature. Etymology shows that it belongs to a stem meaning 'one's own'.

The 3rd person pronoun is formed from the Indo-European stem *ei-*; the nominative forms are: sg. *jìs* 'he', *jì* 'she', pl. *jiẽ* m., *jõs* f. 'they', du. *jiẽdu* m., *jiẽdvi* f. 'they two'.

VERBS

The Indo-European verbal system has been very considerably re-shaped. Synthetic tenses (present, future, imperfect, preterite) occur only in the active, other tenses, likewise the passive, being formed periphrastically with the auxiliary *bū́ti* 'be'. There are three moods: indicative, imperative, subjunctive, with relics of an optative, p. 166.

Thematic conjugation is the rule, but there are traces of athematic forms, e.g. *ẽsti* 'is', OLith. *esmì* 'am', now thematic *esù*. The 3rd person of all numbers is always the same, the form being historically that of the singular. This feature is explained as follows. The plural of inanimates was originally a collective singular, hence the use of the singular verb with the neuter plural subject in Ancient Greek, p. 99. Since the reason for this construction had been long forgotten, other languages removed the apparent anomaly by using the plural verb in such cases also. Lithuanian, however, took the opposite course generalising the singular verb instead.

The preterite stem may differ from the present by ablaut, e.g. *beřti* 'to scatter', 3rd pres. *bēria*, but 3rd pret. *bě̃rė*. Some idea of Lithuanian synthetic conjugation may be obtained from the paradigms below. Conceivably, *beřti* is related to Goth. *bairan*, Lat. *ferre*, etc. 'bear'.

| | INDICATIVE | | | | SUBJUNCTIVE |
	Present	Future	Imperfect	Preterite	Present
Sg.1	*beriù*	*beřsiu*	*beřdavau*	*bėriaũ*	*beřčiau*
2	*berì*	*beřsi*	*beřdavai*	*bėreĩ*	*beřtum*
Pl.1	*bēriame*	*beřsime*	*beřdavome*	*bě̃rėme*	*beřtume*
2	*bēriate*	*beřsite*	*beřdavote*	*bě̃rėte*	*beřtute*

	INDICATIVE				SUBJUNCTIVE
	Present	Future	Imperfect	Preterite	Present
Du.1	bĕriava	beřsiva	beřdavova	bĕrĕva	beřtuva
2	bĕriata	beřsita	beřdavota	bĕrĕta	beřtuta
3rd	bĕria	beřs	beřdavo	bĕrė	beřtų

Imperative sg.2 *beřk*, pl.1 *beřkime*, 2 *beřkite*, du.1 *beřkiva*, 2 *beř-kita*, where *k* is an incorporated particle, p. 166.

Participles include: (active) pres. *bĕriąs* or *bĕriantis*, fut. *beřsiąs*, pret. *bĕręs*; (passive) pres. *bĕriamas*, fut. *beřsimas*, pret. *beřtas*

Old Lithuanian made regular use of a supine *beřtų*, today generally replaced by the infinitive. The ending of the supine (*-tų*) and that of the infinitive (*-ti*) are related formations of Indo-European age. The former continues IE *-tum*, so that Lith. *beřtų* may be directly compared with Skt *bhártum* (infin.) and Lat. *fertum* (sup.). The latter goes back to an IE *ti-* abstract and is possibly a petrified locative. If so, Lith. *beřti* is comparable to Lat. *fertū* (sup.), cf. p. 111.

II: OLD CHURCH SLAVONIC

Two alphabets were used in the writing of Old Church Slavonic texts: the Glagolitic and the later Cyrillic. The first, with more complicated letters, is of disputed origin, the second largely an adaptation of the Greek alphabet. Some contemporary Slavonic languages, such as Russian, still use Cyrillic, but others now employ the Latin alphabet. Old Church Slavonic may be similarly transliterated.

PHONOLOGY

Notes on pronunciation:

č, š, ž, c, ch, j are pronounced [tʃ, ʃ, ʒ, ts, χ, y]; *ĭ, ŭ* denote reduced vowels which may be pronounced as very short *i, u*; *ę, ǫ* are nasalised [ɛ̃, ɔ̃]; *y* is a high central vowel between *i* and *u* (as in Russian); *ě* is a very open *e*; *i* is pronounced [yi] after vowels.

Vowel quantity was not phonemic in Old Church Slavonic and there is no direct evidence for it. On the testimony of certain modern languages, e.g. Russian and particularly Serbo-Croatian, Old Church Slavonic had a movable accent and distinguished acute and circumflex intonation, as in Ancient Greek (pp. 85f.), cf. Russ. *golová* 'head', acc. *gólovu*, Serbo-Croatian *gláva*, acc. *glãvu*, further Lith. *galvà*, etc., p. 125.

By comparison with Lithuanian, Old Church Slavonic has a more advanced phonology involving a large number of combinative changes, only two or three of which can be referred to here.

CONSONANTS

IE *p*: OCS *pluti* 'sail' (vb.), Lith. *pláuti* 'wash', Skt *plávate* 'swims', Lat. *pluit* 'rains', Gk *pléō* 'sail', OE *flōwan* 'flow'

t: OCS *tĭnŭkŭ* 'slender, thin', Skt *tánukas*, also *tanús*, Lith. *tę́vas*, Lat. *tenuis* 'do.', Gk *tanu-* 'long', OE *þynne* 'thin'

k: (1) OCS *krŭvĭ* 'blood', Lith. *kraũjas* 'do.', Skt *kravís* 'raw flesh', Gk. *kréas* 'meat', Lat. *cruor* 'gore', OE *hrēaw* 'raw'
(2) OCS *sĭ* m. 'this', Lith. *šìs* 'do.', Gk *(e)keînos* 'that', Lat. *cis* 'this side of', Goth. *himma* dat.sg., etc. (p. 162) 'this'

kʷ: OCS *kŭto* 'who' (*-to* demonstrative), Lith. *kàs*, Skt *kás*, Goth. *hwas* 'do.', Lat. *quod* 'which'

IE *b*: OCS *bolii* 'bigger', Skt *bálīyān* 'stronger', *bálam* 'strength', Gk *beltíōn* 'better' (for **belíōn* due to influence of alternative form *bélteros* 'do.'), Lat. *dēbilis* 'weak' (p. 87), Mod. Low Ger., North Frisian *pal* 'firm'

d: OCS *domŭ* 'house', Skt *dámas*, Lat. *domus* 'do.', Gk *dómos* 'hut', OE *timber* 'building, timber' (p. 182)

g: (1) OCS *igo* 'yoke', Lith. *jùngas*, Skt *yugám*, Gk *zugón*, Lat. *jugum*, Goth. *juk*
(2) OCS *zǫbŭ* 'tooth', Lith. *žam̃bas* 'pointed object', Skt *jámbhas* 'tooth', Gk *gómphos* 'peg', OE *camb* 'comb'

gʷ: OCS *govęždĭ* 'pertaining to cattle' < **govędo*, cf. Bulg. *govédo*, Latv. *gùovs*, Skt *gaús*, Gk *boûs*, Lat. *bōs* '(head of) cattle', OE *cū* 'cow'

IE *bh*: OCS *brŭvĭ* 'eyebrow', Lith. *bruvìs*, Skt *bhrús*, Gk *ophrûs*, OE *brū*

dh: OCS *děti* 'put', Lith. *děti*, Skt *dádhāmi*, Gk *títhēmi* 'do.', Lat. *faciō*, OE *dōn* 'make, do'

gh: (1) OCS *gostĭ* 'guest', Lat. *hostis* 'stranger, enemy', Goth. *gasts* 'stranger'
(2) OCS *vozŭ* 'carriage', Gk *ókhos* < **wokhos* 'do.', further OE *wægn* 'wain' (Same root as *vesti* 'convey', p. 134)

gʷh: OCS *goniti* 'hunt' (vb.), Lith. *ganýti* 'herd, pasture' (vb.), Skt *hánti* 'slays', Gk *theínō* 'strike', Lat. *-fendō* 'fend', Goth. **gunþs* 'battle' (p. 118)

The sibilant *s* may be preserved: OCS *solĭ* 'salt', Latv. *sāls*, Lat.

sāl, gen. *salis*, Gk. *háls*, further OE *sealt* (lit. 'salted'). The allophone *z* is likewise preserved: *gnězdo* 'nest', p. 91. In many environments, however, IE *s* appears as *ch*, e.g. when intervocalic after *i* or *u*: OCS *tichŭ* 'quiet', Lith *teisùs* 'just', OCS *suchŭ* 'dry', Lith. *saũsas* 'do.', and similarly after *ě*, cf. pl.loc. ending *raběchŭ*, p. 137.

A feature of consonants is their palatalisation before front vowels, to which a number of new phonemes owe their origin, cf. *počiti* 'rest' (vb.) beside *pokoi* 'do.' (noun), *živŭ* 'alive' but Lith. *gývas* 'do.', *myšĭ* 'mouse' (below) from **mychĭ* (*ch* < IE *s*), further *cěna* 'price' beside Lith. *káina* 'do.'

SONANTS

We note that IE *m̥*, *n̥* appear indifferently as *ę*: OCS *desętĭ* 'ten', Lith. *dẽšimt*, cf. p. 192, OCS *pamętĭ* 'memory' (*pa-* prefix), Lith. *atmintìs* 'do.', *mintìs* 'thought'. IE *l̥*, *r̥* appear as *lŭ*, *rŭ*, also as *lĭ*, *rĭ* (interchange of *ŭ/ĭ* also found in other environments), and finally metathesis is commonly found with these sonants: OCS *vlŭkŭ* 'wolf', Lith. *vil̃kas*, Skt *vŕkas*, etc., p. 119; OCS *sŭ-mrĭtĭ* beside *sŭ-mĭrtĭ* 'death', also simplex **mĭrtĭ* (Czech *mrt* 'dead part'), Lith. *mirtìs*, etc., p. 127.

The IE sonants *w*, *y*, where preserved, appear as *v*, *j*: OCS *voda* 'water', Lith. *vanduõ* (*n* secondary), Goth. *wato*, OE *wæter*; OCS *junŭ* 'young', Lith. *jáunas*, Lat. *iuvenis*, Goth. *juggs* (*gg = ng*) 'do.', Skt *yúvan-* 'young man'.

VOWELS

Slavonic is unique in changing IE *a* to *o*; of the other IE short vowels, *e*, *o* are unchanged, but *i*, *u* become *ĭ*, *ŭ*:

IE *a*:OCS *more* 'sea', Latv. *mare* 'land-locked bay', Lat. *mare*, Goth. *marei* 'sea'

     e:OCS *vesti* 'convey', Lith. *vèsti*, Skt *váhati*, Lat. *vehō*, 'do.', Gk dial. *wekhétō* 'let him convey'.

     i:OCS *mĭgla* 'fog', Lith. *miglà*, Gk *omíkhlē*

     o:OCS *oko* 'eye', Lith. *akìs*, Lat. *oculus*, Gk (Hesychius) *ókkon*, (dial.) *óktallos*

     u:OCS *bŭděti* 'be awake', Lith. *budéti* 'be on guard', Skt *búdhyate* 'awakes, recognises', Gk aor. *eputhómēn* 'I learnt'

Note. The reduced vowels *ĭ*, *ŭ* were sometimes confused, cf. OCS *vŭdova* 'widow' for etymologically correct **vĭdova*.

The reflexes of the IE long vowels are as follows: *ā*, *ō* fall together giving *a*, while *ē*, *ī*, *ū* appear as *ě*, *i*, *y* respectively.

IE *ā*: OCS *bratrŭ* 'brother', Lith. (dimin.) *broterělis*, otherwise *brólis*, Skt *bhrătar-*, Lat. *frāter*, Goth. *broþar* 'brother', Gk *phrătēr* 'clansman'

ē: OCS *sěti* 'sow', Lith. *sěti*, OE *sāwan* 'do.', Lat. *sēvī* 'I have sown'

ī: OCS *svinŭ* 'pertaining to swine', Lat. *suīnus* 'do.', Goth. *swein* 'pig'

ō: OCS *darŭ* 'gift', Gk *dŏron*, also OCS. *danĭ* 'tax', Lith. *dúonis*, Skt *dănam*, Lat. *dōnum* 'gift' (*n/r* alternation ultimately due to change noted on p. 98; two forms have persisted in Slavonic thanks to morphological and semantic differentiation)

ū: OCS *myšĭ* 'mouse', Skt *mŭs*, Gk *mŭs*, Lat., OE *mūs* (On *š*, see p. 134)

The IE combinations *aw*, *ow* fell together giving *u*, *ew* became *ju*; IE *ay*, *oy* fell together giving *ě*, *ey* appears as *i*:

IE *aw*: OCS *turŭ* 'aurochs', Lith. *taŭras* 'bison', Gk *taŭros*, Lat. *taurus* 'bull'

ew: OCS *ljubŭ* 'beloved', Goth. *liufs* 'do.', Lith *liaupsě* 'song of praise', Skt *lobhas* 'desire'

ow: OCS *ruda* 'metal' lit. 'red substance (ore)', Goth. *raups* 'red' (ablauting with Gk *ereúthō* 'redden', *eruthrós* red')

ay: OCS *lěvŭ* 'left' (adj.), Lat. *laevus*, Gk *laiós*

ey: OCS *iti* 'go', Lith. *eĭti*, Skt *émi*, Gk *eĭmi*

oy: OCS *vědě* 'I know', Skt *véda*, Gk *oĭda*, Goth. *wait*

The above scheme was, however, frequently disturbed. Due to a peculiar development of Primitive Slavonic age, every syllable in Old Church Slavonic ends in a vowel. This led to a special treatment of IE *aw*, *ay*, etc., when intervocalic. For the sake of argument we shall regard OCS *kujǫ* 'I forge' as reflecting an earlier **kawjom* (cf. Lith. *káuju* 'I forge, strike' < **kawjō*) the syllables being *ku-jǫ*. Similarly OCS *kovati* 'to forge' (Lith. *káuti*) reflects earlier **kawati*, but here the syllabic division had to be **ka-wa-ti*. In this way old *aw* was decomposed, the first element eventually changing to *o* in accordance with rule, the second element becoming consonantal and appearing in the records as *v*. Cognate with the above are OHG *houwan*, OE *hēawan* 'strike, hew' < Pr. Gmc **hauwanan*; further with dental extension Lat. *cūdō* 'strike'. If all these words originally had the same ablaut grade, then OCS *kujǫ*, *kovati* could be referred to earlier **kowjom*, **kowati* with the same net result.

The nasal vowels of Old Church Slavonic, *ę*, *ǫ* naturally presuppose loss of IE *m*, *n*, cf. OCS *zǫbŭ*, *pamętĭ*, pp. 133f.

MORPHOLOGY

We outline below some of the typical features of Old Church Slavonic accidence. As regards the endings themselves, we refer to what was said in connection with Lithuanian, adding the proviso that changes in Slavonic have been considerably more drastic.

NOUNS

Vocalic formations of Indo-European age are:
    ā-stems: (fem.) *rǫka* 'hand'
    o-stems: (masc.) *gradŭ* 'town, garden', (neut.) *město* 'place'
    i-stems: (masc.) *zvěrĭ* 'wild animal', (fem.) *noštĭ* 'night'
    u-stems: (masc.) *synŭ* 'son'
Consonant declension is somewhat better preserved than in Lithuanian, though the terminations often show contamination from the vocalic classes. Examples include:
    n-stems: (masc.) *kamy* 'stone', gen. *kamene*, (neut.) *sěme* 'seed', gen. *sěmene*
    r-stems: only *dŭšti* 'daughter', *mati* 'mother', gen. *dŭštere*, *matere*
    s-stems: (neut.) *ucho* 'ear', gen. *ušese*
    t-stems: (neut.) *telę* 'calf', gen. *telęte*

Paradigm: IE *o*-stem

IE **ekwos* m. 'horse' is absent from Slavonic; we take *rabu* m. 'servant' (an innovating southern form), otherwise *robŭ* < Pr. Sl. **orbŭ* presumably < IE **orbos*, cf. Lat. *orbus* 'orphaned'; further *selo* n. 'field', presumably < IE **selom*, cf. Lat. *solum* 'ground'.

	Singular	Dual	Plural
nom.	*rabŭ*	*raba*	*rabi*
voc.	*rabe*	*raba*	*rabi*
acc.	*rabŭ*	*raba*	*raby*

	Singular	Dual	Plural
gen.	*raba*	*rabu*	*rabŭ*
dat.	*rabu*	*raboma*	*rabomŭ*
loc.	*rabě*	*rabu*	*raběchŭ*
inst.	*rabomĭ*	*raboma*	*raby*

Neuter: Sg.nom.voc.acc. *selo*, Du. *selě*, Pl. *sela*; otherwise as above.

Sg.nom.acc. m. *-ŭ* unexplained, the acc. contrasting with the equally problematic nom.voc.acc. n. *-o*, the prototype of both being theoretically IE *-om*; voc. m. *-e* < IE *-e*; gen. *-a* presumably an original ablative, cf. Lith.; dat. *-u* unexplained; loc. *-ě* < IE *-oy*; inst. *-omĭ* apparently thematic *o* with *mĭ* comparable to Gk *-phi*, p. 130, see pl.dat. below.

Du.nom.voc.acc. m. *-a* < IE *-ō̃*, n. *-ě* < IE *-oy*; gen.loc. *-u* unexplained; dat.inst. *-oma*, cf. Lith. *-am*, Skt *-bhyām*, see pl.dat. below.

Pl.nom.voc. *-i* < *-oi*, pronominal ending, cf. Gk, Lat., Lith.; acc. m. *-y* < IE *-ons*; nom.voc.acc. n. *-a* < IE *-ā*; gen. *-ŭ* unexplained, but perhaps ultimately from IE *-ŏm*; dat. *-omŭ* with *m*-formative as in sg.inst., du.dat.inst. above, cf. Lith.; loc. *-ěchŭ* < IE *-oisu*; inst. *-y* unexplained, but perhaps < IE *-ŏys*.

As we see, the Indo-European case system as such is well preserved, but the individual endings are much changed and details of their evolution often lacking. It should not be forgotten, however, that the Indo-European endings postulated on the basis of a comparison of Latin, Greek and Sanskrit, may not be entirely valid for that part of Indo-European from which Old Church Slavonic descends. The same holds good in principle for any other branch. Doubtless further alternative reconstructions should be posited in view of the dialect differences within Primitive Indo-European speech. Unfortunately the phonologically advanced forms of Old Church Slavonic make any additional reconstructions hazardous. One must be resigned, in a number of instances, to an agnostic 'evolution obscure'.

ADJECTIVES

The prevailing type of inflexion is that of the *ā-/o*-stems: *novŭ* m. 'new', *nova* f., *novo* n. (< **no-wos* with assimilation of *e* < IE **newos*). Present participles are formed with original *-nt*: *bery* 'taking', gen. *berǫšta* (*-y* < IE *-ōns*, *-ǫšt-* < **-onty-* < IE *-onti-*).

The pronominal declension has the same structure and function as in Lithuanian (p. 130), hence *novŭ*, pron.decl. *novyi* < **novŭ-jĭ*, where *-jĭ* was originally a demonstrative pronoun 'that', comparable to Lith. *jìs*. In later Slavonic the semantic distinction between the two declensions was lost, except to a limited degree in Serbo-Croatian. Both may also elsewhere survive, as in Russian, where the convention developed that the simple form can only be used attributively.

Old Church Slavonic forms the comparative with suffixes reflecting IE *-yes* and its ablaut varieties; the stem of the positive may be modified: *novŭ*, comp. *novĕi* < **nov-ĕ-jĭ*. There is no superlative proper.

PRONOUNS

The Slavonic pronoun may be closely compared with Lithuanian, as the examples show.

1st sg. *azŭ* 'I', *mę* or *mene* 'me', pl. *my* 'we', *ny* or *nas* 'us', du. *vĕ* 'we two', *na* 'us two'

2nd sg. *ty* 'thou', *tę* or *tebe* 'thee', pl.nom. *vy*, acc. *vy* or *vas* 'you', du.nom.acc. *va* 'you two'

The reflexive pronoun has acc. *sę* or *sebe*; it refers indiscriminately to all three persons.

The 3rd person pronoun is: (nominative forms) sg. *onŭ* 'he', *ona* 'she', *ono* 'it', pl. *oni* m., *ony* f., *ona* n. 'they', du. *ona* m., *onĕ* f.n. 'they two'. The pronoun is in origin a demonstrative 'that', cf. Lith. *añs*, OLith. *anàs* 'do.'. It has replaced an earlier *jĭ*, etc., preserved in the terminations of the pronominal adjective.

VERBS

The verbal system of the parent language has been even more drastically modified than in Lithuanian. There are only three synthetic tenses, namely present, imperfect and aorist, other tenses and the passive being formed periphrastically with the auxiliary *byti* 'be'; however, perfective presents have future meaning, see below. A solitary relic of the Indo-European perfect is *vĕdĕ* 'I know' originally 'I have seen', p. 115, the perfect in Slavonic being expressed by the present tense of the auxiliary with the past participle ending in *-lŭ*. Of the Indo-European moods, only the indicative and imperative remain.

We have already noticed that the Indo-European verb expressed not only when the action was done, but also how it was done, p. 109. We noted that Latin modified the system by strongly developing the temporal function of the verb. Slavonic, on the other hand, emphasised aspectic distinctions, creating two main categories, perfective and imperfective. The latter denoted the action in terms of its duration, the former in terms of its starting or finishing, e.g. imperf. *padati* 'fall', perf. *pasti* 'fall down'.

Thematic inflexion is usual, but a small number of verbs have athematic forms, e.g. *jesmĭ* 'am', *jestŭ* 'is'. The paradigms below give an impression of synthetic conjugation in Old Slavonic. Ablaut is often visible in the stem formation, e.g. infin. *bĭrati* 'bear, take, collect' < IE *bhr̥-*, 1 sg.pres. *berǫ* < IE *bher-*.

	Present	Imperfect	Aorist
Sg.1	*berǫ*	*bĭraachŭ*	*bĭrachŭ*
2	*bereši*	*bĭraaše*	*bĭra*
3	*beretŭ*	*bĭraaše*	*bĭra*
Pl.1	*beremŭ*	*bĭraachomŭ*	*bĭrachomŭ*
2	*berete*	*bĭraašete*	*bĭraste*
3	*berǫtŭ*	*bĭraachǫ*	*bĭrašę*
Du.1	*berevě*	*bĭraachově*	*bĭrachově*
2	*bereta*	*bĭraašeta*	*bĭrasta*
3	*berete*	*bĭraašete*	*bĭraste*

Imperative sg.2,3 *beri*, pl.1 *berimŭ*, 2 *berite*, du.1 *berivě*, 2 *berita*
Participles: (active) pres. *bery* (p. 137), past (1) *bĭravŭ*, (2) *bĭralŭ*; (passive) pres. *beromŭ*, past *bĭranŭ*

Old Slavonic has a supine *bĭratŭ* 'bearing', the ending of which (*-tŭ*) is related to that of the infinitive (*-ti*). These correspond to Lith. *-tų*, *-ti* respectively, of Indo-European ancestry, as explained on p. 132.

10

CELTIC

Even at the time of the earliest records the two divisions of Celtic were differentiated to a point which excluded any mentionable degree of mutual comprehension. On the other hand, their close affinities are apparent enough to the philological enquirer so that it will be possible, to some extent, to treat them together. The most representative languages are Irish and Welsh.

PHONOLOGY

The phonology of Gaulish appears to have been on a plane roughly comparable to that of Latin. But Gaulish is poorly preserved. It is also unfortunate that the Celtic best known to us, Insular Celtic, is phonologically very advanced with a bewildering multitude of combinative changes, many of them highly sophisticated and not a few still obscure. Nevertheless, it is possible to find numbers of words whose phonetic shape illustrates the spontaneous evolution of Indo-European sounds. But here, too, developments have often been complex, so that only a selection of more significant facts can be noted in an outline account.

NOTES ON PRONUNCIATION

Old Irish. Stress falls on the first syllable, except in certain verbal compounds (see 'Verbs'). The acute accent marks long vowels.

As an approximate rule, it may be stated that *p*, *t*, *c* are voiced when medial or final, i.e. [b, d, g], while *b*, *d*, *g* in these positions are spirants [β, δ, γ]; *ch* is pronounced [χ]; *m* may be a nasalised [β]—it then corresponds phonologically to W *f*.

Welsh. As a rule, stress is now on the penultimate, but in Old Welsh it fell on the last syllable. Vowel length may be indicated by a circumflex.

ll, rh are voiceless *l, r*; the letters *ch, dd, f, ff, ng* are pronounced [χ, δ, v, f, ŋ]; *w* may be a consonant, or a vowel [u]. In Southern Welsh, *i* and *u* have fallen together as *i*, but Northern Welsh *u* is somewhat similar to Russian *y*. In stressable monosyllables, *y* has the same values as *u*, in final syllables it is pronounced [i], otherwise [ə].

MUTATIONS

The remarkable mutations of Insular Celtic, by which initial consonants are frequently changed in connected speech, are the product of secondary evolution. The changes themselves are phonetic in origin, and as such comparable to the rules of sandhi in Sanskrit. But they were later modified by analogy and eventually grammaticalised. The results in the different languages vary greatly in spite of the same underlying principle. The changes are often unmarked in Old Irish; we therefore quote Modern Irish in the examples which follow.

Ir. *bó* (radical form) '(a) cow', but *an bhó* [ən woː] 'the cow', *an bhó dhubh* [γu] (rad. *dubh* [du]) 'the black cow'. This change is known as lenition, and arose when the occlusive in question found itself (originally) between vowels; it is paralleled in W *buwch* '(a) cow', *y fuwch ddu* (rad. *du*) 'the black cow'. There are no such changes, however, with masculine nouns, hence Ir. *capall* '(a) horse', *an capall dubh* 'the black horse', W *ceffyl, y ceffyl du* 'do.'

Another change, very prominent in Irish, is termed eclipsis. This is a nasal mutation, an original final *n* effecting the initial consonant of the following word, as Ir. *seacht mbliana* [ʃaχt mlʹiənə] (rad. *bliana*) 'seven years', W *saith mlynedd* (rad. *blynedd*) 'do.' In positions where eclipsis would occur, *n-* is prefixed to initial vowels in Irish, as *na deich n-aithne* [nə dʹeː ńæńə] (rad. *aithne*) 'the ten commandments', cf. p. 191.

In British, voiceless occlusives became spirants under various conditions, e.g. W *cant* 'hundred', *tri chant* 'three hundred', *ceffyl a chart* 'a horse and cart'. In Cornish and Breton, voiced occlusives may be devoiced, e.g. Co. *ow tybry* (rad. *dybry*) 'in eating', Bret. *ho tent* (rad. *dent*) 'your teeth'.

Notice Ir. *a teach* [ə t′aχ] 'her house', *a theach* [ə haχ] 'his house', *a dteach* [ə d′aχ] 'their house', W *ei thŷ* 'her house', *ei dŷ* 'his house', *eu tŷ* 'their house', both *ei* and *eu* being pronounced [i]. Radical forms: Ir. *teach*, W *tŷ*.

CONSONANTS

IE *p*:Generally lost: OIr. *lán*, W *llawn* 'full', Lat. *plēnus*, Lith. *pìlnas*, Skt *pūrṇás*, Goth. *fulls*, Gk *plérēs* 'do.'; OIr. *súan*, W *hun* 'sleep', Gk *húpnos*, Skt *svápnas*, OE *swefn*, Lat. *somnus* < **sopnos*, OCS *sŭnŭ* < **sŭpnŭ* 'do.', Lith. *sãpnas* 'dream'

t:OIr. *tanae*, W *tenau* 'thin', Skt *tanús*, Lat. *tenuis*, OE *þynne*, Lith. *tévas*, OCS *tĭnŭkŭ* 'do.', Gk *tanu-* 'long'

k:OIr. *cride* 'heart', W *craidd* 'middle', Gk *kardíā*, Lat. *cor*, gen. *cordis*, Goth. *hairto*, Lith. *šìrdìs*, OCS *srŭdĭce*

kʷ:OIr. *cruim*, W *pryf* 'worm', Skt. *kŕmis*, Lith. *kirmìs* 'do.' The Ogham inscriptions, however, preserve IE *kʷ*, written *Q*, in the frequently occurring *MAQ(Q)I*, later *MACI* (indicating loss of original labial) gen. of OIr. *macc*, Mod. Ir. *mac*, OW *map*, W *mab* 'son'.

The different treatment of IE *kʷ* has led to the use of the terms P- and Q-Celtic to denote the two divisions of the Celtic branch (p. 42). The contrast is noticed in several pairs of words, e.g. initially in OIr. *cenn*, W *pen* 'head', OIr. *coire*, W *pair* 'cauldron', OIr. *cruth*, W *pryd* 'appearance', OIr. *crenid*, W *prŷn* 'buys', OIr. *cía*, W *pwy* 'who', OIr. *Cruthen* 'Pict', W *Prydain* 'Britain'.

IE *b*:A possible example of this rare IE sound is W *bustl* 'gall', Lat. *bīlis* 'do.'

d:OIr. *deich*, W *deg* 'ten', Lat. *decem*, etc., pp. 191f.

g:OIr. *gein* 'birth', W *geni* 'be born', Gk *gígnomai* 'become', Lat. *gignō*, OE *cennan* 'beget'

gʷ:OIr. *béo*, W *byw* 'alive', Skt. *jīvás*, Lat. *vīvus*, Goth. *qius*, Lith. *gývas*, OCS *živŭ* 'do.', Gk *bíos* 'life'

IE *bh*:OIr. *bláth*, MidW *blawd* 'flower', OE *blǣd* 'do., plant', Lat. *flōs*, Goth. *bloma* 'flower, bloom', OE *blōstm* 'blossom'

dh:OIr. *dorus*, W *drws* also *dôr* 'door', Gk *thúrā*, Lat. *foris*, Goth. *daur*, OCS *dvĭrĭ*, Lith. (pl.) *dùrys* 'do.'

gh:OIr. *gaim-red*, W *gaeaf*, OW *gaem* 'winter', Gk *kheimṓn*,
Lat. *hiems*, Lith. *žiemà*, OCS *zima* 'do.', Skt *himás*
'snow', ON *gemlingr* 'winterling (yearling)'

gʷh:OIr. *gorad* 'warming', W *gori* 'brooding', Skt *gharmás*
'warmth', Gk *thermós*, Lat. *formus* 'warm', Lith. *garĕti*,
OCS *gorĕti* 'burn'

IE *s* may remain when initial: OIr. *suide*, W *sedd* 'seat', but
usually becomes *h* in British: OIr. *sen*, W *hen* 'old', cf. Skt *sánas*,
Lith. *sēnas*, Gk *hénos* 'do.', Lat. *senex* 'old man'. Intervocalicly
it was lost in Insular Celtic: Gaul. *esox*, OIr. *éo*, W *eog* 'salmon'.
It was often assimilated to other consonants, e.g. OIr. *net*, W
nyth 'nest', cf. p. 180. There are many other special developments
involving the loss of the sibilant, particularly in British, e.g. OIr.
srón 'nose', W *ffroen* 'nostril', OIr. *slúag*, W *llu* 'host', OIr. *siur*,
W *chwaer* 'sister', OBrit. *Uxello-dūnum* 'High Town', OIr. *úasal*,
W *uchel*, cf. Gk *hupsēlós* 'high'.

It may be emphasised that changes in non-initial position were
often quite different from those noted above. Particularly significant is the lenition in intervocalic position found in Insular Celtic,
e.g. Gaul. *Epo-* 'horse', W *ebol* 'colt' (*p* > *b*), OIr. *ech* 'horse'
(*k* > *ch*). This is, of course, the same change as affected initial
consonants when, in connected speech, they came to stand between vowels, i.e. following a word ending in a vowel. See 'Mutations' above.

SONANTS

Initially, IE *w* appears in Irish as *f*, in Neo-British as *gw*, but was
unchanged in the oldest Celtic: OIr. *fén*, W *gwain* 'waggon', OBrit.
co-uinnus 'chariot', cf. OE *wægn* 'wain, waggon'. It is often lost in
other positions, but after consonants it usually became *b* in Irish,
while remaining in British: OIr. *medb*, W *meddw* 'drunk', cf. Gk
methúō 'am drunk'. IE *y* was entirely lost in Irish, but mostly retained in British: OIr. *óac*, W *ieuanc* 'young', cf. Lat. *juvencus*
'young man', Goth. *juggs* 'young'. By a striking change, *y* could
in certain surroundings develop into W *dd*, thus *newydd* 'new',
Gaul. *Nevio-*, *Novio-dūnum* 'New Town', OIr. *naue*, Lat. *Novius*,
Lith. *naūjas* < IE **newyos*, similarly W *Iwerddon*, OIr. *Ériu* 'Ireland'.

The treatment of IE *ḷ, ṛ, ṃ, ṇ* varies considerably. Examples:
OIr. *lethan*, W *llydan* 'broad', Gk. *plátanos* 'plane-tree', *platús*,
Skt *pṛthús* 'broad'; OIr. *marb*, W *marw* 'dead' < Pr. Clt. **marwos*

(with ending from *biwos 'living', cf. OIr. béo, etc.), cf. Skt mṛtás,
Lat. mortuus, OCS mrŭtvŭ (ending from živŭ 'living') 'do.' The
syllabic nasals often fell together as n with varying subsequent developments: OIr. cét, W cant 'hundred', cf. Lat. centum, OE
hund, all presupposing IE *kn̥tom, where n̥ is for still older m̥,
witness Lith. šim̃tas, p. 127.

VOWELS

As far as spontaneous evolution is concerned, the IE short vowels
may be said to have remained without change:

IE   a: OIr. arathar, W aradr 'plough', Gk árotron, Lat. arātrum,
       another formation Lith. arklas 'do.', further OIr. arim, W
       arddaf, Lat. arō, Gk aróō, Lith. ariù, OCS orjǫ, Goth. arja
       'I plough'
     e: OIr. ech, Gaul. Epo- 'horse', Epona (name of goddess), W
       ebol (diminutive) 'colt', Lat. equus, Goth. aihwa- 'horse',
       OLith. ešvà 'mare'
     i: OIr. bith, Gaul. Bitu- (but W byd) 'world' < Pr. Clt. *bitus,
       cf. Gk bíos 'life'
     o: OIr. roth, W rhod 'wheel', Lat. rota, OHG rad 'do.'
     u: OIr. sruth, W ffrwd 'stream' < Pr. Clt. *srutus, cf. Gk hrutós,
       Skt srutás 'flowing'

But in the great majority of cases, combinative changes have
modified the quality of the IE short vowels. In particular, i, u
frequently appear as e, o, often due to a, o (which may have
disappeared) in a following syllable; such lowering is especially
common in Irish. Examples are: OIr. betho gen. of bith 'world',
further OIr. fedb, W gweddw 'widow', Skt vidhávā, Lat. vidua,
Goth. widuwo 'do.'; OIr. srotha gen. of sruth 'stream', further OIr.
domuin, W dwfn m., dofn (< Pr. Clt. *dubnā) f. 'deep', Lith. dùgnas
for *dùbnas 'bottom', dubùs 'deep'.
    Primitive Celtic reduced the five IE long vowels to three, IE ā, ō,
falling together as Pr. Clt. ā, IE ē, ī falling together as Pr. Clt. ī.
In British, Pr. Clt. ā subsequently changed to ō becoming W aw,
and Pr. Clt. ū became ī.

IE   ā: OIr. bráthir, W brawd, pl. brodyr 'brother', Gaul. Brātonos
       'Big Brother', Skt bhrātar-, Lat. frāter, Lith. broterělis
       (diminutive), OCS bratrŭ 'do.', Gk phrātēr 'clansman'
     ē: OIr. rí, gen. ríg, Gaul. -rīx, W rhi 'king', Lat. rēx, cf. Skt

rájā 'do.' (Goth. *reiks*, OE *-rīc* 'do.' must be borrowings from Celtic)

ī: OIr. *rím*, W *rhif* 'number', OE *rīm* 'do.'

ō: OIr. *gnáth* 'known', Gaul. *Epo-so-gnātus* 'well used to horses', W (obsolete) *gnawd* 'customary', Gk *gnōtós*, Lat. *nōtus*, archaic *gnōtus* 'known'

ū: OIr. *rún*, W *rhin* 'secret', OE *rūn* 'do.'

The IE combinations *aw, ew, ow* are partly preserved as diphthongs in Gaulish, but there are instances of the last two falling together as *ou*, with a further change to *ō*. In Insular Celtic all the original diphthongs usually changed to *ō*. This further changed to *u* in Welsh, but remained in early Irish, afterwards commonly becoming *úa*. Occasionally, the original diphthong may be preserved as [au], especially in Irish.

IE *aw*: OIr. *áu, ó*, gen. *aue* 'ear', Lat. *auris* 'do.'

   ew: Gaul. *Teuto-, Touto-, tōtis*, OIr. archaic *Tóthal*, later *Túathal* (*Ó Túathail* 'O'Toole'), *túath*, W *tud*, Lith. *tautà*, Goth. *þiuda* 'people'

   ow: OIr. archaic *bóchaill*, later *búachaill* 'cowherd', W *bugail* 'herdsman', Gk *boukólos* 'cowherd'

The descendants of IE *ay, ey, oy* preserve their diphthongal character somewhat better.

IE *ay*: Gaul. *Aesus, Ēsus*, OIr. *aís*, variants *áes, oís, óes* (in later OIr. pronounced as a monophthong [eː]), W *oes*, another formation *oed* 'age', Lat. *aetās*, also *aevum*, Gk *aión* < **aiwón*, Goth. *aiws* 'do.'

   ey: Gaul. *rēda* 'cart', OIr. *ríad* 'course, drive (subst.)', Gaul. *-vērēdus* 'horse', W (obsolete) *gorŵydd* 'steed'

   oy: OIr. *oín, óen* (thus falling together with the product of IE *ay*), W *un* 'one', OLat. *oinos*, etc., pp. 191f.

MORPHOLOGY

There is evidence pointing to well-preserved declensional paradigms in Gaulish and Old British, but in Neo-British the traditional system collapsed, the only remaining inflexion being that of the plural. Furthermore, the neuter gender was lost. Irish, however, has been more conservative; Old Irish still distinguished five syntactical cases and retained all three genders. But phonetic attrition, syncretism and analogy have produced a very advanced morphology. Nevertheless, typical Indo-European formations are clearly recognisable, though sometimes only after informed close scrutiny. Indeed, the same is even true of Neo-British forms where, in a small minority of cases at any rate, the form of the plural points to the old declensional class.

NOUNS

Old Irish vocalic stems of Indo-European age:

ā-stems: (fem.) *ingen*, Ogham *INIGENA* 'daughter'

o-stems: (masc.) *marc* 'horse', (neut.) *dún* 'fort'

i-stems: (masc.) *cnáim* 'bone', (fem.) *súil* 'eye', (neut.) *muir* 'sea'

u-stems: (masc.) *cath* 'battle', (neut.) *dorus* 'door'

Traces in British include:

ā-stems: see 'Adjectives'

o-stems: W *march* 'horse' (Gaul. *Marco-*) < Pr. Clt. **markos*, pl. *meirch* (*i*-infection) pointing to Pr. Clt. **markī*

i-stems: W *môr* m. 'sea', pl. *moroedd* with ending from IE *-eyes* (cf. Skt *-ayas*, Gk *-eis*, Lat. *-ēs*) proper to masc. and fem., here transferred to a former neuter

u-stems: W *cad* 'battle' (Gaul. *Catu-*) < Pr. Clt. **katus*, pl. *cadau* with ending from IE *-owes* (cf. Skt *-avas*, Gk *-eis*, Lat. *-ūs*), cf. also W *drws* m. 'door', pl. *drysau* with ending from masculine

Old Irish preserves a large number of consonant stems including:

n-stems: (masc.) *cú* 'hound', gen. *con*, (fem.) *Ériu* 'Ireland', gen. *Érenn*, (neut.) *ainm* 'name', gen. *anme*

s-stems: (neut.) *tech* 'house'

r-stems: (masc.) *athir* 'father', (fem.) *máthir* 'mother'

stems ending in other consonants: (masc.) *rí* 'king', gen. *ríg*, (fem.) *nathir* 'snake', gen. *nathrach*, (masc.) *druí* 'druid', gen. *druad*, (fem.) *luch* 'mouse', gen. *lochad*, (masc.) *care* 'friend', gen. *carat*

The British cognates usually preserve some reminiscence of the old stem, as W *ci* m. 'dog', pl. *cŵn*, *Iwerddon* f. 'Ireland', *enw* m. 'name', OW *anu*, OW pl. *enuein* (*u* < *m*), *tŷ* m. 'house', pl. *tai* < Pr. Clt. **tegesā*, *derwydd* m. 'druid', *llyg*, usually singulative *llygoden*, f. 'mouse', pl. *llygod*.

Paradigm: IE *o*-stem

IE **ekwos* 'horse' as reflected in Old Irish:

	Singular	Dual	Plural
nom.	*ech*	*ech*	*eich*
voc.	*eich*	*ech*	*eochu*
acc.	*ech n-*	*ech*	*eochu*
gen.	*eich*	*ech*	*ech n-*
dat.	*eoch*	*echaib*	*echaib*

Sg.nom. < **echos* < IE **ekwos*; voc. < **echi* < IE **ekwe*; acc. < **echon* < IE **ekwom*; gen. < **echi*, cf. Ogham *MAQQI*, Lat. *equī*; dat. < **echu* < Pr. Clt. **ekwū* (Gaul. *Alisanu*) older **ekwō*, presumably a conflation of IE dat., abl., loc. and inst.

Du. *ech* unexplained; *echaib* either simply dat.pl. or genuine dual form comparable to Skt *áśvābhyām*

Pl.nom. < **echi* < Pr. Clt. **ekwoi* with secondary pronominal ending, cf. Gk, Lat., Lith., OCS; voc. appears to continue IE **ekwōs*, thus remaining faithful to the oldest stratum in spite of the innovation in the nominative; acc. appears to continue IE **ekwons*; gen. < **echon*, cf. IE **ekwom*; dat. prototype not determinable exactly, but related to Skt *áśvebhyas*, Lat. *-ibus*; see du.dat.

Example of a neuter: Sg.nom.voc.acc. *cenél n-* 'kindred' < IE *-om*; Du. (as sg.); Pl. *cenél* < IE *-ā*

ADJECTIVES

Most Old Irish adjectives belong to the *ā-/o*-stems, as *find* m.f., *find n-* n. 'white', but *i*-stems are also numerous, e.g. *maith* m.f., *maith n-* n. 'good'. A small number of *u*-stems virtually completes the inventory; an example is *dub* m.f., *dub n-* n. 'black'.

Only meagre traces of the old declensional schemes can be found in British. One important relic is preserved in a few adjectives which distinguish gender like W *gwyn* m., *gwen* f. 'white'. These go back to Pr. Clt. **windos*, **windā* respectively, *i* being regularly lowered to *e* before *ā* in British. Plural forms, indifferent to gender, are in limited use; *hardd* 'handsome' shows *i*-infection in pl. *heirdd*, but terminations are mostly analogical, as *gwynion* with largely generalised *-ion* from the *n*-stems.

The normal comparative suffix in Old Irish is *-(i)u* < IE *-yos*, e.g. *sen* 'old', comp. *sin(i)u*. Traces of this formation are seen in

British, e.g. W *hen* 'old', comp. *hŷn*. The usual comparative
suffix in British is reflected in W *-ach* of obscure origin, e.g. *glân*
'clean', comp. *glanach*; hence also the now common *hynach*
'older'.

The Celtic superlative suffix was *-*esamos* or *-*isamos*, whence
OIr. *-em*, W *-af*, OW *-ham*, e.g. OIr. *sinem*, W *hynaf*, OW *hinham*
'oldest'.

Celtic developed an equative degree, variously formed. Examples: OIr. *sinithir*, W *hyned* 'as old'.

PRONOUNS

Pronouns associated with verbs may be suffixed or infixed. They
often coalesce with prepositions, becoming pure suffixes. Independent nominative and genitive forms occur, but declension in
the normal sense has been lost. The Indo-European reflexive pronoun (Lat. *sē*, etc.) is absent. There is no dual number. But in
spite of multifarious innovations, not a few due to the syntactical
peculiarities of Celtic, the basic Indo-European affinities of the
personal pronoun are still evident. They are best seen in the independent nominative forms which follow:

   Old Irish: *mé* 'I', *sní* 'we', *tú* 'thou', *sí* 'you'
   Welsh: *mi* 'I', *ni* 'we', *ti* 'thou', *chwi* 'you'
The 3rd person retains inflexion for gender in the singular:
   Old Irish: sg. *é* m., *sí* f., *ed* n., pl. *é*
   Welsh: *ef* m., *hi* f., pl. *hwy*
The sg. forms (except W *ef*) go back to Pr. Clt. *is m., *sī f.,
*id n. (cf. Lat. *is* m., *id* n., Goth. *is* m., *si* f., *ita* n., Lith. *jìs* m., etc.)
Of the pl. forms, W *hwy*, MidW *wy* is perhaps closest to Lith. *jiẽ*
m., OIr. *é* to Goth. *ijos* f.

W *ef*, OW *em* is presumed to stand for *hem and to be related
to OIr. *som*, an emphasising particle cognate with Gk *homós*,
Goth. *sama* 'same'.

VERBS

The Old Irish verb is of unique complexity. Many tenses have two
sets of endings, absolute and conjunct, the latter being found
in compounds and certain syntactical connections, as after
the negative, e.g. (absolute) *berid* 'bears', (conjunct) *dobeir* 'bears
towards, gives', *ni beir* 'doesn't bear'. The origin of this twofold
inflexion is problematic; according to a common assumption it

is a special development of the Indo-European primary and secondary endings. The morphology is further complicated by phonetic changes, particularly in relation to compounds. When a preposition is prefixed to a verb, the stress will normally fall on the second element, and the compound is said to be deuterotonic, as *dobeir* 'gives' (above). In a number of syntactical environments, however, as after the negative, the stress falls on the preposition. The compound is then prototonic and may change its phonetic shape, e.g. *ni tabir* 'doesn't give'. Consider the paradigms:

	ABSOLUTE	CONJUNCT	
		(Deuterotonic)	(Prototonic)
Pres.sg.1	*biru* bear	*-biur*	*-bur*
2	*biri*	*-bir*	*-bir*
3	*berid*	*-beir*	*-bir*
pl.1	*bermi*	*-beram*	*-brem*
2	*berthe*	*-berid*	*-brid*
3	*berit*	*-berat*	*-bret*

Following the terminology of Latin grammar, active verbs are said to have active or deponent (i.e. middle) inflexion. The latter is, however, a declining category. It makes great use of an *r*-suffix, e.g. (abs.) *sechithir* 'follows', Lat. *sequitur*. The passive is imperfectly developed. There are separate forms only for the 3rd sg. and pl., all other persons being made by infixing pronouns to the 3rd sg., e.g. (abs.) *bertir* '(they) are borne', *berir* 'is borne', (conj.) *nomberar* 'I am borne' where *no* is a meaningless prefix, *m* the infixed pronoun, *berar* the 3rd sg. verb with initial consonant lenited after the pronoun (not marked in the script), *nonberar* 'we are borne' with non-leniting infixed pronoun *n*.

Most verbs are irregular in the sense postulated for Primitive Indo-European. Normal verbs distinguish five stems: pres., fut., subj., pret.act. and pret.pass. The indicative has five tenses: pres., fut., imperf., pret. (or perf.), conditional. There are two subjunctive tenses: pres. and past. The imperative belongs to the present stem. The imperf.indic. and past subj. as well as the conditional are used with the prefix *no* and have therefore only conjunct inflexion. The preterite is most commonly found with the perfective prefix *ro* which also requires conjunct forms; in this use the tense is known as the perfect. Some preterites show reduplication, as *canid* 'sings', pret. (perf.) *-cechana*, cf. Lat. *canit* 'do.', perf. *cecinit*.

To convey some idea of conjugation, we quote the remainder

of the active tenses of *berid* 'bears', preferring absolute forms where available. For the preterite (perfect), conjunct forms have been taken since the absolute inflexion is poorly attested.

		INDICATIVE			SUBJUNCTIVE	
	Future	Imperfect	Perfect	Conditional	Present	Past
Sg.1	*béra*	*-berinn*	*-biurt*	*-bérinn*	*bera*	*-berinn*
2	*bére*	*-bertha*	*-birt*	*-bértha*	*bere*	*-bertha*
3	*bérid*	*-bered*	*-bert*	*-bérad*	*berid*	*-berad*
Pl.1	*bérmi*	*-bermis*	*-bertammar*	*-bérmis*	*bermi*	*-bermis*
2	*bérthe*	*-berthe*	*-bertid*	*-bérthe*	*berthe*	*-berthe*
3	*bérit*	*-bertis*	*-bertatar*	*-bértis*	*berit*	*-bertis*

Imperative sg.2 *beir*, 3 *berad*, pl.1 *beram*, 2 *berid*, 3 *berat*

Transitive verbs form a past part.pass. with an IE *tyo*-suffix: *brithe* 'borne'. The related *to*-suffix, which forms perfect participles in other languages (p. 111) is used in the stem formation of the pret.pass., i.e. 3.sg. *brethe*, 3.pl. *brithi*. This recalls the Latin analytical perf.pass., e.g. *lātum est* 'it has been borne' (*lātum* < **tlātom*, cf. *tulī* 'I have borne') and some such construction would be the starting point for the Irish tense.

The present participles familiar in other languages are absent from Celtic.

Almost every verb has a corresponding verbal noun; it is fully inflected: *brith* 'bearing', gen. *brithe*, cf. Skt *bhr̥tís* 'maintenance'. With primary verbs the mode of formation varies greatly, but derivative verbs regularly form the verbal noun with a dental suffix comparable to Skt *-tum*, Lith. *-tu̧*, etc., e.g. *marbad* 'killing', *marbaid*, *-marba* 'kills' from *marb* 'dead'. But Celtic never developed an infinitive proper. Periphrastic constructions with the verbal noun are common, e.g. *roboí in cú oca ascnam* 'the hound was attacking him' lit. 'was the hound at-his attacking' (*ascnam* for **acsnam* < **adcosnam* v.n. of *adcosni* 'attacks')

The Welsh verb is formally much simpler than its Old Irish counterpart. It has remained remarkably conservative during the recorded period, so that it will be appropriate for the present purpose to continue to quote standard modern forms.

The same moods are found as in Irish. The Welsh indicative, however, has only four synthetic tenses: pres., imperf., pret. or perf., pluperf. The subjunctive and imperative are in principle as in Irish. Welsh makes abundant use of periphrastic forms involving the verbal noun, e.g. *yr oedd y ci yn ei ymosod* 'the hound was attacking him' lit. 'in his attacking'. Indeed, the present and imperfect are most commonly expressed periphrastically, the synthetic forms generally having the meaning of the future and conditional respectively. Similarly the pluperfect usually means 'would have, could have'.

There is no deponent inflexion. The passive has only a single form for each tense, though a few traces of two forms, as in Irish, are known from medieval sources. In the absence of inflexions pronouns are, of course, necessary: *cerir fi* (where *fi* is the lenited form of *mi*) 'I am loved', *cerir ni* 'we are loved'.

Middle Welsh may distinguish the imperf.indic. and subj., e.g. indic. *karwn* 'I loved', subj. *kar(h)wn*, but today only *carwn* is used, the two tenses now being formally identical.

Sample paradigm

Verbal noun *caru* 'loving'

	INDICATIVE				SUBJUNCTIVE
	Present	Imperfect	Perfect	Pluperfect	Present
Sg.1	*caraf*	*carwn*	*cerais*	*caraswn*	*carwyf*
2	*ceri*	*carit*	*ceraist*	*carasit*	*cerych*
3	*câr*	*carai*	*carodd*	*carasai*	*caro*
Pl.1	*carwn*	*carem*	*carasom*	*carasem*	*carom*
2	*cerwch*	*carech*	*carasoch*	*carasech*	*caroch*
3	*carant*	*carent*	*carasant*	*carasent*	*caront*
Pass.	*cerir*	*cerid*	*carwyd*	*carasid*	*carer*

A past participle comparable to that found in Irish is well known in Breton and Cornish, e.g. Bret. *kared*, Co. *kerys* ($s < t$) 'loved', but Welsh has only petrified relics, now purely adjectives, as *clyd* 'snug, sheltered', cf. OIr. *clithe* 'hidden', *celid* 'hides', Lat. *oc-culit*, further *cēlat* 'do.'

(IE *bher-* survives in compounds in Welsh, e.g. *adfer*, p. 172.)

II

TEXTS ANALYSED AND COMPARED

We have, in the foregoing, seen something of the nature of the affinities between the members of the Indo-European family of languages. We should not forget, however, that even in their oldest known stages, the various groups had already gone far along their separate ways. It was, of course, largely for this reason that the recognition of their common ancestry was so long delayed. To form an impression of the raw material upon which comparative philologists have based their findings, we now consider a parallel text in representative Indo-European languages. The obvious choice is a biblical passage; we take the Lord's Prayer, but omitting the doxology since this is absent from our Old English version. A translation is not an original, and the influence of the Hellenistic Greek is apparent in the Latin and medieval versions, particularly in matters of word order: the Gothic and Slavonic texts were made direct from the Greek, the others via the Latin. We note, too, that the Greek text itself contains an obvious Semitism in the plural use of the word for 'heaven', p. 156. The Sanskrit version was naturally not made until modern times but it is no more artificial than the great bulk of extant Sanskrit literature which was likewise composed only after the language had ceased to be an ordinarily spoken medium.

The linguistic commentary accompanying the texts identifies the forms and supplies etymological notes. References of the type 'Cf. Gk, Skt' mean that the word in question is paralleled in Greek and Sanskrit at the same point in the text. Where there is no mention of the provenience of an item, it is to be assumed that its etymology is unknown or purely conjectural—it will be seen that the origin of a sizeable proportion of the vocabulary is still obscure.

LATIN

9 *Pater noster, qui es in caelis: sanctificetur nomen tuum.*

10 *Adveniat regnum tuum. Fiat voluntas tua, sicut in caelo, et in terra.*

11 *Panem nostrum quotidianum da nobis hodie.*

12 *Et dimitte nobis debita nostra, sicut et nos dimittimus debitoribus nostris.*

13 *Et ne nos inducas in temptationem, sed libera nos a malo.*

9 *pater* m. 'father'. Cf. Gk, Skt, Goth., OE, Ir.

noster 'our', from *nōs* 'we, us' 12, properly an oblique case, cf. Skt. *vayám* 12. Cf. Ir.

quī rel.pron. 'who' from stem of interrogative pron. *quis*, p. 88. Cf. Lith *kasdiĕnĕs* 11

es 'art', cognates in other languages pointing to IE **es-si* > **esi*, e.g. Skt *ási*, Gk *eĩ*, older *essí*. Cf. OE, Ir., W, OCS, Lith.

caelīs abl.pl. of *caelum* n. 'heaven'

sānctificĕtur 3.sg.pres.subj.pass. of *sānctificāre* 'hallow' lit. 'make holy', a Christian coining to render Gk *hagiázō*: *sāncti-*, nom.sg. *sānctus*, in origin perf.part.pass. of *sancīre* 'hallow', supposed to be somehow related to *sacer*, OLat. *sacros* 'holy'; -*ficāre*, in earlier compounds -*ficere* with regular vowel change, from *facere* 'make', a reformation from perf. *fēcī*, cf. Gk aor. *éthēka* 'placed' < IE *dhē-k-* < *dhē-* 'place', Skt *dádhāti*, Gk *títhēmi* OCS *dĕti*, Lith. *dĕti* 'do.,' OE *dōn* 'make, do'.

nōmen. gen. *nōminis* n. 'name', exactly the same manner of formation as Skt. Cf. also Gk, Goth., OE, Ir., W, OCS

tuum 'thy', nom.m. *tuus* < IE **tewos*, as Gk *teós*, also *sós*, Lith. *tãvas*, cf. Lat. *tū* 'thou'. Cf. Gk

10 *adveniat* 3.sg.pres.subj. of *venīre* 'come': *ad* preverb, originally adverb, whence also prepositional usage, Goth. *at*, OE *æt* 'at', OIr. *ad* 'to'; *venīre* < IE *gʷen-*, cf. Gk *baínō* 'go, come', variant root in Skt *gam-* 'do.' < IE *gʷem-*. Cf. Goth., OE

rēgnum n. 'kingdom' derived from *rēx*, gen. *rēgis* 'king', a term found in Aryan and Celtic, cf. Skt, Ir., also OE

fīat 3.sg.pres.subj. of *fīo*, *fieri* 'become, be done', the alternation *i/ī* in the root vowel being unexplained; used as the passive of *facere* (see *sānctificētur* 9), to which it may be etymologically related, cf. Skt *dhīyáte* 'is placed'

voluntās f. 'will' derived from *volō*, *velle* 'be willing, wish', cf. Goth., OE, OCS, Lith.

tua f. 'thy', see *tuum* 9

sīcut 'as', being *sīc* 'so' and *ut* 'as': *sīc* < OLat. *seic* < **sei-ce* (cf. *sīcine* < **sei-ce-ne* 'is it so?'), i.e. OLat. *sei* > *sī* 'if', -*ce* (enclitic demonstrative particle), cf. Gk *sémeron* 11; *ut* presumably for **uta* as in archaic *aliuta* 'otherwise', Oscan cognate *puz*, Umbrian *puze* (*p* < IE *kʷ*) showing that Latin has lost *qu-* from the original interrogative root IE *kʷu-*, cf. *quī* 9

caelō abl.sg. of *caelum* 9

et 'also, and', Skt *áti* 'beyond', Gk *éti* 'further', Goth. *iþ* 'but'

terrā abl. of *terra* f. 'earth, land', Ir. *tír* 'land', W *tir* 'land, earth'

11   *pānem* acc. of *pānis* m. 'bread'

nostrum acc.sg. 'our', see *noster* 9

quotīdiānum acc.sg. of *quotīdiānus* 'daily' from adv. *quotīdiē* *quottīdiē*, presumably a locative, i.e. *quottī + diē*, the first word being apparently an adjective derived from *quot* adv. 'how many', variant cognate formations being Skt *káti*, Gk *pósos* 'do.', cf. *quī* 9; on the second word *diē* 'day', see *hodiē* below

dā 2.sg.imper. of *dare* 'give', cf. Gk, Skt, OCS, Lith.

nōbis 'us', dat. of *nōs* 12

hodiē 'today' < ?**hō diē* loc. 'this day'; at any rate containing an oblique case of *diēs* m. 'day'. Cf. Skt, Ir., W, also OCS, Lith.

12   *dīmitte* 2.sg.imper. of *dīmittere* 'forgive', a calque on Gk *aphíēmi* (q.v.): *dī-* < *dis-* 'away from', *mittere* 'send'

dēbita pl. of *dēbitum* n. 'debt', formed from *dēbēre* 'owe' < **dē-habēre* (*dē* 'from', *habēre* 'have')

nostra acc.pl. 'our', see *noster* 9

nōs acc. 'us', see *noster* 9, cf. Goth., OE, Ir., W, OCS

dīmittimus 1.pl.pres.indic. of *dīmittere* above

dēbitōribus dat.pl. of *dēbitor* m. 'debtor', formed from *dēbitum* above

nostrīs dat.pl. 'our', see *noster* 9

13 *nē* negative particle used in prohibitions, cf. Goth., OE, Ir., W, OCS, Lith., also Gk

indūcās 2.sg.pres.subj. of *indūcere* 'lead into', expressing a command: *in* 'into' 9; *dūcere*, OLat. *doucere* 'lead', cf. Goth. *tiuhan*, OE *tēon* 'do.'

temptātiōnem acc. of *temptātiō* f. 'temptation' from *temptāre* 'tempt'

sed 'but', in Old Latin also a preposition 'without'

līberā 2.sg.imper. of *līberāre* 'deliver' from *līber* adj. 'free', presumably cognate with Gk *eleútheros* 'do.'

ā 'from', a form of *ab*, cf. Skt *ápa* 'away'; cf. Gk, Goth., OE

malō abl.n. (or m.) of *malus* adj. 'evil'

GREEK

(Within a sentence a final acute is turned into a grave accent, indicating a lower tone. In the modern language the grave, like the other accents, simply denotes a stressed syllable.)

9 *Páter hēmõn, ho en toîs ouranoîs: hagiasthḗtō tò ónomá sou.*

10 *Elthátō hē basileíā sou. Genēthḗtō tò thélēmá sou, hōs en ouranõi, kaì epì gẽs.*

11 *Tòn árton hēmõn tòn epioúsion dòs hēmĭn sḗmeron.*

12 *Kaì áphes hēmĭn tà opheilḗmata hēmõn, hōs kaì hēmeîs aphíemen toîs opheilétais hēmõn.*

13 *Kaì mḕ eisenénkeis hēmãs eis peirasmón, allà rhũsai hēmãs apò toũ ponēroũ.*

9 *páter* voc. of *patḗr* m. 'father', the accent of the vocative characteristically falling on the first syllable, cf. Skt. Cf. Lat.

hēmõn gen. of *hēmeîs* 'we' 12

ho m. 'the', *hē* f., *tó* n., properly a demonstrative pronoun 'this, that', as cognate Skt *sá*, *sā́*, *tád*, Goth. *sa*, *so*, *þata*. All oblique cases formed from the IE root *to-* (e.g. acc.sg.masc. Gk *tón*). Cf. Lith.

en 'in', cf. Lat.

toîs dat.pl. of *ho* above

ouranoîs dat.pl. of *ouranós* m. 'heaven', the use of the plural reflecting the Semitic antecedents of the text, cf. Hebrew *šāmáyim* 'heaven', a word treated as a plural

hagiasthḗtō 3.sg.aor.imper. of *hagiázō* 'hallow', a late formation from *hágios* 'holy', cf. Skt *yajás* (subst.), *yájāmi* (vb.) 'worship'

tó n. of *ho* above

ónoma n. 'name', dial. *ónuma*. The word is Common IE, but the details of the Gk forms remain obscure. Cf. Lat.

soũ gen.sg. of *sú* 'thou', its accent has been absorbed by the preceding word; cf. Doric Gk *tú*, Lat. *tū*, Skt *tu* 13, Goth. *þu*, OE *þū*, OIr. *tú*, W *ti*, OCS *ty*, Lith. *tù*

10   *elthátō* 3.sg.aor.imper. of *érkhomai* 'come', aor. root *elth-*

      hē f. of *ho* 9

      basileíā f. 'kingdom, cf. *basileús* 'king', *basílissa* 'queen', doubtless taken from a foreign source

      genēthḗtō 3.sg.aor.imper. of *gígnomai* 'become, am made', aor. root *gen-*, cf. Lat. *gignō*, archaic *genō*, Skt *jánāmi*, OE *cennan* 'beget', OIr. *gainithir* 'is born', W *geni* 'be born', further Gk *génos*, Lat. *genus*, Skt *jánas* 'sort, kind', Goth. *kuni*, OE *cynn* 'kin'

      thélēma n. 'will' from *thélō* (vb.) 'wish', cf. OCS *želěti* 'do.'

      hōs 'as', also *hóste* 'do.', i.e. *hós te* (*te* 'and, also' p. 91) as in Homer, Doric Gk *hóte* 'do.' < **hŏd te*, cf. Skt *yắd* 'in so far as', < IE **yŏd*, abl. of **yos* > Gk *hós*, Skt *yás* 'who' (relative), p. 93; cf. OCS *iže* 9

      ouranōi dat.sg. of *ouranós* 9

      kaí 'and, also', dial. *kás*

      epí 'on', also *épi*. One compares Skt *ápi* 10

      gẽs gen. of *gẽ* f. 'earth'

11   *tón* acc. of *ho* 9

      árton acc. of *ártos* m. 'bread'

      epioúsion acc. of *epioúsios* 'daily', apparently based on *epì tền oũsan* (*hēmérān*) 'on the present (day)', *oũsan* acc.f.pres.part. of *ṓn* m., *oũsa* < **ontyā* f., *ón* n., stem *ont-* < **hont-* < IE *sont-* 'being', cf. Skt *sān*, *sant-* 'do.', Lat. *sōns* 'guilty' (special semantic shift), also *-sēns* 'being', e.g. in *praesēns* 'present'; cf. Lat. *es* 9 *dós* 2.sg.aor.imper. of *dídōmai* 'give', cf. Lat.

hēmîn dat. of *hēmeîs* 'we' 12

sḗmeron 'today', Attic Gk *tḗmeron*, < **kiámeron*, i.e. *ki-* 'this', also in *ekeî* 'there', Lat. *-ce* (cf. *sīcut*, Lat. 10), *cis*, *citrā* 'this side', cf. Goth., OCS, Lith., and **ámĕra* > *hēmérā* f. 'day', further Homeric *hễmar* n., the only known cognate being Armenian *awr* 'do.'

12 *áphes* 2.sg.aor.imper. of *aphíēmi*, 'forgive', aor. root *he-*, *hē-*: *ap-* < *apó* 13, and *híēmi* 'send, throw', aor. *hḗka*, Lat. *jaciō*, *-ere* 'throw', perf. *jēcī* (pres. from perf., cf. *faciō*, *-ere*, see Lat. *sāncti-ficĕtur* 9)

tá n.pl. of *ho* 9

opheilḗmata pl. of *opheílēma* n. 'debt' from *opheílō* 'owe'

hēmeîs 'we', ultimately derived from the IE oblique stem seen in Lat. *nōs* 12

aphíemen 1.pl.pres.indic., see *áphes* above

opheilḗtais dat.pl. of *opheilḗtēs* m. 'debtor' from *opheílō* above

13 *mḗ* prohibitive particle, dial. *mā́*, construction with aor.subj. being traditional, cf. Skt

eisenénkēis 2.sg.aor.subj. of aor.infin. *eisenenkeîn* 'lead into': *eis* 'into' below, *enenkeîn* 'lead'

hēmâs acc. of *hēmeîs* 12 'we'

eis 'into', dial. *ens* = *en* 'in' 9 + *s* after analogy of *ek*, *ex* 'out of', cf. Lat. *ex*, < IE **eks*

peirasmón acc. of *peirasmós* m. 'temptation', late formation from *peirázō* 'tempt', cf. *peirỗ* 'do.', *peîra* 'attempt, experiment', Lat. *experior* 'try', *(ex)perītus* 'experienced', *perīculum* 'danger'

allá 'but' lit. 'otherwise', cf. *állos* < **ályos*, Lat. *alius*, Goth. *aljis*, OE *el(e)-* ('foreign', gen.sg. *elles* 'else'), OIr. *aile* 'other', MidW *eil* 'second'; another formation Lat. *alter*. Cf. IE *-yos*, *-teros*, endings of comparative pp. 105f.

rhŭ̃sai 2.sg.aor.imper. of *rhŭ́omai* 'deliver, protect', aor. root *rhūs-*

apó 'from', also *ápo*, cf. Lat. *ā* 13

toũ gen.m.n. of *ho* 9

ponēroũ gen.m.n. of *ponērós* (adj.) 'evil', cf. *pónos* (subst.), *ponŏ̃*, also *pénomai* (vb.) 'toil'

SANSKRIT

In keeping with the practice of the native script, the words in a sentence are divided when a word ending in a vowel, *ḥ* or *ṃ* (the former an aspirate, substantially as *h*, the latter a no longer determinable variety of *m*) is followed by a word beginning with a consonant. Otherwise, words are mostly written together, the final sound of one merging with the initial sound of the next according to the rules of *sandhi* 'connexion'. Certain final consonants are also affected when standing at the end of a sentence. The nature of these changes—they are, in fact, the phonetic changes made in connected speech—may be seen in the text below, where the undivided words are separated beneath the line and forms altered in the sandhi have been restored.

9 *Bho   asmākaṃ svargastha pitaḥ: tava nāma pavitraṃ*
    (*bhos*) (*asmākam*)   (*pitar*)   (*pavitram*)
   pūjyatāṃ.
   (*pūjyatām*)

10 *Tava rājyamāyātu.   Yathā svarge tathā medinyāmapi*
        (*rājyam ā yātu*)   (*medinyām api*)
   tavecchā   sidhyatu.
   (*tava icchā*)

11 *Śvastanaṃ   bhakṣyamadyāsmabhyaṃ   dehi.*
    (*śvastanam*) (*bhakṣyam adya/adyā asmabhyam*)

12 *Vayañca   yathāsmadaparādhināṃ   kṣamāmahe, tathā*
    (*vayam ca*) (*yathā asmat aparādhinām*)
   tvamasmākamaparādhān   kṣamasva.
   (*tvam asmākam aparādhāṃs*)

13 *Asmāṃśca   parīkṣāṃ mā naya, api tu durātmata uddhara.*
    (*asmāṃs ca*) (*parīkṣām*)   (*durātmatas*)

___

9 *bhos* 'o!' < **bhávas* < *bhágavas* voc. of *bhávān*, *bhágavān* 'fortunate person', used as an honorific title, from *bhágas* 'fortune'

   asmākam gen. of *vayám* 'we' 12; this and other oblique cases (*asmábhyam* 11, *asmát* 12, *asmā́ṃs* 13) ultimately derived from IE oblique stem seem in Lat. *nōs* 12

   svargastha voc. of *svargasthas* 'heavenly' from *svargás* m. 'heaven'

   pítar voc. of *pitá*, stem *pitár-*, m. 'father', cf. Lat. For position of accent, cf. Gk *táva* gen. of *tvám* 'thou' 12

nǎma, stem *nāman-*, n. 'name', cf. Lat.

pavítram n. of *pavítras* 'holy', cf. *pavate* 'purifies', *pūtás* (adj.) 'purified', further Lat. *pūrus* 'pure', Ir. *úr*, W *ir* 'fresh, green' *pūjyatām* 3.sg.imper. from the middle stem *pūjyā-* 'be honoured'

10 *rǎjyam* n. 'kingdom', properly n. of adj. *rǎjyas* 'kingly, royal', Lat. *rēgius* 'do.'. Cf. Lat.

ā 'towards', prefix with verbs of motion

yǎtu 3.sg.imper. of *yǎti* 'comes', cf. Lith. *jóti* 'ride (on horseback)'

yáthā 'as': rel.pron. *yá-* (nom.m. *yás*, see Gk *hōs* 10) and suffix *-thā*

svargé loc. of *svargás* 'heaven', see *svargastha* 9

táthā 'so': demon.pron. *tá-* (nom.m. *sá*, see Gk *ho* 9) and suffix *-thā*; cf. Lith.

medinyām loc. of *medinī* f. 'earth'

ápi 'on', postpositive use of adverb emphasising case-relationship. Out of such use arose the category of postpositions usual in the later Indian languages. Elsewhere, the adverb preceded the noun, hence the parallel category of prepositions. See also 13. Cf. Gk *epí* 7

icchǎ f. 'will', cf. *iccháti* 'wishes', OE *āscian* 'ask', OCS *iskati*, Lith. *ieškóti* 'seek'

sídhyatu 3.sg.imper. of *sídhyati* 'succeeds, is accomplished', cf. *sādhyati* 'goes to a target', *sādhús* 'straight', also Gk *ithús* 'directed to a target, straight' < **hithús* < IE **sídhus*

11 *śvastanam* acc. (n.) of *śvastanas* 'daily' from *svás* properly 'tomorrow', but *sváḥ svás* 'day by day'; an adj. *adyatanas* 'daily' also exists, cf. *adyá* below

bhakṣyám n. 'food', cf. *bhakṣati* 'eats, partakes', Av. *baχšaiti* 'partakes', Mod. Persian *bakhshīdan* 'bestow', *bakhshīsh* 'present, baksheesh'

adyá, also *adyǎ* 'today', doubtless containing a word for 'day', which otherwise occurs with an *n*-enlargement, i.e. *dínam*, see OCS *dĭnĭ* 11. Cf. Lat.

asmábhyam dat. of *vayám* 'we' 12, cf. *asmākam* 9

dehí 2.sg.imper. of *dádāti* 'gives'; the termination *-hi*, a reduced variant of -*dhi*, is regularly used with athematic stems, cf. Skt *ihí*, Gk *íthi*, OCS *idi* 'go!' Cf. Lat.

12 *vayám* 'we', cf. Goth., OE, continuing IE nom., whereas forms like Lat. *nōs* 12 derive from the IE oblique root

ca 'and', cf. Gk *te*, Lat. -*que*, Goth. -*uh*

asmát abl. of *vayám* 'we' above, see *asmâkam* 9; ablative here has the force of 'against'

aparādhinām gen.pl. of *aparādhī* m. 'trespasser', substantivised adj. 'trespassing', see below

kṣamāmahe 1.pl.pres.indic. of *kṣamate* 'forgives'

tvám 'thou', an Aryan innovation (cf. *vayám* above), see *tu* 13

aparādhāṃs acc.pl. of *aparādhas* m. 'trespass', cf. *aparādhyati* 'trespasses': *ápa* 'away', see Lat. *ā* 13, and -*rādhyati* 'accomplishes'

kṣamasva 2.sg.imper. of *kṣamate* above

13 *asmâṃs* acc. of *vayám* 'we' 12, see *asmâkam* 9

parīkṣām acc. of *parīkṣā* f. 'temptation', cf. *párīkṣate* 'tempts'

mâ prohibitive particle; here construed with imper., more usually with an (unaugmented) aorist. Cf. Gk

náya 2.sg.imper. of *náyati* 'leads'

ápi, cf. 10, here in common emphatic function (reinforcing the meaning of the following particle *tu*)

tu 'but', really a special application of 2.sg.pron. 'thou', otherwise now *tvám* 12; cf. Gk. *soũ* 9

durātmatas gen.m.n. of *durātman* 'evil' lit. 'of evil nature': *dur*- < *dus*- 'evil, bad', cf. with similar or related meanings Gk *dus*-, Goth. *tuz*-, OE *tor*-, OIr. *du*-, *do*-, and *ātmán* m. 'body, soul, person, nature'

uddhára 2.sg.imper. of *uddhárati* 'delivers', i.e., *ud* + *hárati*: *ud* 'out', cf. Goth., OE *ūt* 'do.', and *hárati* 'takes'

GOTHIC
(mid-fourth century)

9 *Atta unsar, þu in himinam: weihnai namo þein.*

10 *Qimai þiudinassus þeins. Wairþai wilja þeins, swe in himina, jah ana airþai.*

11 *Hlaif unsarana þana sinteinan gif uns himma daga.*

12 *Jah aflet uns þatei skulans sijaima, swaswe jah weis afletam þaim skulam unsaraim.*

13 *Jah ni briggais uns in fraistubnjai, ak lausei uns af þamma ubilin.*

9   *atta* m. 'father', in origin a baby word which had largely replaced *fadar*; it is widely attested in Gmc, e.g. OHG *atto*, ON *Atte* as personal name, cf. with diminutive suffix Goth. *Attila*, further Lat. *atta*, Gk *átta*; cf. OCS. For other baby words, cf. W, Lith.

unsar m. 'our', formed from *uns* 'us' 11, cf. OE

þu 'thou', cf. Gk *soû* 9

in 'in', cf. Lat.

himinam dat.pl. of *himins* m. 'heaven'; on the use of plural cf. Gk. Cf. OE

weihnai 3.sg.pres.subj. of *weihnan* 'be hallowed', with passive *n*-suffix, cf. *weihan* 'hallow' derived from *weihs* 'holy', cf. OE *wih* m. 'idol'

namo n. 'name', cf. Lat.

þein n. of *þeins* 'thy' from *þu* above, cf. OE

10   *qimai* 3.sg.pres.subj. of *qiman* 'come' < Pr. Gmc **kwemanan*. Cf. OE, Lat.

þiudinassus m. 'kingdom' from *þiudans*, OE *þēoden* 'king', itself a derivative of *þiuda*, OE *þēod* 'people', cf. Ir. *túath*, W (obsolete) *tud*, Lith. *tautà* 'people'

þeins 'thy', see *þein* 9

wairþai 3.sg.pres.subj. of *wairþan* 'become, be done', cf. OE; cf. further Lat. *vertō*, Skt *vártate*, OCS *vrŭtĕti* 'turn', Lith. *veřsti* 'overturn', *viřsti* 'bend'

wilja m. 'will', cf. Lat.

swe 'as', a different ablaut grade *swa* 12, cf. OE

himina dat.sg. of *himins* 'heaven', see *himinam* 9

jah 'and, also', OE *ge*

ana 'on', cf. OE; also Gk *ána* 'on', Skt *ánu* 'towards'

airþai dat. of *airþa* f. 'earth', cf. OE

11   *hlaif* acc. of *hlaifs* m. 'bread', cf. OE

unsarana acc.m. of *unsar* 9

þana acc. of demon.pron. *sa* m., cf. Gk *ho* 9; here used as an article in imitation of Greek

sinteinan weak acc.m. of *sinteins* 'daily': *sin-*, OE *do*. 'ever', and *-teins* 'day', cf. OE *lengten, lenten* 'spring, lent' lit. 'long day'; cf. OCS. See *daga* below

gif 2.sg.imper. of *giban* 'give', cf. OE

uns dat. of *weis* 'we' 12, see Lat. *nōs* 12

himma dat.m. of pronominal stem *hi-*, preserved also in acc.m. *hina*, n. *hita*, < IE *ki-*, cf. Gk *sĕmeron* 11

daga dat. of *dags* m. 'day', cf. OE. For another term, see *sinteinan* above

12   *aflet* 2.sg.imper. of *afletan* 'forgive': *af* 'from' 13, and *letan* 'let, set free, forgive', cf. OE *lǣtan* 'let'

þatei 'that which', i.e. *þat=þata* 'that' (cf. Gk. *ho* 9), and *ei* relative particle

skulans nom.m.pl. of *skula* adj. (weak; a few Gothic adjectives always so declined) 'owing', formed from the same root as *skulan*, OE *sculan* 'owe', cf. Lith. *skolà* 'debt', *skelĕti* 'owe', *skìlti* 'get into debt', and apparently also forms without initial *s* ('*s*-mobile' p. 91). Cf. Lith.

sijaima 1.pl.pres.subj. of *wisan* 'be', pres.subj. stem *sij-*, cf. OE *si* 9, from IE root *es-*; cf. Lat. *es* 9

swaswe 'as', presumably an emphatic reduplication: *swa* 'as', *swe* 'do.' 10, cf. OE

weis 'we', cf. Skt *vayám* 12

afletam 1.pl.pres.indic. of *afletan* above

þaim dat.pl. of *sa*, cf. *þana* 11

skulam dat.pl. of *skula* m. 'debtor', a substantivised adj. (see above), OE *gestola* 'do.'

unsaraim dat.pl. of *unsar* 'our' 9

13   *ni* 'not', cf. Lat.

briggais 2.sg.pres.subj. of *briggan* 'bring, lead', OE *bringan* 'do.'

fraistubnjai dat. of *fraistubni* f. 'temptation' from **fraistan*, cf. ON *freista*, 'tempt', also Goth. *fraisan*, OE *frāsian* 'do.'

ak 'but', cf. OE

lausei 2.sg.imper. of *lausjan* 'deliver, set free' from *laus* adj. 'free', OE *lēas*; other ablaut grades, e.g. Goth. *fraliusan* 'lose', OE *-lēosan*, further Goth. *fralusts* 'loss'. Cf. OE. Other cognates: Lat. *luō* 'pay, atone for', Gk *lúō* 'set free, (middle) ransom', *lúsis* 'release'

af 'from', cf. Lat.

þamma dat.m.n. of *sa*, cf. *þana* 11

ubilin weak dat.m.n. of *ubils* 'evil, bad', cf. OE

OLD ENGLISH
(West Saxon Dialect, end of tenth century)

9 *Fæder ūre, þū þe eart on heofonum: sī þīn nama gehālgod.*

10 *Tōbecume þīn rīce. Geweorþe þīn willa on eorþan swā swā on heofonum.*

11 *Ūrne dæghwāmlican hlāf sielle ūs tō dæge.*

12 *And forgief ūs ūre gyltas, swā swā wē forgiefaþ ūrum gyltendum.*

13 *And ne gelæd þū ūs on costnunge, ac ālīes ūs of yfele.*

9 *fæder* m. 'father', cf. Lat.

ūre 'our', older (m.) *ūser* < **unser*, cf. Goth.

þū 'thou', cf. Goth.

þe relative particle, found in all West Germanic languages, from the stem of the demon.pron. (*sē* m., *sīo* f.) *þæt* n., see Gk *ho* 9

eart 'art', like *earon* 'are', etymologically obscure, being formed from a root not otherwise associated with the Germanic substantive verb; one compares Lith. *yrà* 'is'

on 'on', cf. Goth. *ana* 10

heofonum dat.pl. of *heofon* m. 'heaven', cf. Goth.

sī 3.sg.pres.subj. of *wesan*, also *bion* 'be', cf. Goth. *sijaima* 12

þīn 'thy' from *þū* above, cf. Goth.

nama m. 'name', cf. Lat.

gehālgod perf.part. of *hālgian* 'hallow' from *hālig* 'holy', a derivative of *hāl* 'hale', cf. Goth. *hailags, hails* 'do.'

10   *tōbecume* 3.sg.pres.subj. of *tōbecuman* 'arrive, come': (1) *tō* 'to' 11, (2) *be-* < *bi*, cf. Goth. *do.*, 'by', (3) *cuman* 'come', cf. OHG *koman*, older *kweman*; cf. Goth.

rīce n. 'kingdom' (still in *bishopric*), cf. Goth. *reiki*; it is a derivative of *-rīc* 'king', preserved in personal names, e.g. *Æþelrīc* 'Noble King', cf. Goth. *reiks*. The Gmc term is borrowed from Celtic, cf. Gaul. *-rīx*, p. 144; cf. Lat.

geweorþe 3.sg.pres.subj. of *geweorþan* 'become, be done': *ge-*, cf. Goth. *ga-*, prefix, and *weorþan* 'do.', cf. Goth.

willa m. 'will', cf. Lat.

eorþan dat. of *eorþe* f. 'earth', cf. Goth.

swā swā 'as', reduplication, cf. Goth. *swaswe* 12

11   *ūrne* acc.m.sg. of *ūre* 9

dæghwāmlican strong acc.m.sg. of *dæghwāmlic* 'daily', formed with adjectival suffix *-lic*, originally *līc* n. 'shape, body, (lych)', cf. Goth. *leik* 'do.', from *dæghwām* 'daily', properly an accusative of time: *dæg* 'day' below, and *-hwām* for *gehwām* acc. of *gewhā* 'every', i.e. prefix *ge-* (see *geweorþe* 10) and *-hwā* 'someone; who', Goth. *hwas*, < IE *k^wos*, cf. Lat. *quī* 9

hlāf (> *loaf*) m. 'bread', cf. Goth.

sielle imper.sg. of *siellan*, also *sellan* 'give, sell', Goth. *saljan* 'sacrifice', from Pr. Gmc **salō* f. (> e.g. OE *salu*) 'transfer, sale'

ūs 'us' < **uns*, cf. Goth.

tō 'to', WGmc, e.g. OHG *zuo*, cf. Lat. *dō-*, e.g. in *dōnec* 'until', OIr *do*, OW *di*, OCS *do*, Lith. *da* 'do.'

dæge dat. of *dæg* m. 'day', cf. Goth.

12   *and* 'and', also 'but', perhaps related to Gk *antí* 'against', cf. Lith. *añt* 10.

forgief imper.sg. of *forgiefan* 'forgive': *for* 'for, before', Goth. *faur*, Lat. *por-*, Gk dial. *par-*, further Gk *pará* 'along', and *giefan* 'give', cf. Goth. *gif* 11. See also OCS *priidetŭ* 10

gyltas acc.pl. of *gylt* (> *guilt*) m. 'debt, trespass'

wē 'we', cf. Skt *vayám* 12

forgiefaþ pl.pres.indic. of *forgiefan* above

ūrum dat.pl. of *ūre* 9

gyltendum dat.pl. of *gyltend* m. 'debtor, trespasser', substantivised pres.part. of *gyltan* 'be guilty'

13   *ne* 'not', cf. Lat.

gelǣd imper.sg. of *gelǣdan* 'lead': *ge-* prefix (see *geweorþe* 10) and *lǣdan* 'lead' from *lād* (> *load*) 'journey, leading, carrying', related to (*ge*)*liþan*, Goth. *galeiþan* 'go, travel'

costnunge dat. of *costnung* f. 'temptation' from *costnian*, also *costian*, 'tempt', a derivative of *cost* 'choice, condition', cf. Goth. *kustus* 'test', Lat. *gustus* 'tasting', further OE *cēosan*, Goth. *kiusan* 'choose', Gk *geúomai* 'taste', Skt *juṣáte* 'enjoys', *jóṣas* 'enjoyment'

ac 'but', cf. Goth.

ālīes imper.sg. of *ālīesan* 'deliver, set free': *ā-*, also *ǣ-*, *ō-* < *or-* = OHG *ur*, Goth. *us* 'out of' < Pr. Gmc **uz*, and *līesan* 'deliver, etc.' = Goth. *lausjan* (q.v.)

of 'from', also 'of, off', cf. Lat.

yfele dat.m.n. of *yfel* 'evil, bad', cf. Goth.

LITHUANIAN

Lithuanian is only known from the modern period, the earliest document dating from *c.* 1515. The following version is in contemporary standard language.

9   *Tėve mūsų, kurs esi danguje: teesie šventas tavo vardas.*

10   *Teateinie tavo karalystė. Teesie tavo valia, kaip danguje, taip ir ant žemės.*

11   *Kasdienės mūsų duonos duok mums šiandien.*

12   *Ir atleisk mums mūsų kaltes, kaip ir mes atleidžiame savo kaltininkams.*

13   *Ir nevesk mus į pagundą, bet gelbėk mus nuo pikto.*

9   *tėve* voc. of *tėvas* m. 'father', cf. Goth.

mūsų gen. of *mēs* 'we' 12

kuřs 'who', also *kurìs*, < *kuř* 'where' + *jìs* 'he': (1) *kuř* from the IE interrogative stem (cf. *kasdiēnės* 11) with *r*-element used to form adverbs of place, cognate with Goth. *hwar*, OE *hwǣr* 'where' and presumably with Lat. *cūr* 'why' which will then have originally meant 'where'; (2) *jìs*, cf. with the same meaning Lat., Goth. *is*, Skt. *ayám* (*-ám* secondary), further Pr.Sl. **-jĭ* (in the pronominal declension of adjectives)

esì 'art', cf. Lat.

dangujè loc. of *dangùs* m. 'heaven'

teesiĕ 3.sg.optat. of *bŭti* 'be' (cf. OCS *bǫdetŭ* 10): *te-* (obligatory) optative particle, and *-esiĕ*, cf. *esì* above

šveñtas 'holy', OCS *svętŭ* 'do.'

tàvo gen. of *tù* 'thou', also poss.adj. *tãvas* 'thy', cf. Lat.

vařdas m. 'name', cf. Goth. *waurd*, Lat. *verbum* 'word'

10 *teateiniĕ* 3.sg.optat. of *ateĩti* 'come': (1) *te-* particle, see *teesiĕ* 9; (2) *at-* 'hither', see OCS *otŭ* 13; (3) *eĩti* 'go', cf. OCS *priidetŭ* 10

karalỹstė f. 'kingdom', from *karãlius* 'king', a borrowing via German of Carolus (Magnus) 'Charlemagne', cf. OHG *Karal*. The name was likewise borrowed into Slavonic, cf. e.g. Czech *král*, Russ. *koról'* 'king'

valià f. 'will'. Cf. Lat.

kaĩp 'as', cf. *kóks*, OCS *kakŭ* 'what kind of', further W *pob*, OIr. *cach* 'every'; *p*-suffix perhaps identical with Lat. *-pe* in *nempe* 'certainly', *quippe* < **quidpe* 'because, indeed'

taĩp 'so', cf. *tóks*, OCS *takŭ* 'such', connected with IE pron. *to-*, seen in Lith. *tàs* m., *tà* f. 'this; the same', cf. Gk *ho* 9. For *-p*, see *kaĩp* above. Cf. Skt

iř 'and, also'

añt 'on', cf. Gk *antí* (loc. ending), also *ánta* (acc. ending) 'against, before, in place of, opposite', Skt *ánti* 'opposite', Lat. *ante* 'before', Goth. *and* 'along'. See OE *and* 12

žĕmès gen. of *žĕmĕ* f. 'earth', cf. OCS

11 *kasdiĕnės* gen.f. of *kasdiĕnis* 'daily' from adv. *kasdieñ(ą)*: *kàs* 'each' in origin an interrogative pronoun, cf. *kuřs* 9 and Lat. *quī* 9, and *dienà* 'day', cf. OCS

dúonos gen. (here in partitive use) of *dúona* f. 'bread'

dúok 2.sg.imper. of *dúoti* 'give', i.e. *dúo* plus a (generalised) particle *-k*, older *-ka*, originally having an emphatic function, as Russ. *ka* (common with imperatives, e.g. *idí-ka sjudá* 'come here'), also *-ko*, OCS *-kŭ*, Gk *-ka*, *-ke(n)*, Skt *kám*. Cf. OCS *mùms* dat. of *měs* 'we' 12

šiañdien 'today' lit. 'this day' (acc. of time): *šiañ-* = *šią* from *šìs* m. 'this', OCS *sĭ*, cf. also Lat. *cis* 'this side of', Gmc *hi-*, cf. Goth., and *-dien*, see *kasdiēnės* above

12 *atléisk* 2.sg.imper. of *atléisti* 'forgive': *at-* see *teateiniě* 10, and *léisti* 'allow' < **leid-ti* (2.sg.pres.indic. *léidi*), cf. Goth. *letan*, OE *lǣtan* 'let'

kaltès acc.pl. of *kaltě* f. 'trespass', cf. *kaĺtas* 'guilty', apparently to be connected with forms having initial *s-*, as *skolà* 'debt', cf. Goth.

měs 'we', cf. OCS

atléidžiame 1.pl.pres.indic. of *atléisti* above

sàvo gen. of reflexive pronoun (all persons, genders, numbers), also corresponding poss.adj. *sāvas*, OCS *svoi*, Lat. *suus*, OLat. *sovos*, Gk *heós* < **sewós*, Goth. *swes*, OE *swǣs* 'one's own'; cf. OCS *sę* 9

kaltininkams dat.pl. of *kaltininkas* m. 'trespasser' from *kaltě* above

13 *nevèsk* i.e. *ne* 'not', *vèsk* 2.sg.imper. of *vèsti* 'lead' < **ved-ti* (1.sg. pres.indic. *vedù*), cf. OCS

mùs acc. of *měs* 'we' 12

į 'into', cf. Lat. *in* 9

pagùndą acc. of *pagùnda* f. 'temptation': (1) *pa-* prefix, also *pó-*, and prep. *põ* 'on, in, along, through', OCS *po* 'do.', cf. also Lat. *põnõ* 'I place' < **poznõ* < **po + sinõ* 'do.', cf. supines *situm, positum*; (2) *-gùnda*, cf. *gùndyti* 'tempt'

bèt 'but'

gélbėk 2.sg.imper. of *gélbėti* 'deliver, help'

nuõ 'from'

pìkto gen.m.n. of *pìktas* 'evil, wicked'

OLD CHURCH SLAVONIC

(Tenth century)

9 *Otĭče našĭ iže jesi na nebesĭchŭ: da svętitŭ sę imę tvoje.*

10 *Da priidetŭ cěsarĭstvije tvoje: Da bǫdetŭ volja tvoja, jako na nebesi i na zemlji.*

11 *Chlěbŭ našĭ nastojęštajego dĭne daždĭ namŭ dĭnĭ sĭ.*

12 *I otŭpusti namŭ dlĭgy našę, jako i my otŭpuštajemŭ dlĭžĭnikomŭ našimŭ.*

13 *I ne vŭvedi nasŭ vŭ napastĭ, nŭ izbavi ny otŭ neprijazni.*

9   *otĭče* voc. of *otĭcĭ* m. 'father' < Pr. Sl. **otĭkŭ*, hypocoristic of **otŭ*, cf. Goth.

     našĭ 'our' < Pr. Sl. *do.* < IE **nōsyos*, cf. Lat. *noster* 9; cf. *ny* 13

     iže 'which', consisting of *i-*, a reflex of the IE relative stem *yo-*, cf. Gk *hōs* 10, and *že* emphatic particle, cf. Gk *-ge*, Skt *(g)he*

     jesi 'art' < **esī* for IE **esi*, cf. Lat.

     na 'on' ultimately related to Gk *ána, aná* 'up, on', Goth. *ana* 'on'

     nebesĭchŭ loc.pl. of *nebo*, gen. *nebese* n. 'heaven', cf. Skt *nábhas* 'cloud, sky', Gk *néphos, nephélē*, Lat. *nebula* 'cloud', OHG *nebul* 'mist'. Also doubtless Lith. *debesìs* 'cloud', with *d-* for *n-* perhaps by analogy with *dangùs* 'heaven'. On the semantic variation 'heaven—cloud—mist', cf. Eng. *sky*, a borrowing from ON *ský* 'cloud', cognate with OE *scio* 'do.' and OIr. *céo* 'mist'. Cf. Ir.

     da conj. 'may that'

     svętitŭ 3.sg.pres. of perfective *svętiti* 'hallow' from *svetŭ* 'holy', cf. Lith. *šveñtas* 9

     sę refl.pron.acc., cf. Lat. *sē*, Gk *hé*, Goth. *sik*, further Lith. *sàvo* 12

     imę, gen. *imene* n. 'name', cf. OPruss. *emmens*; cf. Lat.

     tvoje n. 'thy', nom.m.sg. *tvoi*, cf. Lat.

10 *priidetŭ* 3.sg.pres. (future sense) of perfective *priiti* 'come' = *pri* + *iti*: (1) *pri* 'towards', cf. Lith. *priẽ* 'up to, at', ultimately related to the large complex of IE prepositions based on the consonants *pr*, cf. e.g. OE *forgief* 12, and (2) *iti* 'walk, go', 1.sg.pres. *idǫ* (where *d* is a formative element), Lith. *eĭti*, 1.sg.pres. *eimì*, cf. Skt *émi*, Gk *eĭmi*, Lat. *eō* < **eiō*

     cěsarĭstvije n. 'kingdom' from *cěsarĭ* 'king, czar', a borrowing via Goth. *kaisar* of Lat. *caesar*

     bǫdetu 3.sg.fut. of imperfective *byti* 'be', with same formative *d* as in *priidetŭ* above; cf. Lith. *búti* 'be', further Lat. *fuī* 'I was, have been', Gk *phúō* 'I grow', Skt *bhávati* 'happens', OIr. *ro-both* 'was', W *bod*, OE *bēon* 'be'

     volja f. 'will', cf. Lat.

     tvoja f. 'thy', cf. *tvoje* 9

     jako 'as', older *ako*

nebesi loc.sg. of *nebo* 'heaven', see *nebesĭchŭ* 9

i 'also, and'

zemlji loc. of *zemlja* f. 'earth', cf. Lith. *zĕmĕ*, Lat. *humus* 'do.', Gk *khamaí* 'to, on the ground'

11 *chlěbŭ* m. 'bread', most likely loan word from Gmc, cf. Goth. *hlaifs* 'do.' (q.v.)

nastojęštajego gen.sg.m. (pronominal declension) of *nastoję* 'present': *na* 'on' (see 9), and *stoję* pres.part. of imperfective *stojati* 'stand', in ablaut relationship perfective *stati* 'stand, become', cf. Lith. *stóti* 'enter', *stověti* 'stand', further Skt *tíṣṭhati*, Gk *hístēmi* Lat. *stāre*, OHG *stān*, *stēn* 'stand', Ir. *tá*, W *taw* 'is'

dĭne gen. of *dĭnĭ* 'day' below

daždĭ 2.sg.imper. 'give' < Pr. Sl. **dadjĭ*, formed from the reduplicating root *dad-*, cf. Skt *dádāmi*, Gk *dídōmi*, Lith. *dúodu* 'I give'. The corresponding perfective infinitive is *dati* from the root *da-*, cf. Lith. *dúoti*, Lat. *dare*

namŭ dat. of *my* 12, see also *ny* 13

dĭnĭ m. 'day', cf. Lith. *dienà*, Skt *dínam*, Goth. *-teins*, OE *-ten*, further Lat. *nūndinus* adj. '(falling on) the ninth day', an *n*-enlargement of the root seen in Lat. *diēs* 'day'. Cf. Lat., Skt, Goth., OE, Lith.

sĭ m. 'this', *si* f., *se* n., cf. Lith.

12 *otŭpusti* 2.sg.imper. of perfective *otŭpustiti* 'remit, forgive': *otŭ* 'from' 13, *pustiti* 'allow', cf. *otŭpuštajemŭ* below

dlĭgy acc.pl. of *dlĭgŭ* m. 'debt'. Apparently related to OIr. *dliged*, W *dyled* (q.v.). But also Goth. *dulgs* 'debt'. Borrowing?

našę acc.m.pl. of *naši* 9

my 'we', cf. Lith.

otŭpuštajemŭ 1.pl.pres. of imperfective *otŭpuštati* 'remit, forgive', cf. *otŭpusti* above

dlĭžĭnikomŭ dat.pl. of *dlĭžĭnikŭ* m. 'debtor' from *dlĭgŭ* above

našimŭ dat.pl. of *našŭ* 9

13 *ne* negative particle 'not', cf. Lat.

vŭvedi 2.sg.imper. of *vŭvesti* 'lead into': *vŭ* 'into' below, and *vesti* 'lead' < **ved-ti* (1.sg.pres. *vedǫ*), cf. Lith., also W *nasŭ* gen. (syntactically required after negative) of *my* 'we' below

vŭ 'into' before vowels *vŭn*, with regular prosthetic *v* < **ŭn*, cf. Lat. *in* 9

napastĭ f. 'temptation': *na* 'on' 9, and *-pastĭ*, cf. *pasti* 'fall' (vb.), < **pad-ti*, cf. Skt *padyate*, OE *ge-fetan* 'do.', ultimately one with Skt *pắt*, *padás*, Gk *poŭs*, *podós*, Lat. *pēs*, *pedis*, Goth. *fotus* 'foot'

nŭ 'but', likely the same word as Lith. *nù* (interj.) 'well', Gk *nú*, Skt, Goth. *nu* 'now'

izbavi 2.sg.imper. of perfective *izbaviti* 'free, deliver': *iz* 'out of', cf. Lith. *ìš*, Lat. *ē*, *ex*, Gk *ek*, *ex* 'do.', and *bavati* causative of *byti* 'be' (cf. *bǫdetŭ* 10), Skt *bhāvayati* 'causes to be'

ny 'us' acc. of *my* 12, cf. Lat. *nōs* 12

otŭ 'from', cf. Lith. *at-* 'away, back, hither'

neprijazni gen. of *neprijaznĭ* f. 'evil': *ne* negative particle, see above, and *prijaznĭ* 'goodness, kindness', cf. *prijati* 'care for' cognate with Skt *prīyate*, also *priyāyáte* 'enjoys oneself', Goth. *frijon* 'love' (vb.), *frijonds* 'friend', Skt *priyás* 'beloved, dear'

IRISH

The first known version goes back to about the twelfth century. A text of this date still contains many features found in Old Irish. On the other hand, the philological commentary necessary in the case of the text in question seemed to be unduly lengthy for our purpose here. We therefore substitute a version in present-day standard language. There is, however, no corresponding unified pronunciation; we give that of Connemara. Though declensional and conjugational forms have been simplified in the modern period, the vocabulary remains largely traditional.

9 *Ár n-athair, atá ar neamh: go naofar d'ainm.*

10 *Go dtaga do ríocht. Go ndéantar do thoil ar an talamh, mar dhéantar ar neamh.*

11 *Ár n-arán laethúil tabhair dúinn inniu.*

12 *Agus maith dúinn ár bhfiacha, mar mhaithimid dár bhféichiúna féin.*

13 *Agus ná lig sinn i gcathú, ach saor sinn ó olc.*

[9 aːr nɑhif əˈtaː ef ńæːw gə niːfər dǽńiḿ 10 gə dagə də fiəχt gə ńiːntər də hilʹ ef ə talə mar jiːntər ef ńæːw 11 aːr nəˈraːn

læhuːlˊ toːf duːń əˈńu 12 əgəs ma duːń aːr v́iəχə mar wahiḿidˊ
daːr v́eːhuːnə heːń 13 əgəs naː lˊiǵ ʃiń ə gahuː aχ siːr ʃiń oː olk]

9   *ár n-* (invariable) 'our', OIr. *ar n-*, perhaps a form of *nár, nathar* 'of us', reminiscent of Lat. *noster* 9

   athair m. 'father', OIr. also older *athir*, with regular loss of IE initial *p*, cf. Lat.

   atá syntactically 'who is', OIr. *do.* < **ad-tá*: preverb *ad-* 'to' (OW, Lat. *ad* 'to', Goth. *at*, OE *æt* 'at'), and *tá* 'is', W *taw*, lit. 'stands' < IE *stā-*, cf. OCS *nastojęštajego* 11

   ar 'on, in', OIr. *for*, cf. W *ar* 10

   neamh m. 'heaven', OIr. *nem*, cf. W *nêf* 10. Perhaps somehow related to the very widely attested IE root *nebh-* 'cloud, heaven', see OCS *nebesǐchǔ* 9, but Clt. *m* cannot regularly derive from IE *bh*

   go conj. 'that may', OIr. *co n-* 'so that, until', formally identical with *co n-*, older *com-* 'with', W *cym-, cyf-, cyn-, cy-*, cf. Lat. *cum*, older *com*

   naofar, older modern spelling *naomhthar*, pres.pass. of *naomhaím* 'hallow' from *naomh* 'holy', OIr. *noíb*, cf. OPersian *naiba-* 'good, beautiful'

   d' elision of *do* 'of thee', generalised voiced form of archaic OIr. *t', to*, cf. *tú* 'thou', see Gk. *soû* 9

   ainm m.f. 'name', OIr. *ainm n-* n, cf. Lat.

10 *dtaga* eclipsed form of *taga*, pres.subj.sg. of *tagaim* 'come', verbal noun *teacht*, OIr. *techt* ('going'), W *taith* 'journey', OIr. *tíagu* 'go', cf. Gk *steíkhō* 'walk', Goth. *steigan*, OE *stígan* 'go (up, down)', Lith. *staigýtis, steĩgtis* (-*s* reflexive) 'hasten', OCS *stignǫ* 'I come', Skt *stigh-* 'walk'

   do 'thy', see *d'* 9

   ríocht f. 'kingdom', older modern spelling *ríoghdhacht*, derivative of *ríoga* 'royal', older mod.sp. *ríoghdha*, OIr. *rígda*, from *rí* 'king', OIr. gen. *ríg*, W *rhi*, Gaul. *-ríx*; cf. Lat.

   ndéantar eclipsed form of *déantar* pres.pass. of *déanaim* 'do', OIr. (prototonic) *dénim* with (deuterotonic) *dogníu*, containing *do*, archaic *to* 'towards', W *dy-*, and the root *gni-* 'do', cf. W

   thoil lenited form of *toil* f. 'will', formally accusative, OIr. *tol*

   an 'the', OIr. *(s)in(d)*, cf. W *yr hwn* 9

   talamh m. 'earth', OIr. *talam*, cf. Skt *taliman* 'ground' *mar* 'as', MidIr. (*a*)*mar*, OIr. *amal*, archaic *amail*, an (originally dative) form of *samail* 'likeness' with regular loss of initial *s* in pretonic position, cf. Lat. *similis* adj. 'like', further Gk *homalós* 'equal' from *homós* 'do.', Skt *samás* 'equal, same', OCS *samŭ* 'self', Goth. *sama* 'same', related to IE **sems* 'one', see p. 191 cf.; W *fel* 12

dhéantar lenited form of *déantar*, see *ndéantar* above

11   *arán* m. 'bread'. Not attested in OIr., which has *bairgen*, cf. W. The MidIr. paternoster referred to above has *sásad* lit. 'sustenance'

laethúil 'daily', older modern spelling *laetheamhail*, from *lá* m. 'day', OIr. *lae* n. beside fuller form *laithe* < Pr. Clt. **lati*, cf. Gaul. (abbreviation) *lat.*, and suffix *-amhail* formally identical with OIr. *amail* discussed under *mar* 10. See *inniu* below

tabhair 2.sg.imper. of *tabhraim* 'give' (but replaced in the standard language by *tugaim*), containing *to-* (see *ndéantar* 10), and the root *ber-* 'bear', cf. W *-fer* (*adfer* 'restore'), Lat. *ferō*, etc.

dúinn 'to us', OIr. *dún*(*n*), 1st pl. of pronoun (cf. *ár n-* 9, *sinn* 13) combined with *do* 'to' (apparently distinct from *do-*, *to-* referred to under *ndéantar* 10), cf. OE *tō* 11

inniu 'today', OIr. *indiu*, temporal dative (originally instrumental?): *in* 'the' (cf. *an* 10), and *diu* 'day', nom. *die* m. For another word for day, see *laethúil* above. Cf. Lat.

12   *agus* 'and', OIr. *acus*, *ocus*, when stressed 'near' (Mod. Ir. *fogas*), W *agos* 'near'

maith 2.sg.imper. of *maithim* 'forgive', verbal noun *maitheamh*, OIr. *mathem*, a borrowing from W *maddau* 'do.'

ár 'our' (= *ár n* 9), form used before a word beginning with a consonant

bhfiacha eclipsed form of *fiacha*, pl. of *fiach* m. 'debt', OIr. *do*.

mhaithimid lenited form of *maithimid*, 1.pl.pres.indic. of *maithim* 'forgive' above

dár 'to our', OIr. *do ar n-*, cf. *ár* above, *dúinn* 11

bhféichiúna eclipsed form of *féichiúna*, older modern spelling *féiche-amhna*, pl. of *féicheamh* m. 'debtor', OIr. *féchem*, from *fiach* above. The present form, usual in this context, is otherwise replaced in the standard language by *féichiúnaí*, pl. *féichiúnaithe*

féin '-self, -selves', OIr. (inflecting) nom.sg. *féin*, pl. *féisine*; the word is a purely Gaelic development of inherited materials

13 *ná* negative particle used in prohibitions, OIr. *na*, full form *nach-* preserved mainly before appended pronouns, cf. Lat. *neque* 'and not'; cf. W

lig 2.sg.imper. of *ligim* 'let, allow', OIr. *lécim*, cf. Gk *leípō*, also *limpánō*, Lat. *linquō* 'leave', Skt *riṇákti* 'releases', Lith. *lìkti* 'remain', Goth. *leihwan*, OE *līon* 'lend'

sinn 'us' also 'we', OIr. *snisni, sníni, sinni*, emphatic forms of *sní*, itself a stressed form of *ni* 'do.', cf. W *ni* 11; cf. Lat. *nōs* 12

i 'into', before vowels *in*, OIr. *i n-*, cf. Lat. *in* 9

gcathú eclipsed form of *cathú*, older modern spelling *cathughadh*, m. 'temptation' also 'trial, act of fighting' from *cath* 'battle', W *cad*, Gaul. *Catu-*, also in Gmc, e.g. OE *Heaþu-*, OHG *Hadu-*, ON *hǫþ* 'do.'

ach 'but', OIr. *acht*

saor 2.sg.imper. of *saoraim* 'deliver, set free', OIr. *soírim*, from *saor* adj. 'free', OIr. *soír*

o 'from out, of', cf. W *o* < Pr. Clt. **au*, Lat. *au-* (*auferō* 'bear away'), OCS (preverb) *u-*, Skt *áva* 'do.'

olc m. 'evil', OIr. *do.*

WELSH

There are no connected Biblical texts in Old Welsh. Since the literary language of today is not far removed from Middle Welsh, it seemed practical to quote here the standard version in use today; it dates from the sixteenth century.

9 *Ein tad, yr hwn wyt yn y nefoedd: sancteiddier dy enw.*

10 *Deled dy deyrnas. Gwneler dy ewyllys, megis yn y nef, felly ar y ddaear hefyd.*

11 *Dyro i ni heddiw ein bara beunyddiol.*

12 *A maddau i ni ein dyledion, fel y maddeuwn ninnau i'n dyledwyr.*

13 *Ac nac arwain ni i brofedigaeth, eithr gwared ni rhag drwg.*

9 *ein* 'of us', cf. *ni* 11

tâd m. 'father', cf. Lat. *tata*, Gk *tatã*, Russ. *táta*, Skt *tatás* 'do.', in origin a baby word, cf. Goth.

yr hwn 'who' lit. 'this': *yr* 'the' < *yn*, cf. OIr. *(s)in(d)* 'do.', < Pr.

Clt. **sindos* (nom.m.sg.), *hwn* m. 'this', *hon* f., *hyn* n., cf. Ir. *sin* 'do.'

ŵyt 2.sg.pres.indic. of *bod* 'be': *ŵy-* < Neo-Clt. **ei* < Pr. Clt. **esi*, cf. Lat.; and *-t* from pronoun *ti* 'thou', i.e. **ŵy ti* became *ŵyt ti* in the preliterary period, cf. OIr. *at* 'do.'

yn 'in', OW, Gaul. *iň*, cf. Lat.

y 'the', the form before consonants other than *h*, see *yr* above

nefoedd pl. of *nêf* 'heaven' 10

sancteiddier pres.subj.pass. of *sancteiddio* 'hallow', a literary naturalisation of Lat. *sānctificāre*, cf. Lat.

dy 'of thee', a generalised lenited form, cf. *ti* 'thou' and Gk *soŭ* 9

enw m. 'name', OW *anu*, pl. *enuein* (*u* < *m*), cf. Lat.

10   *deled* beside *deued* 3.sg.imper. of *dyfod* 'come': preverb *dy-*, cf. Ir. *do-*, *to-* under Ir. *ndéantar* 10, and *fod* lenited from *bod* 'be', see OCS *bǫdetŭ* 10. The *l*-form is due to contamination by a root *el-* 'go', e.g. pres.subj.pass. *eler* (i.e. impersonal), cf. Gk *elaúnō* 'travel'

deyrnas lenited form of *teyrnas* f. 'kingdom' from *teyrn* 'king', OBrit. (latinising) *Vor-tigernus* lit. 'Over-Lord', OIr. *tigerne* 'lord', originally 'master of the house', OW *tig*, OIr. *tech* 'house', cf. Gk (*s*)*tégos* 'house, roof', *stégei*, Lat. *tegit*, Skt *sthágati* 'covers', Lat. *tēctum* 'roof'. A semantic parallel in Lat. *dominus* 'lord' from *domus* 'house'.

gwneler pres.subj.pass. of *gwneuthur* 'do.', OIr. *gniid* 'does', the *l*-form being regarded as a contamination due to the similarly constructed parts of *dyfod*, above under *deled*; cf. Ir.

ewyllys f. 'will'

megis 'as'

nêf f. 'heaven', see *nefoedd* 9, cf. Ir.

felly 'so' < **evelhyn* < **haval hyn*, cf. Bret. *evel henn* 'so' lit. 'like this', cf. *fel* 12, *yr hwn* 9

ar 'on', Co., Bret. *war*, etymologically identical with the prefix *gor-*, *gwar-*, Co. *gor-*, Bret. *gour-*, Gaul. *ver-* 'over', OIr. *for* 'on' < IE **upor*, cf. Skt *upári*, Goth. *ufar* 'over', further with secondary initial consonant Lat. *super*, Gk *hypér*, *hýper* 'do.'

ddaear lenited form of *daear* f. 'earth'

hefyd 'also' lit. 'likewise', related to *hafal* adj. 'like', see *fel* 12

11   *dyro* 2.sg.imper. of *rhoi* beside fuller form *rhoddi* 'give', *dy-* being a preverb, see *deled* 10

i 'to', MidW *y*, OW *di*, cf. OE *tō* 11

ni 'us' also 'we', cf. OIr. *ni*, stressed *sní* 'do.' Whether Welsh once had such a stressed form is unknown, W *ni* being ambivalent, since OBrit. *sn-* was always reduced to *n-*. Cf. Ir. *sinn* 13

heddiw 'today', older *heddyw*, petrified dative (originally instrumental?): *he-* from the IE demonstrative stem *so-*, cf. Gk *ho* 9, and *-ddyw* lenited form of *dyw* 'day', see *beunyddiol* below; cf. Lat.

bara m. 'bread', OIr. *bairgen* 'do.', further Goth. *barizeins* adj. 'of barley', OE *bere* 'barley', Lat. *far* 'corn', OCS *brašĭno* 'rye meal'

beunyddiol adj. 'daily' from *beunydd* adv. 'do.', a petrified accusative of time (with common lenition of initial consonant), also with radical initial *peunydd* < OBrit. **papon diyen*, i.e. *peu-n-* 'every', cf. W *pob*, OIr. *cach* 'do.' (cf. Lith. *kaĩp* 10), and *-(n)-ydd* (with secondary spirant), radical *dydd* 'day', cf. *heddiw* above

12   *a* 'and', also *ac* 13, cf. Lat. *atque* 'and also': *at*, Gk *átar*, Goth. *aþ-þan* 'but', and *-que* 'and', cf. Skt *ca* 12

maddau 2.sg.imper. of *do.* 'forgive', cf. Ir.

dyledion pl. of *dyled* f. 'debt', OIr. *dliget* 'obligation', further W *dylid* 'one ought', OIr. *dligid* 'merits' later 'owes', cf. OCS

fel 'as', MidW *val*, OW *amal* 'do.', further W *hafal* adj. 'like', OIr. *samail* 'likeness', cf. Ir. *amal* 10; cf. *felly* 10, also *hefyd* 10

y verbal particle, older *yd*, now meaningless but formerly having a relative function, cf. OIr. *-d-* found in relative verbal complexes

maddeuwn 1.pl.pres.indic. of *maddau* 'forgive' above

ninnau 'we too', emphatic form of *ni* 11

'n 'our' = *ein* 9 with regular elision after word ending in a vowel

dyledwyr pl. of *dyledwr* m. 'debtor' from *dyled* above

13   *ac* 'and' = *a* 12, form used before words beginning with a vowel and also before a small number beginning with a consonant, including *na(c)*

nac, except before words beginning with a vowel *na*, negative particle used in prohibitions, cf. Ir.

arwain 2.sg.imper. of *do.* 'lead' < OBrit. **are-wed-no-* (cf. 1.sg.pres. indic. MidW *arwedaf*): *are-* preverb 'in front', *-wed-* 'lead', cf. OIr.

fedid 'leads', OCS *vesti*, Lith. *vèsti* (q.v.), and *-no-*, suffix forming verbal noun

brofedigaeth lenited form of *profedigaeth* f. 'temptation' from *profi* 'tempt, test', a popular borrowing from Lat. *probāre* 'test, find good', *probus* 'good'

eithr 'but', OIr. *echtar* 'outside', cf. Lat. *extrā* 'do.'

gwared 2.sg.imper. of *gwaredu* 'deliver, save', *gwa-* preverb 'under', cf. Ir. *fo* < *uo < IE *upo, Goth. *uf* 'do.', Skt *úpa* 'up to, near', further with secondary initial consonant Lat. *sub*, Gk *hupó*, *húpo* 'under', and *-redu* 'run', i.e. *rhedaf* 'I run', cf. OIr. *rethim* 'do.', further W *rhod*, Ir. *roth*, Lat. *rota*, OHG *rad*, Lith. *rātas* 'wheel', Skt *ráthas* 'chariot' lit. 'wheeled (vehicle)'

rhag 'from' also 'before', a proclitic form, cf. with full stressing (*y*)*rhawg* 'in future'

drŵg m., also adj. 'evil, bad', cf. Ir. *droch-* 'do.'

APPLIED COMPARATIVE PHILOLOGY

It goes without saying that comparative philology often makes important, sometimes decisive, contributions to other departments of linguistics. Its influence is also more widely felt, for it regularly performs ancillary duties for historical and social studies as well. All this we have termed 'applied comparative philology'.

ETYMOLOGY

It is very evident that etymology is an integral part of comparative as of historical philology. It is in fact the corner stone of these studies which have revealed so much of the true nature of the lexicon. We give some representative examples.

Bridegroom is admittedly rather a curious term. The mode of formation is unusual—it contrasts, for instance, in this respect with *bride's maid*—and why should the lucky man be called a *groom* of all things? The difficulties are, however, at once resolved when the etymology of the term is established, as follows. The Middle English form was *bridegome*, which goes back to OE *brȳdguma*, a transparent compound regularly formed according to the rules of composition in Old English: *brȳd* 'bride', *guma* 'man' (cognate with Lat. *homō*). Then, during the middle period, the simplex *gome* dropped out of use, so that the literal meaning of the compound was no longer apparent. At this point, in the sixteenth century, *bridegome* was 'corrected' to *bridegrome*, since there was in the current language another, commonly used, word *grome* '(serving) lad, youth'. Such a 'correction', arising

anonymously in the spoken language, the purpose of which is to
make some sort of sense of a word no longer properly understood, is technically known as a folk etymology. Meanwhile the
Middle English form has become Mod. Eng. *groom* 'servant having
the care of horses'. It is this semantic narrowing which makes
the word bridegroom sound so bizarre if we try to interpret it
literally on the evidence of the modern language only.

OE *brȳdguma* has exact parallels in the other West Germanic
languages and in Scandinavian. Except in Icelandic, the simplex
corresponding to OE *guma* has quite died out, though the compound lives on everywhere unimpaired. None of these languages,
however, know a term corresponding to ME *grome*, and have
thus not been tempted to tamper with the compound even though
the second element is naturally incomprehensible to ordinary
speakers of the languages concerned, e.g. Ger. *Bräutigam*, Dutch
bruidegom, Danish *brudgom*.

Etymology and semantics go hand in hand. On p. 87, Skt
dhūmás, Lat. *fūmus* and Gk *thūmós* were compared as evidence of
a fundamental sound law. The first two mean 'smoke', the third
'passion'. We nevertheless feel confident that the Greek meaning
has developed out of the first. We have, indeed, no difficulty in
accounting for it, for there is a close analogy in our own figurative
use of 'heat, hot air'. The three words are without a doubt etymologically identical and may be safely used as evidence. On p. 88,
we compared Lat. *veniō* 'come' with Skt *gam-* and Gk *baínō*
meaning 'go', again in illustration of an important sound law. It
was later seen that Eng. *come* belongs etymologically to the same
group (p. 164). But perhaps this equation is puzzling, since 'come'
and 'go' are semantically opposites. We discover, however, that
English usage is not necessarily typical. Even the closely related
Germanic languages can occasionally be divergent, e.g. Ger. *sie
kommt auf die Universität* 'she's going to university'. In Russian
we have to expect even less familiar modes of expression: a single
verb often covers both meanings, as *ja idú domój* 'I'm going home',
ja idú íz domu 'I'm coming from home'. Russian possesses more
precise verbal forms as well, e.g. *ja prijdú* (*pri* 'towards' + *idú*)
'I'm coming, arriving', as in Old Church Slavonic, p. 168, and
similarly in Lithuanian, see note on *teateiniĕ*, p. 166.

Returning to the etymological equation Lat. *veniō*, etc. above,
one infers that a root with the primary sense of 'walk', neutral as
to direction, has tended to acquire, in the individual languages,
the specialised sense of 'come' or 'go', though without rigid uni-

formity. It happens, indeed, that both Sanskrit and Greek not uncommonly employ the verbs quoted where English idiom requires 'come'. Similar semantic shifts are seen again between Skt *yǎti* 'comes', also 'goes', and Lith. *jóti* 'ride (on horseback)', p. 157. Changes of sense may be noticeable within a single language. The Old Irish verbal noun *techt* is best translated 'going', but its Modern Irish descendant *teacht* is 'coming'; the word is cognate with Gk *steíkhō* 'walk', etc., p. 87. Finally mention may be made of Welsh *deled* 'let it come' which shows contamination from a root *el-* 'go', p. 174. The contamination may be due to the attraction of opposites, but it could equally reflect a basic semantic affinity.

Eng. *wether* has restricted its earlier sense; OE *weþer* meant 'male sheep' generally, like its cognates OHG *widar*, ON *veþr*. Goth. *wiþrus*, however, renders Gk *amnós* 'lamb'. Pr. Gmc **weþruz* < IE **wetrus* is understandable as a derivative of IE **wetos* 'year' attested, e.g. in Gk *étos* (archaic dial. *wétos*) 'do.'. One may therefore postulate for *wether* a primitive meaning 'yearling' and observe that Gothic has remained most faithful to its source. Lat. *vetus* 'old' is also related to this word for 'year'. It is further thought that the Latin diminutives *vitulus, vitellus* 'calf' (from which ultimately Eng. *veal*, p. 54), in spite of the unexplained radical *i* for expected *e*, must be derived from the same root and thus also have originally meant 'yearling'. With the above may be further compared Skt *vatsás* 'calf', Gk dial. *étalon* 'yearling'.

The Latin verb *canere* 'sing' is paralleled in Celtic, e.g. W *canu*, and presupposes the IE root *kan-*. In Germanic this root would appear as *han-* (p. 118), but one searches in vain for a verbal form like this. But the root is seen to be formally present in Goth. *hana* 'cock', likewise OE *hana* 'do.' which has a feminine derivative *henn* < Pr. Gmc **hanjō* 'hen'. The conclusion is soon reached. Goth. *hana* etc. must literally mean 'singer', in reference of course to its crowing. The correctness of this etymology is further confirmed by the fact that both Latin and Celtic use the verb in question in the sense required: Lat. *gallus canit*, W *y mae'r ceiliog yn canu* 'the cock crows'. It requires no further demonstration that Gk *ēikanós* (*ēi-* 'dawn'), an epithet of the cock, also belongs to the same root. To the above Lithuanian offers an exact semantic parallel: *gaidỹs* 'cock', *gaidà* 'melody', *giedóti* 'sing, crow', cf. also Skt *gấyati* 'sings'. In conclusion, one may infer from the semantics of the names just discussed that Pr. Gmc **hanjō* could not have

arisen until the etymological connections of the masculine form
had been forgotten.

The word for 'nest' in Latin, Celtic and Germanic is explicable
as continuing IE *nizdos < *nisdos* m., *-om* n., e.g. Lat. *nīdus* (loss
of *z* and compensatory lengthening of preceding vowel); OIr. *net*,
W *nyth* < Insular Clt. *niδdos*; OE *nest* < Pr. Gmc *nistan*. The
same may be said of Skt *nīdás*, *nīdám* 'do.'. The term occurs in
Slavonic also, with an unexplained, but at all events secondary,
initial *g*: OCS *gnězdo* (Russ. *gnezdó*). Peculiarly enough, Lithuanian has *lizdas* instead of the expected **nizdas*. Bearing in mind all
the circumstances, one must here assume an exceptional shift of
n to *l*, for some reason unknown; it would be unrealistic to regard
the Lithuanian as an unrelated word. IE *nisdos* is not difficult to
etymologise, for it invites comparison with Skt. *ni-sídati* 'sits
down'. Our word therefore contains the particle *ni* 'down' (preserved as the first part of OE *niþer* 'nether', *niþan* 'beneath') and
the zero grade of the IE root *sed-* 'sit', cf. p. 97. A nest is
literally something to sit down on, a 'seat' in fact. It is a term
which has been very anciently transferred from the human sphere
to the ornithological and has petrified there.

READING OF TEXTS

Since it is often possible, thanks to comparative method, to pre-
dict linguistic forms with great accuracy, manuscript errors can
sometimes be put right by this means. A good example is to hand
from our own historical tradition in the name of Boadicea. One
wonders if her name has been transmitted correctly. But whatever
the form, it is realised that it must have had a meaning as would
befit a queen. Boadicea spoke Old British, of which Welsh is a
linear descendant. There is a Welsh name *Buddug*, simply a
personification of *buddug*, MidW *budic* 'victorious', cf. OIr.
búadach 'do.', a common epithet of heroic figures, from *búaid*
'victory'. This is enough to enable the philologist to postulate
still older forms and, taking also into account the manuscript
variants, he can recognise the spelling Boadicea as corrupt and
confidently amend it to **Boudicā* 'Victoria'.

Under this rubric may be mentioned the interpretation of extinct
languages. The meaning of the Oscan inscriptions has now been
almost fully established thanks to the close affinity with Latin, the
two languages differing about as much as German and Dutch.

The philology of Umbrian has been clarified in much the same way. More spectacular was the decipherment of Old Persian, for in this case an unknown script had first to be recognised for what it is, namely an alphabetic cuneiform. Once this was realised, the decipherment and interpretation followed rapidly, as the language was so close to Avestan and Sanskrit.

But undoubtedly the most remarkable example of the application of the comparative method concerns the identification of an unknown language belonging to an entirely distinct branch of Indo-European, Hittite. The cuneiform records of this language contain among the phonetically written words a number of ideograms. These were at once recognised as they were already known from texts in other languages (Akkadian, Sumerian). Then B. Hrozný, the pioneer decipherer of Hittite, found this sentence: *nu BREAD-an ezateni watar ma ekuteni*, where *BREAD* is an ideogram which can be understood and *-an* a phonetically written termination native to the language of the text. A glance at the sentence shows that two words have identical endings. Possibly they are the same parts of speech. Suppose they are verbs. Which verb is likely to go with 'bread'? Try 'eat'. And, indeed, *ezateni* could conceivably contain the Indo-European root *ed-*, as seen in Lat. *edō*, Gk *édomai*, OE *etan* 'eat'. Suppose the first group of words really means 'now eat bread', what of the second group? It could be a parallel clause to the first. Utterly unexpected though it seems, *watar* looks uncommonly like 'water'. If it is not a coincidence, then *ekuteni* will presumably mean 'drink'. All this makes perfect sense as a ritual direction: 'now eat bread, then drink water', and we accept it as a first translation. Much philological detail remains to be filled in, but to all appearances this is an Indo-European language. As we know, Hrozný's premise was long since transmuted into philological certainty, and the meaning of the passage above can now be shown to be 'now you eat bread and drink water'.

MATERIAL CULTURE

Linguistic evidence is often highly significant in questions of material culture. To take a simple example. An examination of the English names for berries shows that they are Germanic, but the names of fruits, with the sole exception of *apple*, are loan words, the oldest borrowed from Latin. One infers that our ancestors had been familiar from time immemorial with berries of various sorts, but that before contact with Roman civilisation the only fruit they ever tasted was the wild crab apple. It alone is seen to have been indigenous, the pears, cherries and the rest being later introduced from kinder climates.

By the same token, it is not difficult to see that many other arts beside horticulture were brought to the Germanic peoples by the Romans. Many of the terms used in connection with houses built of brick or stone are from Latin, as *wall, tile, mortar, kitchen*. But purely Germanic words tell a different story; *hurdle, wattle, wicker, thatch* afford a glimpse of a less pretentious homestead, where *timber* was the essential building material. OE *timber* also means 'building', cf. OHG *zimbar* 'building, timber' (Mod. Ger. *Zimmer* 'room', *Zimmermann* 'joiner'). In these forms, *b* is intrusive, cf. Goth. *timrjan* 'build'; we postulate Pr. Gmc *tem(b)-ran* n. The root is identical with that of Gk *démō* 'build', with a different grade of ablaut *dómos* 'hut', Lat. *domus*, Skt *dámas*, OCS. *domŭ* 'house'. We conclude that the IE *domos* was a very modest abode.

One can, it seems, go back further still. The Old English antecedents of Eng. *door* are *duru* f. and *dor* n., parallel to OHG *turi* f., *tor* n. (Mod. Ger. *Tür* 'door', *Tor* 'gate'). There is no doubt that the first of these doublets is, in origin, nothing more than the plural of the second. Old Norse has only the one form: *dyrr* f.pl. Why should the door of the Germanic hut have been designated by a plural form? They would scarcely have been double doors. And the phenomenon is not confined to Germanic. It is found in the cognate Lat. *forēs*, Gk *thúrai* f.pl., which occur much more frequently than the corresponding sg. *foris, thúrā*, and in OCS *dvĭri*, Lith. *dùrys* f.pl. An explanation is forthcoming if we look to a more primitive dwelling than a hut and assume that the term was originally applied to the two flaps which form the door of a tent. Language has been described as the oldest living witness to history.

The word *hammer* occurs in all the Germanic languages, except Gothic (in the surviving texts of which no reference to a term of this nature is made), e.g. OE *hamor*, OHG *hamar*, ON *hamarr*. In Old Norse, however, the meaning is not only 'hammer', it is also 'stone'. How is this wide difference of meaning to be accounted for? It is not easy to imagine how a word primarily meaning 'hammer' could acquire the sense 'stone', but it is not so difficult to envisage semantic development in the other direction, for 'hammer' is seen to be explicable as a particularisation of the sense 'stone' on the assumption that it was originally a stone implement. The first hammers had stone heads; the word in this sense goes back to the Stone Age.

We are now in a position to consider cognates in other Indo-European languages and compare first OCS *kamy*, gen. *kamene* 'stone'. Assuming an IE *r/n* declension (p. 98), afterwards variously reformed, Germanic generalising *r*, Slavonic generalising *n*, the words in question can be intimately connected. In fact, evidence for an ancient *r/n* alternation is seen in Sanskrit: *áśman-* 'stone' beside *aśmarás* 'stony'. Further, with *n*: Lith. *akmuõ*, gen. *akmeñs* 'stone', Gk *ákmōn* 'anvil', the latter another particularisation of the original sense. It will be noted that the Slavonic and Germanic forms contrast to some extent with the Aryan, Baltic and Greek, the former suggesting an IE root *kōm-* and *kom-* respectively, the latter *akm-*. Such differences are attributable to dialect variation within Primitive Indo-European.

One of the commonest seabirds in British waters and the North Atlantic today is the fulmar, which now nests on well nigh every cliff along our coasts. Until about 1870, the fulmar was one of the rarer birds, its only breeding sites being on St Kilda in the Hebrides and on Grímsey off the north coast of Iceland. The case of this bird is of interest to ecologists who would like to know how old the two traditional colonies are. But historical records refer only to the recent past. Comparative philology can, however, throw light on the position long before, as follows. The name *fulmar* is Norse, first occurring in a stanza of a tenth-century Icelandic poet. The name must have been bestowed by fowlers visiting nesting sites, for ON *fúlmár* lit. 'foul mew' i.e. 'stinking gull' can only refer to the bird's habit of squirting regurgitated oil at intruders. The same name was used by the St Kildans, from whose dialect the word passed into Standard English; it must go back to the Norse occupation of the island in Viking times. The fulmars were thus certainly breeding there, as on Grímsey, a millennium ago, and of course were being taken by fowlers. It appears certain that the colonies were stationary on these two islands until recent times, so that their remarkable expansion must be due to some purely modern development, presumably the abundance of offal as a consequence of intense trawling.

LAW AND SOCIETY

An examination of the Old Welsh Laws, compiled in the tenth century, reveals that the fundamental legal terms are nearly all native Celtic despite the veritable flood of Latin loan words which poured into the Celtic dialects of Britain during the Roman occupation. One concludes that native institutions, at least in the West, were but slightly affected by Roman law. In other words, the tribes concerned were not subjugated, but retained their autonomy.

One of the Latin loans is of particular interest here. There are in the Laws two words for 'witness': *gwybyddiad* lit. 'knower' and *tyst* borrowed from Lat. *testis*; the form *gwybyddiad* shows the influence of *gwybod* 'know' which incorporates the stem *bod* 'be', the older simplex being seen, for instance, in *gŵyr* 'knows'. Irish legal tracts, more archaic than the Welsh, also have two terms for 'witness', a native one *fíadu* also lit. 'knower', cf. *-fitir* 'knows', and *teist* from Latin. The legal tradition of the two countries has preserved no reminiscence of any difference in the meaning of these terms, but there must have been one because in Irish sources they are sometimes listed separately. Both the native Welsh and Irish words are referable to IE *weid-* 'know from seeing', cf. for the sense Lat. *vidēre*, OCS *viděti* 'see', Gk *eîdos* for **weîdos* 'appearance', W *gŵydd* 'presence', OIr. *fíad* 'in the presence of'. This linguistic material suggests a solution of the legal problem. The native Celtic terms will properly denote eye-witnesses, who in the earlier period alone were entitled to testify. According to the more advanced Roman law, other forms of evidence, as for example testimony as to character, were admissible. At some stage the Celtic courts adopted such practices too, and the Latin term would be borrowed to distinguish a witness giving evidence of this sort from a witness who could testify to what had actually been done in his presence.

Comparative philology shows that the words *father* and *mother* are part of the basic Indo-European word stock, but curiously there is no such common term for 'parents'. To express this concept, Sanskrit may simply link the terms for 'father' and 'mother' in a special formation *pitárā-mātárā* or *mātárā-pitárā*; elliptic use is also possible: *pitárā* 'father (and mother)', *mātárā* 'mother (and father)'. Some languages use terms meaning literally 'bearers' as Lat. *parentēs*, Goth. *berusjos*, but more have 'begetters' as Gk *goneîs*, Russ. *rodíteli*, W *rhieni*, Ir. *tuismitheoirí*. Others employ words meaning 'elders' or 'ancestors', thus Ger. *Eltern*, Icel. *foreldrar*; in Lithuanian they are called *tėvaĩ* properly 'fathers'. The absence of a Common Indo-European term for parents can only mean that the society in question had no need for such a term. It looks as though the concept of the rights and duties of parents as a team, so to speak, was preceded in older society by a concept of the rights and duties of father and mother separately.

Other linguistic evidence points in the same direction. The Greek words for 'brother' and 'sister' are *adelphós* and *adelphḗ* respectively. It is not difficult to imagine that these terms are connected with *delphús* 'womb'. Etymology confirms this supposition by revealing cognates in Sanskrit. Applying the regular sound changes, Gk *delphús* can be closely compared with Skt *gárbhas* 'do.', the prototypes being IE *g^welbhus*, *g^welbhos*. Further, the Sanskrit compound *sagárbhyas* 'full brother' enables us to analyse Gk. *adelphós* (Homer *adelpheós*) correctly: it has been dissimilated from *$*hadelpheós$. The prefix is IE *sm̥-* 'one', normal grade *sem-* (cf. Lat. *semel* 'once', and p. 191). The basic sense of the compound is therefore 'belonging to one womb'. It is a formation of Indo-European antiquity, from a time when society needed a term for 'uterine brothers and sisters', i.e. not the children of parents, but the children of a specific mother.

It may seem perfectly natural that feminine forms should be derived from masculines and not vice versa, e.g. Ger. *Erbe*, Russ. *naslédnik* 'heir', *Erbin*, *naslédnica* 'heiress'. After all, it is a man's world. But there is one, sad exception: the word *widow*. In all Indo-European languages, the feminine form is primary, the masculine *widower* always secondary, and only the former is of Indo-European age. It is widely attested: Skt *vidhávā*, OCS *vŭdova*, Lat. *vidua*, Goth. *widuwo*, OIr. *fedb*, W *gweddw*, doubtless to be compared with Lat. *dīvidō* < *$*dis-vidō$ 'divide', giving a basic meaning 'deprived'. Examples of derived masculines are Ger. *Witwer* from *Witwe*, Fr. *veuf* analogically after *veuve*, Russ. *vdovéc* from *vdová*. It is not hard to account for the unique primacy of the feminine form. In a patriarchal society, the status of the woman depends upon that of her husband. Hence widowhood automatically leads to changes in her social position. The man's standing, however, is not so affected if the wife dies.

There are words of Indo-European age for the relatives of the husband (i.e. his father, mother, brother, sister, brother's wife), but the corresponding terms for the wife's relatives are indefinite and vary much from language to language. Indo-European society was thus markedly patriarchal, the wife entering the husband's family. Doubtless a reminiscence is preserved in Lat. *domum dūcere* 'marry' lit. 'lead home', a term used only of the man. Compare also Ger. *heimführen* with the same sense, in (literary) use to this day.

LINGUISTIC TABOO

No account of lexical evolution would be complete without a reference to linguistic taboo. The names of unpleasant or feared objects are particularly susceptible, and may be replaced entirely by quite different words. We saw on p. 52 that Lat. *ignis* 'fire' has not survived in Romance. To the mind of pre-scientific man, a fire is an awesome, magical thing, and such associations were felt as being implicit in its very name. As a consequence, a stage may be reached when the name is consciously avoided and then a so-called noa word is taken in its place. In the present example, *focus* properly meaning 'hearth' provided the harmless euphemism.

The supposed baleful influence of the moon is clearly reflected in Eng. *moonstruck*, paralleled in Late Lat. *lunaticus*, and the name of the moon has frequently been changed. A most striking change has taken place in Faroese, where in certain phrases one hears not *máni* 'moon', but *sól* 'sun', e.g. *í minkandi sól* 'in the waning moon'. Since obviously the sun doesn't wane, confusion of sense is not possible and the harmful word is thus eschewed in the critical contexts—the period of the waning moon being regarded as especially dangerous. In many languages the noa word has completely dislodged an original term. Eng. *moon*, like Faroese *máni*, continues the Indo-European name for this luminary, but its cognate Gk *mene* early passed out of use, so that the normal word in Ancient Greek is *selēnē*. In Modern Greek, however, the term is *phengári*. We can now make an inspired guess at the reason for these changes. The inherited *mēnē* was tabooed and replaced by *selēnē* lit. 'shiner'. Then in due course the euphemism, no longer understood as such, itself fell under taboo and yielded to *phengári*, also literally meaning 'shiner'. Latin keeps the Indo-European term only in *mēnsis* 'month', but 'moon' is *lūna*, a word connected with a root meaning 'light'. The same formation appears in Slavonic, sometimes in its primitive sense of 'light', but often as a term for the moon. In this case, the noa term (OCS *luna*) has not driven the inherited term (OCS *měsęcǐ*) out of use. It is possible that the noa word was preferred by the lower classes, the more educated having less compunction about using the traditional word. Anyway, at some stage a compromise was reached. In Russian, for instance, *luná* and *mésjac* are both commonly used of the moon, in some usages interchangeable, at other times differentiated idiomatically or stylistically.

The names of animals have often been tabooed. A favourite device was to create a general term instead of the specific name. The Scottish Gaels call a hare *maigheach* lit. 'one in the *magh* (field)'. Since many sorts of animals live in fields, the designation is strangely vague; precisely this vagueness betrays its origin as a noa word. The hare was formerly regarded as a demonic creature and much superstition attached to it. With these things in mind, we may consider the provenance of Eng. *hare*. Among the oldest Germanic forms are OE *hara*, OHG *haso*, both weak decl. masc. pointing to Pr. Gmc stems *hazan-*, *hasan-* respectively, voicing of original *s* to *z* being explained by Verner's Law (p. 118). Two cognate names for the hare have been found in Baltic and Celtic, languages traditionally in contact with Germanic. The first is fairly evident: Old Prussian *sasins* (Baltic *s* usually represents IE *k*). The second has been recognised in Welsh *ceinach*, where -*ach* is a common suffix, leaving *cein*- which through the intermediary stages **kani-*, **kahnī-* can regularly derive from IE *kasnī-*. Whereas the formations are not identical in detail, there is agreement in essentials, namely an IE base *kas-* with an *n*-enlargement. This base and enlargement have been further identified in Lat. *cānus* 'grey-haired, aged', regularly explicable as IE **kasnos*, parallel to Lat. *cascus* 'aged' < IE **kaskos*, with *k*-enlargement. There is yet another parallel: OE *hasu*, ON *hǫss* 'grey' < Pr. Gmc **haswaz* < IE **kaswos*, this time with *w*-enlargement. Unless all appearances are deceptive, the above names of the hare derive from the colour. The hare is the 'grey one', a term as imprecise as the 'one in the field', and coined for the same reason, more than two thousand years ago.

I 3

INDO-EUROPEAN AND NON-INDO-EUROPEAN

Indo-European is now the largest and most widely diffused linguistic family in the world. This position has been achieved as the result of upwards of four millennia of expansion from an area thought to have lain in Central or Eastern Europe. In the course of its advance, many non-Indo-European languages must have been wiped out. And indeed, occasional survivals, exotic enclaves surrounded by Indo-European speech, give some idea of the nature of the languages which have perished. Examples are the minor groups of pre-Aryan speech scattered throughout central and northern India in the remoter hilly and jungle districts. In the far north of India, in an almost inaccessible area beneath the peaks of the Karakorum and Hindukush, a language of unknown affinities, Burushaski, is spoken by less than twenty thousand villagers. There is one such isolated language in Europe; this is Basque, spoken by perhaps half a million in the mountains at the angle of the Bay of Biscay, partly on the French, but mainly on the Spanish, side of the frontier.

But all has not been success story. Indo-European has sometimes had to yield ground. Hungarian, a language of the Finno-Ugrian division of the Uralic family, has established itself in Central Europe on traditionally Indo-European territory after migrating from the Volga region. The spread of Turkic languages in Central Asia was effected mainly at the expense of Indo-European (Iranian, Tocharian). A member of this family, Ottoman Turkish, dislodged Indo-European (Armenian, Greek, Iranian) from most of Anatolia and crossed the Bosporus to set up a permanent bridgehead on the European bank.

There are a number of linguistic families which, in view of their wide distribution and long recorded history, may well be compared with Indo-European. One thinks at once of Semitic. Its earliest known branch, Akkadian (formerly called Babylonian-Assyrian), is attested on cuneiform tablets going back as far as 2500 B.C. Another ancient Semitic language is Hebrew, known chiefly from the Old Testament. Hebrew became extinct by the second century B.C. at the latest, but through a unique combination of circumstances has, since the eighties of the last century, been successfully restored as a spoken tongue, a development unprecedented in linguistic history anywhere. The most used Semitic language today is Arabic, which spread rapidly from Arabia in the seventh and eighth centuries. Its chief early document is the Koran (seventh century).

With such a rich tradition, the comparative philology of Semitic has been built up on similar lines to Indo-European. Yet there is a marked difference of degree. Broadly speaking, the Semitic languages are all much of a muchness; they are more the analogue of, say, the Germanic or Slavonic group, than of the whole, diverse Indo-European family. This circumstance was being exploited by the end of the ninth century by Arabic-speaking Jewish scholars who brought their knowledge of this language to bear upon their Hebrew studies. They practised a comparative philology advanced enough to give scientific results, as when a number of lexicographical cruces in Hebrew were clarified in the light of Arabic cognates.

Semitic has certain important features in common with Indo-European, notably the use of ablaut which has come to dominate the entire morphology. Attempts have sometimes been made to show that the two families have most likely evolved from a common stock. But a convincing number of grammatical correspondences, etymologically underpinned, which, at the present stage of knowledge, alone can unequivocally demonstrate genetic affinity, are not forthcoming.

The great majority of linguistic families in the world, however, have more modest historical records. In fact, most of them have only been committed to writing in recent times. This applies, for instance, to the great Bantu family which extends over most of Black Africa. Needless to say, the comparative philology of such families is grievously hampered by the absence of early monuments and cannot develop as fully as it does for such historically well attested families as Indo-European or Semitic.

The evidence of known languages can throw no light on the problem of ultimate origins. Comparative philology is only able to state that the multifarious languages of the world can be classified in distinct families having no recognisable genetic affinity to each other. These families are, naturally, of varying sizes. Sometimes a single language is seen to constitute a family on its own, as Burushaski or Basque.

Languages from the various families are seen to have influenced each other whenever they have been in contact. Comparative philology has revealed a significant interchange between Indo-European and Uralic, especially the Finno-Ugrian division of the latter. The Finno-Ugrian languages contain a number of words which have been borrowed specifically from Aryan, e.g. Finnish *sata* '100', Mordvin *śado*, Hungarian *száz*, cf. Skt *śatám*. Such borrowing could only have taken place when the Aryans were still in Eastern Europe. It dates from the period of Primitive Finno-Ugrian, so that one thinks in terms of not later than 2000 B.C. Such observations confirm, incidentally, that Aryan as a type of Indo-European had developed characteristic forms before its speakers left Europe.

The differences between the various linguistic families are legion and often so profound that even the grammatical concepts of one may be largely irrelevant in another. We cannot elaborate on these matters here, but we have at least room to illustrate the enormous difference between the families in respect of word material and to offer one sample text. We therefore propose to consider the cardinal numbers 1 to 10 in representative Indo-European languages—comparative philology shows that numerals belong to the more stable entities in language—and to contrast them with the corresponding numbers in certain non-Indo-European languages. These we shall choose from among those spoken in Europe, as follows: Basque, Hungarian, Turkish, Maltese (an independent form of Arabic). As our text, a version of the Lord's Prayer in the last named will afford a further glimpse of a linguistic constellation beyond our own.

Indo-European

The numerals 1 to 4 characteristically inflect for gender and case. The other numerals may in some languages inflect for case, but this is a secondary development, though it began in Late Indo-European. In the following summary statement we confine ourselves to the nom.masc. form of the first four numbers and to the primary, indeclinable form of the rest. We begin with Sanskrit, Greek and Latin and attempt a reconstruction of the Primitive Indo-European prototypes.

	Skt	Gk	Lat.	Pr. IE
1	*ékas*	*heîs*	*ūnus*	**oykos, *oynos*
2	*dvaú*	*dúō*	*duo*	**dwõ(w)*
3	*tráyas*	*treîs*	*trēs*	**treyes*
4	*catvắras*	*téttares*	*quattuor*	**kʷetwŏres*
5	*páñca*	*pénte*	*quinque*	**penkʷe*
6	*ṣáṭ*	*héx*	*sex*	**seks*
7	*saptá*	*heptá*	*septem*	**septṃ*
8	*aṣṭaú*	*oktố*	*octō*	**oktõ(w)*
9	*náva*	*ennéa*	*novem*	**newṃ*
10	*dáśa*	*déka*	*decem*	**dekṃ*

Notes. (1) Cuneiform Aryan *aika-*; Gk *heîs* for **hems* < IE **sems* (cf. p. 185), but *oinós* '1 (on dice)'; OLat. *oinos*. (4) Gk, Lat. *-tt-* exceptional, but Gk (Doric) *tétores*. (5) Lat. *qu-* for original *p-* (assimilation), doubtless supported if not initiated by preceding *quattuor*. (6) Skt *ṣáṭ* < **ṣáṭṣ*; Gk dial. *wéx* points to alternative IE **sweks*. (7) Position of accent in Skt and Gk presupposes (Late?) IE **septṃ́*, which cannot, however, be original since stress appears on a reduced syllable. (9) Gk *ennéa* < **ennéwa* explicable as a mixture of regular **néwa* and a variant with metathesis **énwa* attested as *ena-*.

The Gothic numerals may illustrate the Germanic forms: they show close conformity to the Primitive Indo-European prototypes just postulated: 1 *ains*, 2 *twai*, 3 **þreis*, 4 *fidwor*, 5 *fimf*, 6 *saihs*, 7 *sibun*, 8 *ahtau*, 9 *niun*, 10 *taihun*. Here 2 has a plural instead of the original dual ending; in 5 the second *f* is due to the first, and *f* in 4 is due to 5.

Celtic follows suit: OIr. 1 *oín*, 2 *da*, 3 *tri*, 4 *cethir*, 5 *cóic*, 6 *sé*, 7 *secht n-*, 8 *ocht n-*, 9 *noí n-*, 10 *deich n-*, MidW 1 *un*, 2 *deu*, 3 *tri*, 4 *pedwar*, 5 *pump*, 6 *chwech,* 7 *seith*, 8 *wyth*, 9 *naw*, 10 *dec*.

Notes. (4) W *p* regular for IE *kʷ*. (5) Both languages show the same assimilation of initial consonants as Latin. (6) Both languages presuppose IE **sweks*, as Gk dial. *wéx* above. (7) W shows exceptional retention of original *s-* instead of commoner secondary *h-*. In the Irish forms 7 to 10, *n-* may appear prefixed to the following word; it is a relic of IE *ṃ* in **septṃ* etc., and analogically added to 8.

Baltic and Slavonic forms are: Lithuanian 1 *víenas*, 2 *dù*, 3 *trỹs*, 4 *keturì*, 5 *penkì*, 6 *šešì*, 7 *septynì*, 8 *aštuonì*, 9 *devynì*, 10 *dẽšimt*, Old Church Slavonic 1 *jedinŭ*, 2 *dŭva*, 3 *trĭje*, 4 *četyre*, 5 *pętĭ*, 6 *šestĭ*, 7 *sedmĭ*, 8 *osmĭ*, 9 *devętĭ*, 10 *desętĭ*.

Notes. Lith. 1 has prosthetic *v*-, comparable in principle to Eng. *one* [wɔn]. OCS divided *jed-inŭ*, the first element being interpreted as an interjection 'look', the second descending from IE *inos, an ablaut variety of *oynos '1'. Lith. 4, etc. with -*ì* show a peculiar Baltic development, where 7 to 9 further take an *n*-suffix. Lith. 6 has initial *š* (for expected *s*) by secondary assimilation. OCS 5 to 9 have been refashioned, perhaps through involvement with the ordinals. In both groups 9 has irregular *d*- for original *n*-, clearly in anticipation of *d*- in 10, the forms of which presuppose an Indo-European variant **dekm̥t*.

Non-Indo-European

	Basque	Hungarian	Turkish	Maltese
1	*bat*	*egy*	*bir*	*wieħed*
2	*bi*	*kettő*	*iki*	*tnejn*
3	*hiru*	*három*	*üç*	*tlieta*
4	*lau*	*négy*	*dört*	*erbgħa*
5	*bost*	*öt*	*beş*	*ħamsa*
6	*sei*	*hat*	*altı*	*sitta*
7	*zazpi*	*hét*	*yedi*	*sebgħa*
8	*zortzi*	*nyolc*	*sekiz*	*tmienja*
9	*bederatzi*	*kilenc*	*dokuz*	*disgħa*
10	*hamar*	*tíz*	*on*	*għaxra*

The immense phonic differences between Indo-European and these representatives of various linguistic families are not deceptive. Only occasional reservations are necessary. As seen above, the Uralic languages have anciently been influenced by Indo-European. A very early borrowing from the latter is represented by Hung. *hét* '7' < IE **septm̥*. It seems, too, that Hungarian *tíz* '10' is a later loan word from a lost Iranian language of Southern Russia, cf. Ossetic *dæs* 'do'. Lastly, Turk. *beş* 'five 'is a borrowing from Iranian. But otherwise there is an unbridgeable gulf between the forms of the numerals in the distinct linguistic families. The irreducible lexical differences in such a basic category as that of the numerals have, among other things, led philologists to speak of families of languages as being genetically unrelated.

Text
(Matt. vi.9–13 in Maltese)

9 *Missierna li   inti fis-smewwiet: jitqaddes   ismek.*
father-our who thou in-the heavens be-hallowed name-thy

10 *Tiġi saltnatek.   Ikun li   trid int, kif fis-sema,*
come kingdom-thy will-be which want thou as in-the heaven
hekkda fl-art.
so   on-the earth

11 *Ħobżna   ta' kull jum agħtina illum.*
bread-our of every day give-us today

12 *U   aħfrilna   dnubietna kif naħfru   lil min hu ħati*
and forgive-us sins-our   as we-forgive to who he guilty
għalina.
in-respect-of-us

13 *U la ddaħħalniex   fit-tiġrib,   iżda eħlisna*
and not lead-us-(thing) into-the temptation but deliver-us
minn kull deni.
from all evil

A Basque version with linguistic analysis is given in W. J.
Entwhistle, *The Spanish Language*, 1936, pp. 32–3.